Broadcast Journalism
1979–1981

The Eighth Alfred I. du Pont/
Columbia University Survey

The Alfred I. du Pont/Columbia University Survey and Awards in Broadcast Journalism

Broadcast Journalism
1979-1981

The Eighth Alfred I. du Pont/
Columbia University Survey

edited by

MARVIN BARRETT

EVEREST HOUSE
Publishers
New York

LIBRARY OF CONGRESS CATALOGING IN PUBLICATION DATA:

Main entry under title:

Broadcast journalism, 1979–1981.

(The Eighth Alfred I. duPont-Columbia University survey)
Includes index.
1. Broadcast journalism—United States.   I. Barrett, Marvin.   II. Series: Alfred I. duPont-Columbia University survey; 8th.
PN4784.T4A43   8th   PN4888.B74   070.1'9'0973   82-5067
ISBN 0-89696-160-5   AACR2

Contents

PART I

The State
of
the Art

1

Introduction: 157 Million Eyewitnesses to History

JANUARY 20, 1981. Inauguration Day. Whatever importance history might assign to that date, it unquestionably represented a peak experience in the short, hectic life of broadcast journalism.

From Tuesday dawn until the early hours of Wednesday, January 21st, the day was uniquely television's, and television was uniquely given over to reporting its dramatically unfolding events. For months broadcasters had been participating in the two stories which converged on that bright winter morning—one relating to the last steep climb to the heights by a political late starter, the other concerned with the grueling 14½ month captivity of 52 Americans held prisoner by a small, unpredictable group of zealots half a world away. Without TV cameras and newsmen both stories would undoubtedly have been different, perhaps drastically so, a suspicion that underlined the predominantly electronic character of the day. There was also the possibility, only hinted at by the presence of a brash electronic newcomer on the scene, that never again would broadcasters have another such opportunity to influence matters of national and global import or bring them to so obviously a made-for-TV climax before such a massive and undistracted audience.

Of the two intersecting events, the easy, predictable one was the swearing-in of the President of the United States, the fortieth such occasion since the founding of the Republic and the ninth to be seen on network TV.

Here was the quintessential electronic inauguration. The President-elect, Ronald Reagan, had, after all, spent a large portion of his professional career as a broadcaster. He had started out as an aspiring young sports announcer in Depression-era radio; then—after a stretch as a second-string Hollywood star—he had spent more than a decade in the schizophrenic world of prime-time commercial TV as a highly effective entertainer and corporate spokesman.

The experience had served Reagan well when in 1966, at the age of 55, he had decided to run for public office. Already the practice of politics was molding and revising itself to suit the demands of the electronic media. On his first try the former film and TV star was elected governor of California, the nation's most populous state. He won a second term and then started the abrupt ascent to the country's top office. Now that he had reached the final political eminence, Reagan had to be acknowledged as the television candidate par excellence, surpassing all his predecessors in his ability to accommodate himself to, and, when necessary, manipulate to his own ends the unpredictable and frequently treacherous medium. Previous presidents had won the office in spite of TV. With TV now at the apogee of its reach and power, the timing for a video pro like Reagan was perfect. Not only did he answer the country's apparent need for a conservative leader, he matched almost exactly the specifications dictated by the nation's 80 million home screens.

TV's requirements had become increasingly demanding. Thanks to the medium's determination to be there first, the functional opening of the presidential campaign had been pushed all the way back to the heretofore obscure Iowa caucuses in January of the election year. A presidential finalist had to last through 36 primaries (up from 29 in 1976), survive the gavel-to-gavel coverage of the conventions, and then the campaign proper, including debates and many other TV-oriented trials.

During those ten months of 1980, broadcast journalists communicated in painful detail, and frequently seemed actually to promote, a great deal of political confusion and distress. (See special report on page 163). Like no other candidate so far visible, Reagan had managed to rise above the turmoil, or simply ride it out.

After the stunning defeat of President Carter and his party, there seemed no reason to believe that Reagan's unflappable performance would stop. No startling innovations or disturbances appeared likely to mar the serene surface of the inaugural. Indeed, a great deal of money and effort had been invested in insuring the smooth, telegenic course of the day's events. The budget allotted by the Presidential Inaugural Committee to the celebration was estimated at approximately $10 million, triple what Jimmy Carter had spent four years earlier, ten times the tab for the first day of Camelot.

Nor were the networks stinting on the occasion. They had invested nearly half a million dollars alone in the booth set up adjacent to the West Front of the Capitol. Interrupting the line of vision of a good portion of the dignitaries congregated in the seats facing the inaugural site, the gleaming steel-and-glass structure was conspicuous proof, if any was needed, of the priority that politicians now gave to TV and the importance the networks still assigned to the coverage of the nation's premier political ritual. Another similarly elaborate installation had risen on the grass of Lafayette Park at the White House end of Pennsylvania Avenue.

To man these and dozens of other stations throughout the nation's capital, a broadcast news army invaded Washington in the days immediately preceding the ceremony—probably the largest and certainly the most richly rewarded group of journalistic talent to be congregated for that purpose in history.

Conspicuous among these well-heeled troops were the myrmidons of Roone Arledge, the gung-ho leader of ABC News. At the same occasion four years before, ABC was still running a weak third among the networks in news prestige. All that had changed. This time ABC's coverage would be the most elaborate of any inaugural by any network to date.

The redesigned ABC was already off to a headstart the night before by carrying for two hours the pre-inaugural gala staged in suburban Maryland by perennial presidential crony Frank Sinatra with Johnny Carson, Elizabeth Taylor, Bob Hope, Charlton Heston, and Donny and Marie Osmond among the volunteer talent. ABC collected $580,000 for its air time from the Presidential Inaugural Committee. In its turn the Committee peddled 12 minutes of commercials at $250,000 per minute. With 19,000 seats going for up to $150 each, the Committee cleared nearly $2 million to help offset the whopping bill the following day's festivities were scheduled to run up.

As for the inauguration itself, ABC would give its viewers eyewitness accounts from more than two dozen correspondents at 20 locations throughout the nation's capital. There would also be reports (so advance announcements proclaimed) from the West Coast, Plains, Georgia, "and other cities around the country."

Anchorman Frank Reynolds, flanked by special guest commentator George Will, would be stationed in the Capitol booth. In Lafayette Park opposite the White House would be Barbara Walters, Ted Koppel, Charles Gibson, and Bettina Gregory. Correspondents James Wooten, Susan King, and Ann Compton shared responsibilities for covering the Capitol. Sam Donaldson would be waiting at Blair House where the President-elect and his wife were spending the night. Later, with correspondent Brit Hume, Donaldson would float along the parade route. Bill Greenwood at the White House would move, at the appropriate moment, to the Ellipse. Barry Serafin and Sander Vanocur were assigned to President Carter's departure from Andrews Air Force Base, and Al Dale would be waiting for the Carters when they arrived in Plains. Standing by on the West Coast were Stephen Geer in Los Angeles and Ken Kashiwahara in San Francisco.*

To accommodate the inaugural coverage, ABC's *Good*

---

*Conspicuous by their absence were star reporter Geraldo Rivera and anchorman Max Robinson, representatives of minorities that had given small support to the winning candidate.

Morning America would be expanded to three hours and the whole day cleared of the usual games and soaps from 10 A.M. to 4:30 P.M. There would be recaps of what had happened on *World News Tonight,* and after a four-hour break for the normal prime-time entertainment, a special ABC News *Nightline* would be devoted to the nine inaugural balls. Ted Koppel and Barbara Walters would be back to anchor the party coverage with supplementary frills and thrills provided by the *Washington Post*'s social arbiters Sally Quinn and Maxine Cheshire and *Los Angeles Herald-Examiner* columnist Wanda McDaniel.

At NBC things were to be a little more laid back with John Chancellor, Roger Mudd, Tom Brokaw, and Jane Pauley scheduled to lead the troops through the day's maneuvers. The *Today* show would be bumped up to three hours and a special on the balls, hosted by Jessica Savitch, would be inserted in the late-night schedule.

Although CBS pretended to equal enthusiasm, it just wasn't the same. On the leading news network, this was to be the eighth and last time Walter Cronkite would stand surrogate to the nation on this hopeful occasion. It was also likely to be his last big assignment as the nation's favorite anchorman and most trusted citizen.

With Cronkite's departure, an era not only for CBS but for the whole broadcast journalism community was obviously coming to an end. And arriving on the scene to dramatize the change was a new and rambunctious presence, Ted Turner's Cable News Network. Barely half a year old, with 24 hours to fill seven days a week, CNN had assigned its entire 60-person Washington bureau plus anchors and crew from Atlanta to the occasion.

With characteristic indifference to the opinions of others, Turner had chosen as his star newsman prickly Dan Schorr, who just four years before had left his 23-year slot at CBS with noisy recriminations on both sides. George Watson, Turner's first Washington bureau chief, had departed ABC when the network had asked him to move over for Watergate investigator Carl Bernstein. And one of CNN's co-anchors, Don Farmer, was an ex-ABC national correspondent.

Turner, the new technology's most flamboyant and outspoken entrepreneur, not only was grabbing up network talent, but had boasted to the world that he would show the networks how electronic news really should be done. "We are going to do news," said Turner, "like the world has never seen news before."

Although the rest of the industry scoffed and pointed to the formidable losses Turner was suffering getting his operation under way, a certain uneasiness prevailed beneath the broadcasters' business-is-better-than-ever bravado. Despite the indignant protests and frantic lobbying of the old timers, cable, with a conspicuous boost from the outgoing administration, was growing at an alarming rate. Nor was there any reason to believe that the new administration would do anything to slow it down.

If Cronkite's passing from the scene did not, after all, herald the beginning of the end of an era (there were already signs that his withdrawal would be a gradual and incomplete one), Turner's arrival very well might.

And then with everyone primed for the grandest inaugural celebration in history, all of a sudden the nation's attention was elsewhere. On a collision course with the painstakingly planned, elaborately staged ritual was one of the breaking news stories of the decade—the long-awaited release of the American hostages in Iran. The circumstances, however, remained as uncertain and subject to last-minute reversal and disaster as those of the inauguration were staid and predictable.

The unpremeditated contrasts and ironies of the day began to unfold. The events of the inaugural, intended to be all sunlit pomp and circumstance, were interrupted by shots of night-time airdromes in faraway lands where a small band of happy and exhausted men and women was being shunted from continent to continent. For more than 157 million Americans who watched at least part of the day's events, emotions of relief and joy were mixed with darker feelings.

A handful of scruffy students and bearded, fist-shaking fanatics who for 14½ months had appropriated to their own infuriating uses the media of the most powerful nation in history had, at the very last minute, managed to insert them-

selves into and upstage democracy's most sacred ceremony.
And the instrument that made it possible for them to achieve
this absurd, exasperating triumph was, once again, TV.

As impossible as it seemed to predict the behavior of this
raggle-taggle band, all three networks and CNN had been
more than ready for such an appropriation of their resources.
Although the broadcasters had been inattentive and sometimes laggard in their coverage of the earlier stages of the
revolution in Iran, they had, despite their enormous advance
commitment to Reagan's inaugural, managed to deploy substantial forces in Europe, Africa, and the Middle East to accommodate the Iranians' terminal whim.

In Algiers, where the final negotiations were taking place,
so many newsmen milled about outside the American Embassy that traffic came to a standstill. In Frankfurt, near the
military hospital at Wiesbaden, Germany, where the hostages
were expected to make their first extended stop, a special
studio had been built and more than 600 journalists and
supporting crews had congregated.

Satellite space to beam the unfolding events back home had
been booked since mid-November. Network news bureaus
had been shifted from capital to capital. ABC had personnel
posted in Zurich, Geneva, and the Azores. CBS had kept a
crew in Germany since October in anticipation of some resolution of the crises.

In America TV crews from all three networks were ready to
hold the hands of the prisoners' families and record their
reactions upon seeing their loved ones freed—on TV, natu-
rally. ABC alone had 80 staffers assigned to 16 separate hostage families. One farm in Minnesota where the in-laws of a
hostage lived had 50 reporters on the scene with another 50 in
regular phone communication.

Only at the dark Teheran airport, where the planes had
waited to load up the Americans and take off, did there seem
to be no live representation of network broadcasters. The
chilling pictures of the hostages running the gauntlet of jeer-
ing Iranians to the plane's gangway came from Iran State
Television and were not shown in the United States till the
next morning. Nor were the networks, for all their resources,
able to avoid considerable confusion as to exactly when the

hostages were clear of Iranian airspace or where they were heading. ABC's Sam Donaldson, tagging the President as he left the West Front of the Capitol following the swearing-in, wagged his microphone in the new chief executive's face and told him and ABC's home viewers ecstatically, "They're free. They're free."

The actual release was nine minutes later, at 12:33 P.M. EST. Entertaining a group of senators and congressmen at lunch in the Capitol's Statuary Hall, the new President, a half hour later, marked the moment by coming forward, facing his guests, the cameras, and an estimated 43 million Americans and saying: "Some 30 minutes ago the planes bearing our prisoners left Iranian air space and are now free of Iran. So we can all drink to this one. To all of us together doing what we all know we can do to make this country what it should be, what it can be, what it always has been."

And so it went throughout the day. As the parade featuring dozens of marching bands, 500 horses, and the entire Mormon Tabernacle Choir singing "Battle Hymn of the Republic" escorted the new President to his residence for the next four years, the hostages' two Algerian transport planes were winging toward Athens for refueling. While former President Carter returned to Plains with wife Rosalynn and a teary daughter Amy, and while the Reagans took their place at the reviewing stand to watch such entries in the Inaugural Parade as the Dixon, Illinois, high school marching band, Alaskan dog sled teams, and the Appaloosa Horse Club, the hostages departed Athens for Algiers.

The first glimpse of the released hostages for millions of American viewers came when they deplaned in rain-slick, floodlit Algiers. That 90-minute stopover miraculously coincided with TV prime time, effectively wiping out most of what was left of the networks' entertainment schedule and drastically reducing ad revenues and increasing costs.*

---

*Although the networks refused officially to divulge exactly how much advertising revenue they may have lost that night, James Rosenfield, president of CBS' TV division, estimated that his network alone may have lost up to $2 million. Rosenfield also put combined network costs of covering the entire hostage homecoming over a period of several days at roughly $10 million.

One by one the hostages came through the plane hatch. First out was Bruce Laingen, head of the American mission in Iran, followed by the two female hostages, Elizabeth Ann Swift and Kathryn Koob. At the bottom of the ramp they were greeted by chief U.S. negotiator Deputy Secretary of State Warren Christopher. Emerging from the plane smiling and crying, the hostages embraced old friends and moved about in cheerful confusion. One after another the names and faces of all 52 came on the air. Then while the Reagans and the TV cameras were going from one inaugural ball to the next, the hostages' planes flew north from Algeria and there was another arrival at the snow-covered Rhein-Main Air Force Base in West Germany. Outfitted in fur-lined Air Force flight jackets, the travelers were whisked in waiting buses to the Wiesbaden military hospital 20 miles away, where they were greeted by cheering crowds of patients leaning out of windows waving American flags. With the first light of dawn the hostages, turning their backs on the TV cameras, were bundled through the hospital gates to banks of phones to call their anxious families and then to their waiting beds. Finally, on day 445, the 52 captive Americans *were* free.

By 1:30 A.M. EST the President and Mrs. Reagan had left the last ball for their first night in their new home. The inaugural parties were winding down. At 2:10 the networks had departed, ending what Jeff Gralnick, ABC's executive producer for special events, called "the single most complex day in broadcast history."

Ted Koppel, after a very long day, which began with ABC cameras taping the final hectic hours of the Carter presidency and ended when ABC *Nightline* terminated its record two-and-a-half-hour watch, was more explicit:

There are times, and today was one of those times, when television approaches the truly magical; when it becomes the sort of instrument that, fifty or sixty years ago, would have been regarded as supernatural.

Consider what we've all seen today, whom we've heard, and where we've been. If you were there at the inauguration of President Reagan, for example, you saw him from only one angle in only one location. If you were at home, watching television, you saw him at church, at Blair House, with the Carters at the White House, inside

Congress, outside Congress, riding up Pennsylvania Avenue, and down Pennsylvania Avenue, and throughout it all, you were in Germany and Algiers; you were in the homes of a dozen different hostages' families; you were in Plains, Georgia, and at Andrews Air Force Base.

You watched a magnificent parade, and you attended not one but eight or nine inaugural balls, and you saw the hostages the instant they disembarked in Algiers, the moment that they landed in Germany.

And all of it you saw as it was happening.

This has been, without question, one of the more memorable days in our nation's history, and television, much maligned television, which frequently does numb the brain and dull the senses, today produced a technological miracle. Never has any generation of Americans had greater reason to claim that they were eyewitnesses to history.

And the people who devised television's unbelievable technology deserve some credit.

TV Guide, looking back on the day in relative tranquility ten days later, wrote:

That sense of national unity can no longer be created without television. And the news divisions of the major networks—as well as PBS, scores of local stations, and the around-the-clock coverage provided by the innovative Cable News Network—rose to the occasion admirably. They showed that television can help us achieve something precious: a realization that in spite of all our problems and differences, we can still react to events as a united people, as Americans.

But as Ted Koppel said in the final moments before he signed off, "The crisis is over. The story, of course, is not."

2

Other
Vietnams?
Broadcasters
Abroad

WHILE RECORD-SIZE ABC task forces were being deployed across the nation and around the world to cover the twin stories of January 20th, a whole other ABC team was working day and night to wind up an extraordinary two-month investigation into the precarious, behind-the-scenes negotiations that led to the hostages' release.

On Thursday, January 22nd, forty-eight hours after the hostages were freed, *America Held Hostage: The Secret Negotiations,* went on the air in two blocks, the first preempting the entire sixty minutes of the ABC magazine *20/20,* the other taking over the time assigned to *Nightline,* ABC's late-night news program, and extending its usual half hour to two hours and six minutes.

The amount of time devoted to a single aspect of an important story was in itself rare. The investment of network money and staff in an investigative project that at any moment could dry up or self-destruct was unheard of.

The resulting program, according to *American Film,* "was not only the finest thing of its kind ever done on television, but the most impressive example of reportorial initiative and organization since Woodward and Bernstein developed the Watergate story."

For once, a worthwhile documentary beat out the entertainment competition in the ratings as 32.5 million Americans tuned in. Six nights later the proud network appropriated its entire prime-time evening schedule to repeat an updated version of the program and accommodated 16.9 million more Americans, making this the most viewed documentary in ABC's history.*

The significance of *America Held Hostage: The Secret Negotiations* was double. First, it confirmed an opinion long held by supporters of TV news that the networks and frequently local TV stations, when given the opportunity, were capable of original and significant work—the equivalent of the best print journalism could offer. Second, it was one more demonstration that the TV audience was willing and eager to tune in such coverage.

Indeed, the overall network commitment to the hostage story from the outset was formidable. Besides the saturation coverage of their day of release and heavy coverage on the nightly news throughout the crisis,** there was a total of 21½ hours of additional programming on the subject of Iran on NBC, 28½ hours on CBS. The highest total of 71 hours belonged to ABC, which, four days into the crisis, added a special late report five nights a week to cover the story. This program became *Nightline*, the first expansion of evening news on the commercial networks since 1963. And *Nightline* soon began stealing the audience from its entertainment competition, including the supposedly unbeatable Johnny Carson.

*Its combined gross audience of nearly 50 million did not compare to the 69 million viewers of *Dallas* on November 21, 1980, the night J.R.'s would-be assassin was identified, nor the 68 million who watched the Super Bowl, but it was considerably larger than the 40 million drawn by the 1981 Academy Awards.

**The story led off all three network newscasts for 43 days running, sometimes occupying as much as two-thirds of their allotted time, according to Professor William Adams of George Washington University, author of the book *Television Coverage of the Middle East*. Professor Adams also notes how little attention the networks devoted to Iran before the hostage crisis. In 1973, for example, each network gave Iran only an average of four-and-a-half minutes on the nightly news over the entire year. In 1974, each devoted an average of six minutes to Iran. By contrast, in 1980 the networks devoted over 700 minutes to news about the hostage crisis.

Nor did all this attention go unregarded. In the month after the hostages were taken, total news viewing increased by 3.6 percent and remained at abnormally high levels for the entire year.*

Coming at the end of such a massive 14½-month commitment to a single subject, and after the emotional binge attending the hostages' release, ABC's early return to the story with a three-hour documentary might have seemed too much, too soon. And the tale to be told was not only long and complicated, it was deeply disturbing, challenging many of the simpler assumptions that day-by-day coverage by the media had encouraged.

For remarkably, despite all the attention given the hostage story on TV, until the airing of ABC's blockbuster there had been no single program or sustained sequence that exploited the full arsenal of the networks' formidable news resources. Nor were TV viewers given any idea of the complexity of the behind-the-scenes maneuvers during the long months of waiting.

ABC's three hours had certainly not been quickly or easily come by. The blockbuster had begun as a glint in the sharp reportorial eye of ABC Paris Bureau Chief Pierre Salinger shortly after the invasion of the American Embassy by the Iranian students on November 4, 1979. It became a candidate for a major TV report nearly a year later when Salinger shared his conviction with the ABC brass that an untold and possibly very important story lay behind the grim and disturbing events coming to a climax in Teheran.

Salinger's point of entry into the story was a radical Parisian lawyer and an Argentinian businessman who had made contact with the Iranian revolutionary leaders during their years of exile in France. The two men claimed they had been acting as go-betweens for the U.S. government and Iran since the early days of the crisis. Confirmation of their claims by the eminent Egyptian journalist and politician Mohammad Heikal persuaded Salinger that the real story of the Iran crisis and

*However, in the last quarter of 1980, after the elections were over and the hostage negotiations were bogged down, the viewing audience for all newscasts returned to normal pre-hostage crisis levels.

what was being done to end it deserved deeper investigation.

Salinger's bosses at ABC not only agreed but gave him the sort of instant massive backing seldom offered by network TV to a story that promised to be both precarious and controversial.

The report from the outset was given special handling so far as budget and air time were concerned. The staff ended up roughly six times as large as that assigned to the ordinary hour-long documentary.

Av Westin, vice president of program development at ABC News, was put in charge. Under him were two executive producers, two senior producers, four field producers, two reportorial producers, with the supporting staff growing to 90. Over the weeks of digging and reporting, producers and correspondents traveled to Iran, Ireland, Panama, Spain, Austria, Germany, Turkey, Pakistan, Algeria, France, Egypt, Italy, and Sweden. Like some secret military operation, the project was given the code name "Tango Delta" and its production facilities were open only to those with special network clearance.

As the story built, its fate began to parallel that of the hostages. No release, no program—an unusual example of journalistic restraint. All along the line were surprising and, to many, alarming confirmations of the importance of the press in not only reporting the story but affecting its course. Heikal, one of the Mideast's premier journalists, was heavily involved as a go-between. Eric Rouleau of *Le Monde* sat in on the most intimate of Iranian conferences and was asked to help out in contacts the principals were afraid to make, and Salinger himself was called on to establish secret contact with Iranian leaders so that discussions could go on. Right from the start the fact that representatives of the media, with no diplomatic training, could barge in where State Department officials were reluctant and often unable to tread had been deeply troubling. What became evident as the Salinger story unfolded was that the journalistic presence penetrated to the deepest levels. Journalists, in fact, were frequently called on to make up for the impotence and incompetence of statesmen and their surrogates.

With brevity and skill, the ABC program reminded the

viewer of the surface events that had taken up so much of the day-to-day attention of the media and then showed what really was happening behind the scenes. By the time the program was over, black and white were thoroughly blurred and no special interest—religious, corporate, political, racial, military, or sociological—emerged blameless.

The Salinger diagnosis was a subtle, disquieting display of the disparity between appearance and reality, a distinction seldom made on the TV screen. Most disturbing of all was the revelation of a proposal from the U.S. side that cynically took into account TV's central position in the crisis. According to a scheme allegedly devised by Assistant Secretary of State Harold Saunders, Iranians were to take the hostages to the site where the U.S. rescue attempt had aborted in the desert of Tabas on April 24, 1980. There, within sight of the derelict U.S. helicopters and other grim reminders of the raid, the Iranians would mount "a media show." The hostages would be paraded before an international battery of TV cameras. Then, in exchange for their acting out a pantomime intended to demonstrate Iran's moral superiority and the humiliation of the United States, they would be released. Heikal, a Muslim and a friend of the Iranian revolution, was asked to serve as middle man in setting up this sorry spectacle. He refused to have any part of it and withdrew from the negotiating process.

Episodes involving UN Secretary General Kurt Waldheim and the double shuffling surrounding the dying Shah's flight from Panama to Egypt did little to reassure the viewer of either side's competence or humanity. They did, however, illuminate the background for the endless delays leading up to the hostages' final release.

When his distressing and convoluted tale was finally told, Pierre Salinger commented:

There are those Americans who believe the United States should have walked away from the hostage crisis. They point out that the Iranians are used to haggling in the bazaar. And their argument is it takes two to haggle. And if the United States had refused to deal, the Iranians would've come running after them.

But the Americans are not used to the idea of sacrificing human life. And this negotiating tactic would have been unacceptable to the majority of the American people.

So we negotiated. And, in the end, we freed the hostages. Their return home was a victory of the human spirit but not a victory for America.

Such a low-keyed, rational voice on that particular subject had not been heard in the land for many months.

The media pursued the hostages for a while following their return to native shores. There was an unedifying scramble at West Point where the 52 returnees had their first meeting with their families. Intended to take place in seclusion on the cloistered grounds of the U.S. Military Academy, the event became a media riot when 1,000 members of the international press descended on the small Hudson River community of Newburgh, seven miles away. Scaffoldings were erected, hill-tops were occupied, helicopters commandeered in the hope of getting a telescopic view of familiar faces. Chambermaids and waitresses at the Hotel Thayer within the Academy grounds were importuned to pass on any comment they might have overheard while making beds or serving meals.

The following week local stations were covering homecom-ing celebrations across the land. There were a few scattered reports of books and magazine articles to be written and movie or TV rights to be peddled. Hostages and their families made the obligatory appearances on talk and panel shows, describ-ing the trauma of reentry. Gradually the principals faded from the nation's TV sets.

In June, five months after the hostages' return, Bill Moyers presented his *Reflections on Iran,* the last edition of his distin-guished PBS *Journal* before his return to CBS. If *America Held Hostage: The Secret Negotiations* wrote a meticulously detailed conclusion to the 444 days of captivity, Moyers' reflections represented the beginning of wisdom so far as TV and Iran were concerned.

Far from being a rehash of material better forgotten on a subject already horrendously over-exposed, *Reflections* was a level-headed introduction to realities that, in the general ex-citement surrounding the hostage crisis, had been ignored or glossed over. It was also a sober challenge to the journalistic community to be better prepared in the future.

"Our joy at their return," Moyers stated at the opening of

the program, "relieved the poison of resentment that had built up during their captivity. But it also overwhelmed any desire to ask if there was something to be learned from the long ordeal and the events that precipitated it. As are all such events, this one was made of many parts. There was reality—*two* realities actually: Iran's and ours. And there was also the *perception* of reality, again from two viewpoints—theirs and ours. The perceptions became so beclouded that reality drifted out of focus."

Moyers was not easy on himself or his fellow journalists. Surprise in Iran, according to Moyers, was the rule rather than the exception. "We were surprised that politics and religion were so tightly meshed in Persian life. We were surprised when one of the best-equipped armies in the world could not keep the Shah in power. We were surprised that revolutionary fervor permeated the whole society. We were surprised they hated us so. We were surprised because neither we nor the Shah could in the end control events."

Moyers reaffirmed television's involvement in the U.S. government's disastrous policy, "which saw Iran and the Shah as one and the same. A policy reinforced for years by images from the media so superficially drawn as to make a heresy of subtlety. The lens through which Americans long viewed Iran was a cloudy lens, taking one-dimensional snapshots of a complex culture. . . . And when revolution came, television presented Iran in storybook terms, condensing the story into comic-strip symbols of good and evil. The coverage was stark, emotional, simplistic . . . incessant."

Moyers' was not the only criticism of TV's behavior before and during the nation's Iranian ordeal. The Monday morning quarterbacking on TV's day-to-day coverage was unprecedented in its scope and vehemence. But not all of the vehemence was justified.

True, months and years prior to the overthrow of the Shah, as Moyers pointed out, signals from the Persian Gulf had been ignored or misread.

The invasion of the U.S. Embassy brought American newsmen out in force. But once there, the journalists were attacked for their intrusive presence. The escalation of a stu-

dent sit-in into an international incident of frightening pro-
portions was blamed on TV brashness and overkill. TV's
coverage of Iran was given credit for President Carter's returning popularity. Thanks to Teddy Kennedy's negative remarks about the Shah, TV and Iran got partial credit for the
Massachusetts senator's elimination as a contender for the
Democratic nomination and, finally, TV and Iran were supposed to have contributed decisively to Carter's precipitate fall
from the voters' favor and the Republicans' landslide victory.
Without the media's meddling and misrepresentation, went
the reasoning, none of these things would have happened.*

There was also much criticism of the saturation coverage of
Iran, the densest in TV history.

"Television played it like a soap opera, and made it the
greatest soap opera of the year," said former Under Secretary
of State George W. Ball. "Television has played this situation
up so that it has become the central issue of American policy,
which I think is absurd."

TV Guide accused the networks of a cynical ratings race,
which led to a frantic scraping of "the bottom of the Iranian
news barrel for another morsel to titillate the morbidly çuri-
ous and the unquestioningly naive."

Ron Nessen, press secretary to President Ford and one-time
NBC correspondent, went even further. "In Iran," he said,
"television refused to accept responsibility for its role. Television is an element of the story and to pretend otherwise is
sophistry. These kinds of stories require a degree of responsibility that television so far has not displayed. They require
self-discipline. There is a general rule in television. If it can be
done, you do it. This needs to be re-examined."

National Security Adviser Zbigniew Brzezinski suggested
that the U.S. press "should be controlled." Looking back,
Hodding Carter, Assistant Secretary of State for Public Affairs during the crisis, said of press coverage, "Had we been
doing serious diplomatic business rather than political postur-

*Actually the media were charged with a double responsibility—first, for
keeping the hostages alive and relatively unharmed by their insistent reminders to the world; second, for prolonging the hostages' imprisonment
and complicating their final release, again by their constant attention.

ing it would have been disastrous. We never had time to think. We were responding to partial tests and partial responses. It was inherently distorted and inherently anathema to anyone who wanted an orderly negotiating process. . . . I have a feeling that when all was said and done, the smartest thing would have been, whatever the political cost, to have just shut up. Just shut it down."

But at what point could the government, or the media, have put a lid on the hostage story? Given the quick and vivid concern of the American people, probably never. Nor would it have been possible to justify such a silence when its principal motivation would be to cover up the ineptness of government and media alike. Indeed, *The New Yorker* magazine, in its lead item of the June 2, 1980 issue, charged the media with deliberately clamming up in the wake of the ill-fated U.S. rescue attempt:

One of the most striking features of the news these days is an absence. Since the disastrous mission to release the American hostages in Iran, coverage of the hostages, which once blanketed the news columns and the airwaves almost to the exclusion of any other news, has evaporated. In an instant, the frantic urgency about their release dissipated, and they seemed to disappear from the face of the earth. Gone were the interviews with their friends and relatives, gone the impromptu delegations of clerical would-be peacemakers, and gone the whole sideshow of eccentric free-lance meddlers, including the congressman who went to Iran to conduct his own negotiations and the American Indian who wanted to mix up his cause with the highly publicized hostage question. Gone, too, were reports of the "rising impatience" of the American people, which was thought to have so much to do with the decision to launch the rescue mission, and which was supposed to play such an important role in the fluctuating popularity of the various Presidential candidates, according to the polls. Now the time that was said to be "running out" politically for the Carter Administration if the issue was not resolved has lengthened again, and appears to stretch out into the indefinite future. . . .

. . . the news media may have abandoned the hostage issue because of a well-founded, if largely unarticulated, suspicion that their own disproportionate coverage of it, together with the Presidential campaign, had generated the terrifying vortex of political pressure that brought on the tragic rescue mission and came near to dragging the nation into a catastrophe.

The New York Times answered in a sharp editorial:

Our colleagues at *The New Yorker* magazine complained this week not
about Iran but about being "used" by American news media. They
accused the media of suddenly ignoring the hostages on cue from
the President "because of a well-founded . . . suspicion that their
own disproportionate coverage . . . had . . . brought on the tragic
rescue mission and came near to dragging the nation into a catastrophe." What a mighty misreading of the nature of news and what a
disproportionate allocation of guilt. A magazine should know there
are truths beyond the front page and that there can be catastrophe in
failures of moral judgment as well as military operations.

The dip in Iran coverage, if it actually happened, was of
short duration.

Walter Cronkite, who had sustained his share of criticism
for his gong-ringing for 444 numbered nights and who also
had the uneasy distinction of being considered the father of
"TV diplomacy," once again spoke with the voice of firm
reason. "We can't be asked to abstain from journalistic practices because a story will complicate diplomatic practices. That
is a diplomatic problem; it's not our problem. We have to be
responsible, of course. But within the ethical framework of
responsibility, we have to pursue the story. It would be terrible
if, through self-interest or government interest, we didn't get
a clear picture."

Edward Said, a Columbia University professor and a
member of the Palestine National Council, saw things in a
broader context in his book, *Covering Islam.* Said wrote: "The
Iranians as well as the United States government were per-
fectly aware that statements made on television were aimed
not only at people who wanted the news, but also at governments, at partisans of one faction or another, at new or
emerging political constituencies."

Barry Rosen, press attaché at the U.S. embassy in Teheran,
mentioned another more elementary problem.

I don't feel that they [the media] were ready to really understand
what was going on in Iran . . . couldn't deal with the situation. . . .
They could deal with a middle-class society, or a society that looked
somewhat like the United States, and they could fit predispositions

into that. But when it came to Iran or many Third World countries in general, I would think they come in with predispositions that do not fit the country itself.

Such a barrage of criticism took on added weight when one considered that Iran was only one among dozens of countries in both hemispheres that Americans were seeing dimly and partially—countries, large and small, remote and close by, any one of which could, like Iran, become overnight the gateway to global disaster.

Practicing diplomacy, as Cronkite said, was not TV's duty nor its talent. But television, as the nation's principal source of news, had a formidable duty to keep the public informed of what might be coming next, and where. As Iran so clearly demonstrated, the network news departments could hardly keep up with the explosions when they occurred, let alone anticipate or explain them.

2.

On September 21, 1980, a full-scale war erupted between Iraq and Iran. Despite 11 months of bug-eyed concentration on the immediate vicinity, only one American newsman, Larry Pintak, a radio stringer hired by CBS just two months earlier, was anywhere near the scene. A week later CBS took a full-page ad in *The New York Times*, proclaiming in scare headlines FOR MORE THAN 3 DAYS YOUR ONLY PIPELINE TO THE PERSIAN GULF WAR WAS CBS NEWS. The copy beneath read:

The world was caught by surprise. But not CBS News. . . . All airports were closed. Communications to the outside world disrupted. It was more than three days before other Western newsmen were able to penetrate the area.

In pointing out its scoop, CBS News was only underlining a frightening inadequacy of U.S. journalism—its inability to cover all the places that returning Cold War politics and modern technology (including TV itself) might suddenly promote to life-and-death importance. Actually for the first

27 days he was in Iraq, ostensibly reporting the war, Pintak was forced to remain near phone lines and Telex machines and thus never could file firsthand reports of actual combat. Nor was it likely that Iraq, a staunch ally of the Soviet Union with strict censorship and scarcely more friendly to the United States than its adversary, Iran, would have permitted free access to the front lines. Difficult as this coverage was, there were other places more inaccessible to broadcast newsmen and perhaps even more crucial to the future of the United States.

A year after Russian tanks rolled into Afghanistan, two segments of network magazine shows remained the only substantial TV attempts to tell U.S. viewers exactly what was going on in a war that had been the occasion for a dramatic change in America's foreign policy.*

For *60 Minutes,* Dan Rather disguised himself as an Afghan tribesman and made a courageous if frustrating foray into the hills beyond the Khyber Pass. Nine months later Betsy Aaron, accompanied by producer Joseph DeCola of NBC *Magazine,* went deeper, stayed longer, and came back with a slightly clearer sense of a grim conflict not likely to be soon resolved. Still it was a small part of a big story.

Like Afghanistan, a large percentage of the earth's land mass (including vast areas of the Soviet Union and China) was to all intents and purposes off limits to American newsmen or accessible to them only under the most rigidly controlled conditions. In 1981, according to the annual estimates published by Freedom House, only 24 percent (37 countries) of the nations of the world had "generally free" broadcast media. Another 20 percent (31 countries) were "partly free." Most of the remaining 56 percent, even when friendly to the United States, had little or no conception of, or sympathy for, the news requirements of visiting U.S. journalists.

In Egypt and Israel, both perceived as solid U.S. allies, there

*The first TV newsman to penetrate into Afghanistan after the Russian incursion was reporter Jon Snow of Britain's Independent Television News. In early January 1980 he filed a seven-minute piece on rebel forces harassing Russian convoys in Western Afghanistan that was made available in the United States to clients of United Press International Television News (UPITN).

were accusations of bias and acts of overt hostility toward representatives of the U.S. media, official and unofficial.

On September 9, 1981, shortly after he arrested 1,536 Egyptian dissidents, the United States' great and good friend Anwar el-Sadat launched an on-camera diatribe against ABC reporter Chris Harper, waving over his head confiscated cassettes containing Harper's interview with a known critic of Sadat's regime. The next day Harper was given 24 hours to leave the country.

In Israel the confiscation of film and tapes, the destruction of equipment and attacks on TV personnel had been reported more than once. The official justification evoked similar objections to TV's presence during the U.S. urban riots of the '60's. "As soon as a camera appears, a rock is picked up," explained Zev Chafets, head of the government press office. "TV cameras tend to have an inciting effect very often, particularly in the case of political demonstrators who are anxious to make a point. It is very well known that cameras need pictures and rock throwing needs pictures."

Whether U.S. TV crews were welcome or unwelcome, discreet or provocative, trouble was erupting around the globe with increasing frequency and with little consideration for the convenience of U.S. reporters and their assignment editors.

On two days selected at random in early June 1981, acts of terrorism or violence or their immediate aftermath were reported by *The New York Times* in Chad, South Africa, Greece, Sri Lanka, Yugoslavia, Bangladesh, Uganda, Cambodia, Italy, Spain, West Germany, Turkey, Namibia, Vietnam, Korea, Chile, Taiwan, Argentina, and Belgium. This did not count the continuing agonies of El Salvador, Ireland, Israel, Lebanon, Afghanistan, Poland, and, of course, Iraq and Iran.

Leaving out coverage of those long-standing conflicts, in the week leading up to and following the two days of incidents reported in the *Times* only four of the 19 hot spots listed got even cursory mention on the network evening newscasts. What the surrounding circumstances were and what might come next, no person dependent on the nightly TV news for his information was likely to ever know.

Time was admittedly scarce on the regular evening newscast for secondary foreign news. However, there remained other broadcasts on which overseas coverage still could command attention. These included documentaries, special reports, magazine and panel shows, and other assorted outlets for news and public affairs information scattered through the network schedules. Of the established network documentary series, however, none paid unusual attention to international stories. From September 1979 to September 1981, out of 31½ prime-time documentary hours aired on CBS, only seven were devoted to foreign news. ABC *Closeup* had 24 programs in the same period, nine of which were on international subjects. And NBC had only three *White Papers* on international subjects during the two years. Special reports on international affairs in the same period (excluding the massive live coverage given such events as the assassination attempt on the Pope, Sadat's murder, Iran, and the Royal Wedding) accounted for 8⅔ hours on CBS, 5¼ on NBC, and 2¾ on ABC. The audience for these programs had undoubtedly increased. Still, underpromoted and lacking a regular slot, they could not, except on rare occasions, compete with entertainment programming. They showed up regularly in *Broadcasting* magazine's weekly listing of The Final Five in their Ratings Roundup.*

For the magazine programs, which, at least on two networks, commanded high ratings, the record was a little better. 75 out of 314 segments of the prime-time winner *60 Minutes,* aired between September 1979 and September 1981, dealt

---

*In February 1981, ABC News President Roone Arledge, echoing a suggestion made by CBS Chairman William Paley in his autobiography two years earlier, called on all three networks to exempt documentaries and news specials from the weekly prime-time ratings race. "Serious news programs are a public service that rarely attract a large audience, and they shouldn't have to compete with light-entertainment programming," said Arledge. "Right now, each network is penalized in the weekly averages if it puts on a serious news program." Arledge's proposal was greeted warmly by NBC President Fred Silverman. But CBS News President William Leonard dismissed the idea as unnecessary, saying, "I don't think we have to distort the normal system of measuring in order to do what we should properly do anyway." Although ABC followed through on the idea, NBC, CBS, and, most important, A.C. Nielsen, continued rating the news.

with international stories, but these included such fluff as a profile of the Ritz Hotel in Paris, and, from Switzerland, "The Best Restaurant in the World." On ABC's *20/20* the score was 55 out of 283. On the less successful *NBC Magazine* 50 out of 356 stories dealt with foreign subjects.

On the Public Broadcasting Service, WGBH's exemplary *World* series, which was 100 percent devoted to international concerns, was cut back in 1980-81 from 13 to five hours because of lack of support from PBS's Station Program Cooperative. Two more shows were added in 1981-82 when the cooperative's support returned. But the series still remained well below the 13-hour commitment of its premier year.

The *MacNeil/Lehrer Report,* with 260 half hours at its disposal each year, devoted 74 of them to foreign affairs topics in 1979, 55 in 1980, and 55 through September 1981.

ABC's *Directions,* after a 19-year run, still included some of the most informative coverage of remote potential trouble spots on the air.

CBS's *Sunday Morning* had devoted 17 of its 104 "cover stories" to international subjects in the two-year period under consideration.

Of the 313 "special segments" on NBC's *Nightly News,* 106 were devoted to the international scene. Of the 116 extended series and "enterprisers" on CBS's *Evening News,* 28 came from overseas. ABC's *World News Tonight* broadcast 154 "special assignments" in the two-year period, 44 of which were on foreign subjects.

Face the Nation had 110 guests over the two years; only 13 came from abroad. *Meet the Press* had 112 interviews, 10 of which were with foreign leaders. And *Issues and Answers* had 133 guests, 28 of whom were foreigners.

The striking exception remained ABC's *Nightline,* which had been put on the air to accommodate the nation's acute concern for the hostages. Once the crisis was over, it continued to allot 36 percent of its time to overseas stories.

National Public Radio, which in addition to extensive coverage of international news on its daily programs—the two-hour *Morning Edition* and 90-minute *All Things Considered*—

also produced a weekly half hour devoted entirely to foreign
affairs. Called *Communique,* the program aired at 6:30 P.M.
every Friday and featured documentaries as well as discussions of major international events with newsmakers and
journalists.

But of all the programs and segments devoted to foreign
news, most did not venture beyond the closed circle of developed nations or those few Third World nations that had
been rendered familiar by long-standing crises.

And even with the familiar there was no guarantee that
conscientious coverage would result in local approval. Indeed
the more accurate and hard-hitting the reporting, the more
inevitable seemed the response of "no fair" from one side or
the other—or, likely as not, from both.

In the Middle East the pro-Israel bias of the American
media had long been taken for granted by all parties to the
conflict, including the reporters themselves. John Weisman,
reporting in *TV Guide* on the hard time the media gave the
Palestinians, quoted NBC correspondent Steve Mallory as
saying ". . . Arabs are the people you see wearing kaffiyehs
and riding camels, right? And those aren't your neighbors in
California or Kansas."

To further substantiate his thesis, Weisman tabulated 38
reports of raids and reprisals by both Israelis and Palestinians
between July 1980 and April 1981, 24 of them Israeli raids
against Palestinian targets in South Lebanon. "Only three of
these reports—for a total of one minute, ten seconds—
showed pictures of the effects of the Israeli attacks," wrote
Weisman. "None showed any Palestinian victims. . . . Of the
14 reports of Palestinian raids and attacks on Israel during the
same period, 11 included pictures of Israeli victims and the
filmed reports totaled some 17 minutes." Even allowing for
such contributing circumstances as lack of safe access to Palestinian communities, the complex situation in Lebanon (there
were more than 40 distinct armed groups in Beirut alone
and 92 recorded Lebanese political parties) and a handy
satellite station in Tel Aviv to get the Israeli story out cheap-
ly and easily, there was still a striking imbalance. This could
only be partially justified by the prevalent U.S. conviction

that the terrorist Palestinians were getting what they asked for.

The biases of public and newsmen alike were somewhat shaken in June 1981 when the Israelis bombed Iraq's unfinished nuclear plant in Baghdad, risking, in the opinion of many, World War III. Six weeks later Israeli jets attacked downtown Beirut in reprisal for a Palestinian rocket attack that had left three Israelis dead. 300 Arab civilians, many of them women and children, were killed and 800 wounded. Meanwhile all through the summer President Reagan's campaign for AWACS for Saudi Arabia raised the specter of Israeli interference and latent anti-Semitism. If Israel got plenty of attention from U.S. TV, the young nation was becoming less and less pleased with more and more of the kind of attention it was getting.

Ireland was almost as close to the hearts of some Americans as Israel was to others. Also the media, particularly TV, had been acknowledged a heavy participant in the last dozen years of the troubles in Northern Ireland. As early as 1968 the IRA was said to have been given a new lease on life by the tactics of civil rights activists in the United States, which the Irish saw in graphic detail on their TV screens and began to emulate.

There was no question that over the intervening years TV coverage—when it was available—had kept matters stirred up not only in Ulster but in Great Britain and across the ocean where Irish-American partisans were numerous and voluble.*

*BBC had self-imposed restrictions on coverage of the ongoing crisis. Before approaching any members of eight outlawed paramilitary groups in Northern Ireland, a BBC reporter had to get prior permission from top broadcasting executives. Britain's commercial TV companies were regulated by the Independent Broadcasting Authority. Its mandate apparently included censoring a 20-second sequence in a Granada Television program about propaganda in Northern Ireland showing the dead body of a hunger striker in his coffin. IBA said the sequence "crossed the dividing line between reporting propaganda and adding to it." The company refused to cut the sequence, and so the program never aired. Even more restrictive was the government of Southern Ireland which prohibited by law the broadcasting of "any matter which is an interview, or report of an interview, with a spokesman or spokesmen for" any illegal group in Northern Ireland and a few legal ones as well.

With the hunger strike of Bobby Sands in 1981, the IRA, already sophisticated in its manipulation of the media, found its most potent weapon to date. Camera crews from four continents, 16 from the U.S. networks alone, descended on Belfast to join the Sands death watch. A full-scale civil war did not materialize as some had hoped with his death, but the unprecedented media attention was widely criticized. "Television has many deaths to answer for," said an editorial in the *Spectator*. "Recent media coverage has transformed the morale of the IRA and served as chief recruiting officer."

America, with its strong ties to both Ireland and England, gave "the troubles" particularly extensive coverage, not only on the evening news but on panel and entertainment shows where members of the families of the IRA prisoners were dispatched from overseas to make guest appearances.

At least three local stations in the United States—WNEW-TV and WOR-TV in New York and WCCO-TV in Minneapolis—sent correspondents to do first-hand reports on Ulster. WNEW's Bob O'Brien had been sent to Northern Ireland four times since 1977. He brought the first American cameras into Long Kesh prison and spent a full month in Belfast during the peak of the hunger strike in May 1981, filing an eight-part series on *The 10 O'clock News* and making a half-hour documentary that aired in prime time. The reports were syndicated to 18 cities around the country.

The British were quick to blame TV for the persistence of a situation that could be traced back through history for 800 years. But it was also TV that gave Anglophilia its greatest boost in years when, 11 weeks after Sands' death, the Prince of Wales married 20-year-old Lady Diana Spencer in St. Paul's Cathedral in London. 68 million Americans wallowed in this irresistible combination of spectacle and sentiment, snobbery and coziness to which all three networks, beginning as early as 4:30 A.M., devoted many happy hours.*

Seductive or harrowing, the British Isles and the Middle East had people and customs that a sizable number of Ameri-

---

*CBS had 5 hours, ABC 6, and NBC 7½. All three networks not only had specials the night before the ceremony but hour-long wrapups in prime time afterwards.

can viewers could empathize with. In much of the Third World, however, this bridge of tradition and understanding did not exist. There had been several attempts to correct the situation, the most conspicuous being UNESCO's push for a "New World Information Order." This plan to return the control of the international press to its national components, ostensibly in the interest of fairness and balance, had a sinister ring to most Western newsmen. But there was undoubtedly justice in the undeveloped countries' contention that much of the news offered to them by the big international news agencies had no interest for most of their population, and that the news the same agencies took out from the Third World was deficient in understanding and sympathy, accentuating violence and disaster.

In both his heritage and the circumstances of his life, Prince Karim Aga Khan straddled East and West—or North and South as the haves and have nots of the world now divided themselves.* In an address to the International Press Institute in Nairobi, Kenya, the Prince stated the Third World position with considerable eloquence.

A complaint that the North reports the South superficially, condescendingly, sometimes inaccurately, and without proper social, cultural, economic, and political background often has real validity. To put it another way, there are problems of credibility, on all sides. It is here that questions of repeated editorial sloppiness or misunderstanding can result in accusations of evil intent. It is here that this whole debate can quickly descend to emotion, anger, and stalemate. Yet it is on this very tender area of editorial content that I feel we must see some quick, significant, and visible progress. It is what brought the Third World together on this issue in the first place.

Many of these countries thought that the industrialized world, largely because of its press, was receiving a distorted image of their young nations and their cultures. They felt their problems were being magnified, their accomplishments diminished, their aspirations ignored. They felt as though they were in a nightmare, screaming to be heard, but making no sound. The channels and the content of international communications were a monopoly of the North, or so it seemed, and in this respect many people in developing countries felt as powerless as they had under colonial rule.

*The religious leader of the Ismaili sect of 20 million Muslims, the Prince also owned a leading East African newspaper, *The Daily Nation.*

Ladies and gentlemen, no matter what has happened to this debate at the international level, these basic feelings have not changed. As a Muslim, one of 700 million, I live in daily astonishment about the incomprehension of Islam and its peoples.

Some Western media have perpetuated misconceptions which stick like shrouds to the bones of historical skeletons, but in most civilizations the dead are buried. . . . The fact is that the quality of reporting from abroad is often unacceptably low, and there is need to rethink how to select and train these all-important foreign correspondents and foreign editors and sub-editors.

In his last sentence the Prince struck a nerve. The increasing power and importance of the individual newsman was generally acknowledged, but the idea of licensing journalists to insure their professional competency as one might a physician or a lawyer remained antipathetic to the Western press. Other ideas for controlling international news and subjecting editorial decisions to government bureaucrats in the supposed interest of accuracy and balance were equally unwelcome.

In recent years, non-American news agencies such as Visnews and UPITN had made reasonable attempts to modify the mixture of their news feeds to answer the specific needs of each national client. Older services such as AP, UPI, Reuters, and Agence France Presse had done less.

When the MacBride Commission presented its report and recommendations on a "New World Information Order" to the General Conference of UNESCO in May 1980, there were cries of protest not only from journalists but advertisers as well.

Leonard Matthews, president of the American Association of Advertising Agencies, denounced the report as "a calculated attempt to set the stage for a nightmarish system of trade barriers, propaganda agencies, managed news, thought-conditioning, and advertising bans." Matthews saw the "New World Information Order" as a "frontal attack or privately owned mass media" that could lead to government control of both news and advertising or no advertising at all.

The Voices of Freedom conference was held at Talloires, France, in May 1981. Leaders of independent news organ-

izations from 20 countries adopted the Declaration of Talloires, a free-press counterattack that concluded: "We reject
the view of press theoreticians and those national or international officials who claim that while people in some countries
are ready for a free press, those in other countries are in-
sufficiently developed to enjoy that freedom. . . . We believe
that the ultimate definition of a free press lies not in the
actions of governments or international bodies, but rather in
the professionalism, vigor, and courage of individual journalists. Press freedom is a basic human right. We pledge
ourselves to concerted action to uphold this right."

As of November 1981, the matter remained unresolved and
was, perhaps under the prevailing circumstances, unresolva-
ble.

"There are two systems of journalism in the world and I
don't think it is possible for them to get together," said Stanley
Swinton, vice president and assistant general manager of the
Associated Press (quoted in *Television/Radio Age*). "There's the
Soviet concept—the press is a tool of the government, it works
for the government, its employees are government servants.
There's the Western concept that the press pinpricks, it inves-
tigates to find out what goes wrong. I just don't think you can
bring these two together because there's a fundamentally
different perception of journalism."

The Soviet view of journalism had been getting increasing
attention, thanks mainly to the growing currency of the term
"disinformation," a transliteration of the KGB term *dezinfor-
matsiya*. The word, which was popularized in the 1980 novel
The Spike, by journalists Arnaud de Borchgrave and Robert
Moss, came to be bandied about the halls of Congress,
the columns of *The New York Times,* and the corridors of the
White House.

It was, according to Senator Jeremiah Denton, (R.
Alabama), Chairman of the Subcommittee on Security and
Terrorism, who got his definition from John Barron's book,
KGB, "not only forgeries, literary hoaxes, and disseminations
of false information but also the commission of physical acts
such as sabotage and murder for psychological effect." A State
Department report issued in October 1981 expanded Bar-

ron's description: "The approaches used by Moscow include control of the press in foreign countries; outright and partial forgery of documents; use of rumors, insinuations; clandestine operation of radio stations; exploitation of a nation's academic, political, economic, and media figures as collaborators to influence policies of the nation."

Senator Denton saw a dangerous bridge between the Russians and "a story-hungry and sometimes gullible press." But in hearings of his subcommittee held in April 1981, the senator's evidence of disinformation tended to be nebulous at best. Almost equally difficult to pin down were the accusations of Arnaud de Borchgrave, former *Newsweek* chief foreign correspondent, who testified before Denton's subcommittee. Nonetheless, the Senate Republican Conference—funded entirely with taxpayer money—sent a tape to 290 radio stations around the country in which de Borchgrave, being interviewed by Senator Denton, accused *Mother Jones,* the *Village Voice,* the *Soho Weekly News* and *Progressive* magazine of disseminating KGB disinformation. Neither the senator nor the ex-*Newsweek* correspondent provided specific examples.

Whether they could be considered agents of disinformation or legitimate subjects for journalistic enterprise, an increasing number of Russians had appeared on American TV in the past two years. There were efforts to prevent such interchanges, most notably the refusal by the State Department to extend the visa of Georgi Arbatov, the Kremlin's top expert on the United States, so he could appear on a debate on *Bill Moyers' Journal* on April 10, 1981. Arbatov left and Moyers tried to arrange for three Soviet guests to appear by satellite from Moscow, but the Soviets withdrew from the debate in protest. Another example was the Cable News Network's half-hour program from the Soviet Union, *Moscow Live,* launched in the fall of 1981. CNN planned originally to have officials of both the Soviet Union and the United States on the show and to beam it to audiences in both countries, but the Soviets would not allow the program to be shown on Russian TV and some U.S. State Department officials, including Secretary of State Alexander Haig, refused to appear.

The whole concept of disinformation, according to Harry Rositzke, a former CIA operative familiar with the technique, was fraught with peril.

"To magnify Soviet disinformation efforts in America," Rositzke wrote in *The New York Times,* "not only weakens the image of the American media but also enhances the KGB's reputation for omnipotence, always welcome in Moscow. . . .

"There is an even greater danger. If we interpret an American journalist's contact with a Soviet official, KGB or not, as somehow sinister, or if we interpret any news item or opinion not fitting the current conservative caste of thought as somehow inspired by Moscow, we are on the road to the self-delusion of the '50s." Rositzke did not mention another danger, the frequently thinly disguised disinformation efforts by the U.S. side.

If there was a textbook case, which illustrated the present-day difficulties facing the U. S. media in their foreign news coverage, it lay in the tiny Central American nation of El Salvador.

Hodding Carter in his latest role as host of the new PBS review of the media, *Inside Story,* explained why El Salvador was of sudden interest:

Most people first paid attention to El Salvador because of violent death—the assassination of the Roman Catholic archbishop of El Salvador, the murder of three American nuns and a lay worker, the murder of two American land reform experts. But what finally turned El Salvador into consistent front-page news was President Reagan's decision to sharply increase military aid to the government of El Salvador, a policy President Carter had embraced just before leaving office. . . .

Carter went on:

Adequately covering a place like El Salvador is hard, because a civil war is even more dangerous for reporters than a conventional war. Because the press doesn't devote enough resources to foreign coverage, and because most reporters sent in for quick coverage don't understand the country's language, history, and culture, the result is confusion—a confusion compounded by films that produce more ideological heat than factual light.

Secretary of State Alexander Haig had cautioned: "Communist countries are orchestrating an intensive disinformation campaign to cover their intervention while discrediting the Salvadoran government and American support for that government."

The administration further stimulated interest by issuing in February 1981 a White Paper that purported to prove direct outside intervention from Cuba, Nicaragua, and ultimately the Soviet Union.*

In March of 1981 there were 100 foreign newsmen roaming the streets of San Salvador, the nation's capital, and venturing into the perilous countryside when they dared. Not only were the three networks substantially represented, CBS with three teams, NBC and ABC with two each, but PBS was there and CNN was covering its second war (after Iran-Iraq).

What followed was a scramble that reflected little credit on either the media or the administration. As a demonstration of the U.S. government's ability to direct media attention where and when it desired, the blanketing of El Salvador was disconcerting.** As an instance of the confusion and contradictory signals that could come from such a media concern, the rush was equally upsetting.

In March 1981 the network newscast coverage of El Salvador totaled 59 reports lasting a cumulative 134½ minutes. By April, when the temper of the public toward intervention in El Salvador had been demonstrated as uncertain, the number of network reports had dropped to 16 for a total of 29½ minutes. In May and June the validity of the State Department White Paper was seriously questioned, most conspicuously by Jonathan Kwitny in *The Wall Street Journal*.

Meanwhile the American public had been told that El Salvador was another Nicaragua, another Cuba, another Viet-

*When asked if the White Paper was a return to the domino theory, Haig told ABC News, "I wouldn't call it necessarily a domino theory. I would call it a priority target list—a hit list, if you will—for takeover of Central America."

**Another notable example of such manipulation was President Carter's promotion and then sudden silence about the crisis over alleged Soviet ground troops in Cuba in September 1979.

nam; that the right-wing military was murdering the civilian population; that the left-wing guerrillas and terrorists were doing the same; that President José Napoleón Duarte was a hero; that he was a tool in the hands of the hard-line right; that he was a dupe of the left; that the administration White Paper was definite proof of the implication of the Soviet Union; that the White Paper was a tissue of lies and forgeries woefully misinterpreted.

PBS' *El Salvador: Another Vietnam*, the result of a six-day visit by a group of independent filmmakers, saw the military as the unquestioned heavy in El Salvador, even if this documentary couldn't quite bring itself to espouse the guerrillas' cause.

Said the narrator, leaning heavily on the Vietnam parallel:

Agrarian reform was designed by U.S. advisers, financed by the U.S. government, and is being implemented by the Salvadoran military. . . . Land titles have been given to only 500 peasants, most of them members of ORDEN, the rural paramilitary death squad. Only 15 percent of El Salvador's farmland has been converted to cooperatives and agrarian reform has become little more than a pretext for terrorizing the countryside—what U.S. advisers in Vietnam called "pacification." . . . The entire population has become a target for the Salvadoran Army.

ABC's *20/20* took a less outspoken, more humanitarian approach. "What really bothers me," Democratic Congresswoman Barbara Mikulski of Maryland told ABC's cameras, "is that American military aid has been used to kill people, to spy on people, and to hurt people, and I don't believe that the people of the United States want to see their money being spent to help a military kill and rape women."

Sander Vanocur, ABC's diplomatic correspondent in Washington, resisted the Vietnam metaphor:

To pursue comparisons between Vietnam and El Salvador diverts attention from the real purpose of present American policy, which is to use El Salvador as a pawn, a symbol in a new international chess game of geopolitical power, a game in which the United States intends to block Soviet and Cuban activities in the Third World, whenever and wherever it can. This doctrine, which can be called "The Haig Doctrine," will be a major undertaking, especially if after

El Salvador it's applied to some nation far from our shores, some place like Angola. Then comparisons between that and Vietnam can be properly raised. But for the moment, such comparisons are not very useful. El Salvador is not another Vietnam.

CNN reporter Mike Boettcher, who delivered a series of short, telling vignettes on the war to his comparatively small cable news audience, said, "In El Salvador most victims of the unrest die from isolated acts of terrorism and not on the battlefield. . . . In the mountainous countryside radical death squads are terrorizing the people. . . . Hidden in these hills are training camps where radical leftists are trained to fight radical rightists. Murder has become a way of life in this rugged country."

The conservative press watchdog, Accuracy in Media, bought the Vietnam analogy, at least with a reverse twist. Reed Irvine, AIM's chief, wrote:

The same techniques that were used to defeat us in Vietnam are being used to try to keep us from saving El Salvador. The battlefield is in the media. And the cards are stacked against us. Just how badly stacked they were was brought home to me as I watched Walter Cronkite interviewing President Reagan on CBS television. Uncle Walter, who contributed a great deal to our defeat in Vietnam, was doing his level best to push the idea that El Salvador posed the threat of another Vietnam. Reagan wasn't buying that. But even the President can be overwhelmed by the steady drumfire of the media when they are out to make a point.

Irvine dismissed the PBS documentary as "unbalanced leftist propaganda" and accused *20/20* of being an "obvious disinformation channel. . . ."

Perhaps the most reasonable reporting on El Salvador came, surprisingly, from a local station—KING-TV Seattle, home town of Mark Pearlman, one of the murdered land reformers. Reporter Don McGaffin and cameraman Randy Partin spent three weeks traveling to mountainous jungle villages, and were captured and held for 36 hours at gunpoint by guerrillas. McGaffin's summing up would not please partisans of either side. "Communism is not here yet and there is certainly no democracy," said McGaffin. "El Salvador's President José Duarte is probably the only moderate in the country. Those on the right support the various armies. Those on the left are guerrillas who live in the hills and who seem dedicated to destroying the country. Between the left and the right they've effectively destroyed the middle."

The McGaffin reports ran for a week in five segments totaling 37 minutes on KING's early evening news, then were edited into a prime-time documentary. "Now that we have more time for news," said McGaffin, "I think it is important that more and more local stations report on things outside their area."

Indeed, a growing list of local stations were sending reporters overseas. In addition to KING, WBAL Baltimore sent a crew to El Salvador, landing an interview with President Duarte, and KMOL San Antonio visited not only El Salvador but also central Mexico to inform its 50 percent Hispanic audience of similar problems arising there. WTVJ Miami, WGR Buffalo, and WPXI Pittsburgh all sent crews to Poland to cover the confrontation between the labor union Solidarity and the government. KTRK Houston accompanied city officials to Germany to study mass transit systems in several cities. WBBM Chicago and WKYC Cleveland both took their cameras to Japan to explore production techniques in that country's seemingly miraculous auto industry. WABC New York did a series following up on the earthquake that destroyed several mountain villages in southern Italy. WBBH Ft. Myers, Florida followed the path of one Haitian refugee who fled his poverty-stricken homeland in a leaking boat and ended up unemployed and disappointed in southern Florida. And KGO San Francisco hired a 747 to fly its cameras and $300,000 worth of supplies and food it helped raise in the Bay Area to starvation-ravaged Somalia.

In commenting on El Salvador, Hodding Carter brought up questions that extended beyond the problems of collecting information in out-of-the-way places and getting it on the air.

Who are the enemies of the people of El Salvador? Whatever the answer to that question, the enemy of dependable judgment everywhere is ignorance. And it's up to the press to do battle with that enemy. It should devote more reporters, more time and space: more depth and breadth to the complexities of foreign news. . . . The press can well afford it. But an open secret in the press today is that it is doing less rather than more about foreign coverage. That is because it would rather give people news they want than news they need. And if that philosophy prevails, the press will inevitably continue to dance too often to the government's tune. The result: We will be unprepared when one of a dozen other possible El Salvadors explodes tomorrow.

The solution Carter presented to his viewers was not a simple one:

What can you do about it? It is difficult to fully understand what is happening in El Salvador if you depend upon only one source of information. The press does not speak with one voice. No one has a corner on wisdom, about El Salvador or anything else. There may be people who don't want to be disturbed by the facts. They think they already know the truth. But if you aren't one of them, you must prod the press for better foreign coverage, and prod yourself into looking harder at what is already available.

Hodding Carter was simply asking, in different words, the questions being asked with increasing frequency about the news business in general. Whom am I to believe? Who is telling the truth?

Among the public and newsmen alike, credibility had become the most talked-about issue in journalism.

3

Broadcaster vs. Broadcaster: Credibility I

O_N APRIL 20, 1981, WBBM-TV, the CBS owned-and-operated station in Chicago, took an unprecedented action. It preempted a full hour of its precious Monday evening prime time to air what might seem to some a low inside blow at its network competition, to others an unwarranted exposure of everyone's dirty linen. Actually it was an attempt to consider, in full public view, matters that had been bothering TV journalists and their critics for many seasons.

The program, entitled *Watching the Watchdogs*, was anchored by WBBM's top investigative reporter Bill Kurtis. (For his statement on matters discussed in this chapter see page 223). Kurtis concentrated principally on a year-old segment of ABC's network magazine *20/20*, which had just been awarded an Emmy for investigative reporting. The segment, called "Arson for Profit," purported to reveal the misbehavior of a Chicago landlord and his associates who were alleged to have bought and burned buildings to collect the insurance. 29 fires and 10 deaths, according to the ABC report, had resulted.

Despite its award, *20/20's* 30-minute treatment of a familiar subject seemed fairly typical of TV magazine fare. But Kurtis' accusations against it were grave. Not only was the segment inaccurate and misleading, he claimed, but the man-

47

ner in which the facts were gathered and their presentation on the screen were highly questionable. "Have the demands for investigative reporting," Kurtis asked, "produced pressures and techniques which are doing more to distort the truth . . . than reveal it? We feel the time has come to look at ourselves and the techniques we use. And there is no better place to do that than Chicago."*

The techniques Kurtis questioned had unpleasant labels: the ambush interview, entrapment, misrepresentation, invasion of privacy, the use of undercover reporters. Most of these practices, in Kurtis' view, were aimed not at uncovering essential information but at getting dramatic, audience-grabbing pictures on the tube.

As an example of the ambush interview, a favorite among TV's investigative brotherhood, Kurtis showed *20/20* star Geraldo Rivera surprising his target landlord as he came out of a restaurant, bombarding him with unwelcome questions and getting a deadpan denial of any guilt. No fair, said Kurtis. The landlord, however shady, should have been given adequate warning.

Kurtis also showed *20/20* Producer Peter Lance misrepresenting himself as a potential purchaser of a derelict building and entrapping an insurance inspector by giving him $100 on camera in exchange for a favorable report.

Kurtis pointed out other flaws. The credentials of the arson expert invoked by *20/20* were faulty. The landlord, claimed Kurtis, did not receive insurance payments on some of the buildings that *20/20* said he had. And the insurance inspector, who had approved the landlord's properties and was given the $100 by Producer Lance, had never before taken a bribe,

---

*WBBM was not the only Chicago station to offer an extended critique of TV news. Three-and-a-half months before, WTTW-TV, Chicago's public TV station, gave its first airing to an hour-long independent production called *Six O'Clock and All's Well*. Begun in 1977 by New York University senior Robert Spencer, the documentary was completed in 1979 and had made the rounds for nearly two years before finding a broadcast outlet. It was a devastating inside look at how one local TV news show (in this case ABC's flagship New York station WABC's *Eyewitness News*) was put together.

according to his former employers, thus raising the possibility that *20/20* rather than uncovering corruption, had created it.

As the *coup de grâce* Kurtis reported that, "After a 16-month investigation involving six agencies, federal, state, and private; after agents reviewed thousands of real estate records, bank accounts, tax and fire records, in addition to having all the research material turned up by the Better Government Association* and *20/20*, a federal grand jury did not find enough evidence of arson for profit for even one indictment."

The final irony was that Producer Lance had refused to be interviewed, a gesture usually assumed by investigative reporters to be an admission of guilt.

Kurtis presented further examples of entrapment, invasion of privacy, and misrepresentation, including some from his own network, and pointed out a possible motive for such behavior that involved all broadcasters, network and local alike. "During the ratings period," Kurtis said, "the television stations are at each other's throats, hoping to turn up shocking exposés at just the right moment to draw the attention of the audience."

Finally Kurtis invoked the late Edward R. Murrow, who had said, "If it [TV] is to serve and survive, it must hold a mirror behind the nation and the world. . . . The mirror must have no curves and must be held with a steady hand."

"We conclude this report," Kurtis went on, "in the same spirit . . . hoping the examination of the investigative techniques we have seen in the last hour will help keep the hand of broadcasting steady and the mirror straight."

Although the program was broadcast only locally, the ABC network was every bit as righteously indignant as an entrapped landlord. Labeling it "irresponsible" and "scurrilous, shoddy journalism," ABC promptly issued a point-by-point rebuttal of WBBM-TV's charges and in less than a

---

*The BGA, which helped *20/20* gather its evidence, is a nonprofit agency that has been investigating public and private misbehavior in Chicago for the past 50 years. Other BGA and *20/20* collaborations included investigations of abortion clinics, shelter care homes for former mental patients, hazardous cargoes, and unnecessary surgery.

month was back with its own reflections on the WBBM attack. Also an hour in length, the rebuttal was broadcast in the *20/20* time slot on ABC's owned-and-operated station in Chicago.

"Tonight we will show that in fact. . . . it was WBBM and Bill Kurtis who were wrong," said *20/20* host Hugh Downs. "We will review some of the evidence [as] we presented [it] in our original broadcast. And we will present new evidence that has surfaced *since* our story first went on the air. Evidence that Bill Kurtis chose to ignore."

In addition to reaffirming the original premise that the landlord selected was indeed guilty of arson for profit and giving new proof that should have been of interest not only to WBBM but to the municipal authorities as well, ABC went on to point out—with considerable justification—that indictability is not necessarily a criterion for a viable journalistic investigation.

Rivera's "ambush interview," Downs claimed, had been followed by three attempts to set up a formal sitdown interview with the aggrieved landlord "in which his story could have been told in full. He declined."

ABC also showed an example of "an ambush interview" conducted by *Watching the Watchdogs* Producer Scott Craig the previous year.

WBBM, Downs said, had indulged in selective editing, another accusation frequently made against TV investigators, and pointed out that one of the most flagrant examples of TV invasion of privacy involved WCBS, WBBM's sister station in New York, which had been ordered by a jury to pay $250,000 in punitive damages for barging unannounced into a flossy New York restaurant cited for municipal code violations.*

To top it all off, Reporter Kurtis and Producer Craig had refused to be interviewed for ABC's rebuttal.

Hugh Downs concluded, ". . . We welcome any responsible, thorough, well-documented criticism of our work. Tonight we have examined WBBM's work and we found . . . several factual errors and a number of partial truths and, as we

---

*Upon appeal the case was dropped by the restaurant with WCBS paying no damages.

showed, considerable selective editing. We found that the men who were watching the watchdogs, themselves deserved to be watched."

If it weren't a matter of one distorted and unsteady mirror facing another with an endless corridor of imperfect reflections resulting, it was certainly a classic example of people domiciled in glass houses heaving stones at one another.

The interchange couldn't have taken place at a more appropriate moment. The week before Kurtis and WBBM had gone on the air with their indictment of ABC's Emmy Award winner, Janet Cooke of the *Washington Post,* the winner of a Pulitzer Prize for feature writing, had, in one tumultuous 48-hour stretch, lost her prize, her job, and her reputation by admitting, under duress, that her winning story of Jimmy, an eight-year-old Washington heroin addict, had been a figment of her imagination. Hard upon Cooke's, the *Post*'s and Pulitzer's moments of truth, Teresa Carpenter of the *Village Voice,* Cooke's replacement as Pulitzer winner, was in her turn accused of misrepresentation in her account of the murder of Allard Lowenstein, one of her prize-winning submissions. Then in early May one of the New York *Daily News'* favorite reporters, Michael Daly, resigned under pressure after quoting an outspoken and apparently imaginary British Tommy in a column filed from strife-torn Belfast. Two weeks later ABC's flagship station in New York dismissed five employees, including the station program director and a top producer, for concocting phony letters to be answered on three of its local shows.

This cluster of misadventures may not have permanently compromised the media's credibility. However, it did indicate that the honeymoon between the public and journalism's growing horde of gumshoes and muckrakers, including the most conspicuous practitioners of all—the stars of the top-rated network magazine show—might be drawing to a close. Reportorial behavior that at one time might have been considered clever and resourceful was now looked upon as vaguely disreputable. And television, journalism's dominant medium, was perceived as the principal offender.

For over a decade TV had built a reputation as the revealer

of disturbing and frequently unwelcome truths. Beginning
with the civil rights disturbances of the '60's, carrying on
through Vietnam and Watergate to the point where the
environmental crusade met the energy crisis head-on at
Three Mile Island, television had become not only the nation's
number one source of news but its principal fault finder and
bearer of bad tidings.

Calling television to task for its journalistic behavior and
challenging its credibility had begun long before the video
magazine became the most widely distributed news purveyor
in history. As early as 1970 the National Commission on the
Causes and Prevention of Violence had questioned TV's performance from one side, and Spiro Agnew had attacked from
the other. The Nixon Administration chose broadcast journalism as one of its principal and possibly most vulnerable
adversaries and set out to subvert it. By 1971 such programs as
The Selling of the Pentagon on commercial TV and *Banks and the
Poor* on public broadcasting had also raised hackles in the
military and business communities. The TV investigator was
under serious fire and noticeably losing ground.

Watergate changed all that, not only discrediting the
media's most conspicuous detractors but boosting investigative journalism to an unheard-of prominence. But after half a
dozen years of having its own way, television was long overdue
for reassessment. So its critics contended.

4 ✍

Business
vs.
Broadcasters:
Credibility II

A YEAR BEFORE Chicago's Bill Kurtis delivered his unkind cuts against ABC, Kaiser Aluminum & Chemical Corporation had taken a full-page ad in 12 newspapers to protest a *20/20* segment entitled "Hot Wire" in which Geraldo Rivera accused the company of intentionally marketing unsafe aluminum wiring and withholding information about the product's performance. Headed TRIAL BY TELEVISION, the ad began:

The American system of justice is founded on a simple principle: The accused has the right to be fairly heard in his own defense, and to confront and cross examine his accuser.

This principle, more than any other, defines the difference between freedom and tyranny.

Yet today, here in America, charges are aired before tens of millions of people without fair opportunity for the accused to respond.

They call it "investigative" television journalism. We call it "Trial by Television."

Much of investigative television journalism is solid and responsible reporting—but much is not. Many producers of "news magazine" programs too frequently select story segments with their minds already made up about the points they want to make. Then they proceed to select the facts and quotes which support their case. "Interview" opportunities are sometimes provided the "accused."

But the edited "interview" format puts the producer (i.e. the accuser) in full control of deciding what portions, and how much, of the accused's defense the public will be allowed to see.

Rarely does this result in balanced and objective coverage.

The television production team becomes the accuser, judge, and jury. With no real recourse for the accused to get a fair hearing in the court of public opinion. Yet the viewing public is led to believe that the coverage is balanced and objective. This is a deceptive and very dangerous practice.

"Trial by Television," like the kangaroo courts and star chambers of old, needs to be examined. If we decide, as a society, that we are going to try issues, individuals, and institutions on television, then some way must be found to introduce fairness and balance.

Kaiser proposed to do something about it. Namely:

1. Demand a satisfactory retraction from ABC-TV.
2. Ask the FCC under its "Personal Attack" doctrine to order ABC-TV to provide Kaiser with time and facilities to present its side of the story to the same size audience in a prime-time segment.
3. Ask the chairman of the House Subcommittee on Communications to "consider congressional hearings to examine the implications of this increasingly insidious and dangerous practice."

The ad concluded: "America was conceived to prevent tyranny by providing checks on the power of any institution. Today, a new power is dispensing its own brand of justice—television. There's only one check against it. You." There followed an invitation to the reader to write his congressman or Kaiser to express his shared concern.

Kaiser was not the only target of the TV magazines to fight back. When *60 Minutes* came to investigate Illinois Power Company's embattled Clinton atomic energy plant in September 1979, the utility had the foresight to have its own cameras on the scene. Eight days after Harry Reasoner's blistering report on Clinton's pyramiding costs—"Who Pays? You Do"—aired on the CBS network, IP had completed its own 42-minute tape, including the original *60 Minutes* segment. "*60 Minutes*/Our Reply" gave IP's side of the story complete with documentation of what it claimed were seven out-right CBS errors and several misleading statements. IP's show was available to anyone who was willing to send a blank vid-eocassette in exchange.

In January 1980 Mike Wallace acknowledged on the air two factual errors in the original report. However, that did not diminish the number of requests for IP's version, which by the fall of 1981 totaled more than 2,500 from corporations such as General Electric and General Motors, chambers of commerce, other utility companies, and journalism schools in the United States and overseas. A bid to air the show on Ted Turner's Atlanta superstation WTBS, with a potential national audi-ence of several million, was turned down at the last minute because of copyright problems. However, blank tapes con-tinued to arrive at IP's headquarters at the rate of 25 a week through 1981.

Another utility, Pacific Gas and Electric, whose controver-sial Diablo Canyon nuclear facility was scheduled for investi-gation by *60 Minutes,* attempted to go IP one better, not only demanding the right to tape all interviews independently but
· to select any subject raised in the program and comment on it on the air unedited. *60 Minutes* acquiesced to PG&E's cameras being on hand but refused the demand for the unedited comments. There was no PG&E cooperation thereafter, and as of December 1981 the Diablo Canyon segment had yet to go on the air.*

"The Uranium Factor," an ABC News *Closeup* examining the uranium industry in New Mexico, was aired in April 1980. In rebuttal, some outraged locals, calling themselves Ameri-cans for Rational Energy Alternatives, produced their own videotape entitled "Uranium: Fact or Fiction." The videotape dismissed the ABC documentary as inaccurate and unneces-sarily alarmist. It was available on loan for a $15 fee for postage and handling from The Media Institute in Washing-

*PG&E had a longstanding record of challenging the media, the most conspicuous instance being its attack on documentarian Don Widener and his hour-long program *Powers that Be.* Widener sued for libel, and after being awarded a record $7.75 million judgment against the utility, he finally collected a scaled-down $300,000.

ton. By October 1981, 325 copies had been distributed to
journalism schools from coast to coast and it had been aired on
eight TV stations, both public and commercial.

Most conspicuous and consistent among those business
spokesmen tilting at TV's antennae was Mobil Oil's Vice President
Herbert Schmertz, who began publicly talking back to
the networks in 1974. Since then Schmertz had been challenging
the media's facts and accusing them of everything from
bad faith to bad journalism—which in his eyes included selective
editing, superficiality, a flagrant antibusiness bias, and just
plain stupidity. Among his recurring complaints was the fact
that although he could air his challenges and grievances in
newspapers and magazines, in speeches and public hearings,
he was not permitted to do so on the networks. "The most
powerful communications medium yet devised," said one of
Mobil's full-page ads, "will let you sell dog food and blue jeans,
but never an idea dealing with a controversial subject of public
importance. Not even an argument about such an idea. Not
even facts if they are remotely connected with such an idea. To
the television networks, controversial issues are objects of
taboo that may be approached only by a special tribe: their
own broadcast journalists." (For a further sampling of
Schmertz's views, see page 214).

Schmertz was spending $7.5 million a year on issue advertising,
a large part of which went to correct and scold the media.
This jumbo expenditure bought Mobil, according to the
Sierra Club's Michael McCloskey, a reputation as "the most
antagonistic and outspoken of the oil companies. . . . Abrasive,
high-profile . . . bound to have its way at any cost." Nor
were Schmertz and his fellow businessmen isolated voices of
protest.

John McKinney, the belligerent and beleaguered head of
Johns-Manville, the nation's leading producer of asbestos,
which had been repeatedly pilloried in recent years as a
leading cause of lung cancer, took out after his principal tormentors
in a freewheeling interview in *The Wall Street Journal*.
He dismissed the lawyers of people claiming asbestos-related
illnesses as "ambulance chasers," the government regulators

who had projected that 13 to 18 percent of all cancer deaths would be asbestos-related in the next 30 to 35 years as "charlatans and pipsqueaks who have to go up on the Hill for their budgets and show they've slain some dragons," and reporters simply as "incompetent and dishonest."

"We used to go on all shows, no questions asked," according to Johns-Manville spokesman Curtis Linke, "but now we will not grant interviews, or appear, or be quoted unless we have established ground rules in advance. We must know the format, the other guests, and the general line of questioning, and if any of those things change, we can cancel out or simply walk off the program. We've sunk so low in public opinion polls that we have nothing to lose anymore. We can afford to take that tough stance."

Following the Janet Cooke hoax, the Gallup organization ran a poll on the news media and found that for honesty and ethics the respondents placed journalists fourth in a field of seven, well below clergymen, physicians, and police, a little above businessmen, and far above congressmen and advertising executives. 33 percent thought reporters often made things up.

Daniel Schorr, who had spent four years on the road following his separation from CBS News, reported back:

The public is almost in a state of rage against the news media . . . when they talked about the press once, and the power of the press, it was very white hat . . . power of the press was the power against evil. Power of the news media has a completely different meaning to most people. It is a power to manipulate *them*. It is a power that is used against them. . . . Once the government was the chief source of complaint. The government was on their backs. . . . Now, oddly enough, they're beginning to substitute the news media as the hate object instead of the government.

Gallup and Yankelovich polls reported a mounting percentage of citizens who wanted laws to force the communications media to be more accurate and to be more fair.

Although a *Television/Radio Age* poll of TV news directors

reported that half felt that such episodes as the WBBM—*20/ 20* hassle had definitely hurt TV news credibility, there were others such as Mary C. McCarthy, news director of WFBC-TV, Greenville, South Carolina, who felt such an encounter was "a very healthy form of media criticism, as well as competition. . . . The hard light of competitive, deep-searching criticism is one which will benefit the viewers."

Eric Sevareid projected the problem onto a wider stage: "The normal, conventional, traditional messages from government, the church, educational institutions, have become in this country rather faint and confusing and contradictory. They've lost their force. So the press, print and broadcast, have come to occupy a position larger than what their rightful size ought to be. They're too big for their britches. And with this has come a great deal of personalization of journalism, and a certain arrogance going with it."

The objects of all this analysis and indignation were not unmoved by such attacks. Already in November 1980 ABC had caused a flurry in the TV news community by offering Kaiser Aluminum four unedited minutes on *20/20* in response to the corporation's complaints of unfair treatment. (Kaiser had originally demanded ten.) Such a capitulation had no TV precedent, and an unidentified ABC producer was quoted by *The Wall Street Journal* as saying, "All something like this can do is harm our credibility."

Three months later the powers that be at ABC reneged on their commitment to Kaiser. In February 1981 the network announced, "We believe that *Nightline,* not *20/20,* is the appropriate forum for a full airing of both the subject of aluminum wiring safety and the broader issues of 'response time' and 'access.'"

Pushed out of the prime time where the original attack took place, Kaiser said nothing doing. Instead, it filed a $40 million suit for slander and announced that it would request the FCC to order ABC to provide "appropriate response time." Kaiser's action prompted sharp editorial comment in *Broadcasting* magazine:

A considerable peril to journalistic independence is implied if a corporation that feels wronged in a news broadcast can run to a receptive FCC with complaints of unfairness or unjust criticism; especially if, as in Kaiser's case, the corporation has refused to be interviewed in the preparation of the offending newscast. Let the FCC begin routinely acting as referee in disagreements between journalism organizations and journalism subjects, and the enfeeblement of journalism is inevitable.

The FCC shuffled Kaiser's petition and eventually sent it back, asking Kaiser to make a stronger case. Kaiser complied, adding extensive documentation of the network's treatment of the aluminum wiring controversy in the past.

On July 24, 1981, nearly 16 months after the offending broadcast, Kaiser's four minutes finally got on the air. It was not, however, on *20/20* or *Nightline* but on a one-hour ABC program called *Viewpoint,* which anchorman Ted Koppel introduced as "an experiment in television news . . . an attempt to give a few of our critics a forum on network television in which they can respond to real or perceived injustices done to them by network television." The program was aired at 10 P.M. EDT, at the heart of network prime time.

Kaiser had to share the spotlight with other malcontents— blacks, Arabs, women against ERA, and big business in general (which was represented by cameo appearances by Hooker Chemical's ex-president Don Baeder, Chase Manhattan's David Rockefeller and Mobil Oil's peripatetic Schmertz). Kaiser's four minutes were followed by nearly seven minutes during which Geraldo Rivera contradicted most of the principal points Kaiser tried to make.

Nonetheless Kaiser was delighted. It withdrew its FCC complaint against ABC, let its $40 million suit fall dormant and took full-page ads in *Broadcasting* and *The Columbia Journalism Review* proclaiming GOOD NEWS:

ABC-TV, in what we considered to be a milestone of responsible broadcast journalism, has developed an innovative technique to allow the other side to be heard in a balanced and fair way. . . . We were pleased to be a part of that program and to have the opportunity to present in our own way our response to the charges made against us by *20/20* before a prime-time audience.*

Only the first edition of *Viewpoint,* however, would be in prime time. The next *Viewpoint* was aired in October 1981 in the *Nightline* slot and, henceforth, would be seen there four times a year.

Two months after the first *Viewpoint* aired, CBS' *60 Minutes,* another major offender against fairness—or so many in the business community contended—opened its 1981–82 season with a forum on the problems brought up by Kurtis and Kaiser. Again on hand was Mobil's vice president, Herb Schmertz, along with Ellen Goodman, columnist of the *Boston Globe,* Eugene Patterson, editor of the *St. Petersburg Times,* and *60 Minutes* executive producer Don Hewitt. Although the squaring off between business and broadcasting was less overtly an issue this time, the problems of what is permissible in pursuing a story were discussed with surprising frankness.

Mike Wallace introduced the evening:

Investigative reporting conjures up images of going undercover, going underground, using anonymous sources, confronting the object of one's inquiry with surprise witnesses and surprise documents. And investigative reporting raises serious questions. Is it right to confront reluctant witnesses with cameras and microphones? Should we withhold vital information from a prospective interviewee? Is it proper to pose as someone other than a reporter to get a story? Is it fair for us to set up our own enterprise—a bar, a clinic, a "sting" operation, in effect—to lure unsuspecting

---

20/20 remained the target for most objections to ABC news and public affairs. Also on the first *Viewpoint* was an editorial blast against the ABC magazine program for a piece in which it joined forces with local law enforcement authorities to uncover fraudulent insurance sales in Iowa. Written by Michael Gartner, editor and president of the *Des Moines Register and Tribune,* the complaint was read on the air by Ted Koppel: "I am aghast, appalled, and disgusted. For decades, news organizations, print and broadcast, have been babbling in the courts to establish the principle of independence. In case after case, we have argued that we gather information solely for our own purposes. Now, along comes ABC, which willingly acts as an investigative arm of a government agency, gathering evidence for the state of Iowa, and demolishing in one swift stroke the wall that should exist between the press and the government."

subjects before our cameras? Is it appropriate, is it fair, to infiltrate a factory, a labor union, to find out what is really going on inside . . . ?

The guests were then shown various clips from *60 Minutes* broadcasts that illustrated some of the program's most controversial techniques. The discussions that followed were heated. Of a *60 Minutes* researcher who falsified her identity to prove how easy it was to get a U. S. passport, Ellen Goodman said:

You're saying that in the pursuit of deceit, deceit is okay; that, as journalists, we have the right to use untruths because we are going for a greater truth. . . . Was the pursuit of the story, was the untruth that you were covering, great enough to warrant behaving illegally? Was there no other way to pursue that story?

Patterson added:

There are ways to have covered this story. The Passport Office investigative force probably had case history after case history that *60 Minutes* could have followed up on.

Hewitt's reply:

Which is the more honest reporting—taking the word of people who said this happened to them, or going out and showing it happen? . . . I think it comes down to that.

Following a clip in which a *60 Minutes* soundman posed as a wealthy leukemia victim in order to infiltrate a phony California cancer clinic, Patterson objected:

It's a good story, it's great television, it's terrible journalism. The way you go at that story before you, as a last resort, go phony . . . is to find people who have been victimized by that cancer clinic, which is the way journalism operates. . . . Why couldn't you make your story out of those people?

Hewitt's answer:

Because, whereas newspaper readers are convinced when they read interviews with people, television viewers, to be convinced, want as much documentation as you can give them. This is the only way that we could document that what we were being told by those people was, in fact, true, and the only way we could convince viewers that it was, in fact, true.

Later Hewitt summed up:

I think this probably all comes down to a very simple proposition: Does the end justify the means? We are in the business of providing our viewers with documentary evidence of wrongdoing, misdeeds, and we can do it better this way than we can if Mike Wallace gets on camera and says, "Let me tell you what happened to me last week in Chicago."*

If no one finally won the debate, there seemed to be general agreement with Schmertz who said, "This was a very important show . . . a landmark show. . . . The fact that *60 Minutes* is eager to . . . sit and examine these kinds of things, I think, is an amazing development."**

Meanwhile other opportunities for business to state its case were opening up. According to an Opinion Research Corporation survey quoted in a Mobil ad, 85 percent of the American public thought corporations should be allowed to present their views on controversial issues in TV commercials, a 13 percent increase in two years. The TV Bureau of Advertising reported that 89 percent of TV stations were willing to accept advocacy advertising, up from 50 percent five years before. Already an estimated $100 million was being spent on issue advertising annually. All this despite the fact that until the summer of 1981 none of the three networks would permit such messages on the air.

As of July 1, ABC opened its schedule to issue advertising on an experimental basis. The ads would be limited to 60

---

*If Hewitt wanted further justification, he could have pointed to one of the big TV stories of the year, the ABSCAM scandals in which impersonation and deceit were the principal tactics used in getting evidence against eight members of Congress and other politicians who proved susceptible to the blandishments of FBI operatives posing as Arabs.
**Despite ABC's *Viewpoint* and this *60 Minutes* edition on CBS, as of November 1981, NBC had no announced plans for giving time to its critics.

seconds each (two per customer per week) and be excluded from the immediate vicinity of the news.

TV Guide applauded ABC's initiative. "Television ought to function as an open marketplace of ideas," the magazine editorialized. "The more divergent the views expressed on the air, the better informed a viewer will be. Besides, if you can endure the relentless barrage of commercials touting Brand X or Brands Y and Z, then you should be able to sort through more soberly argued broadsides on the economy, abortion, energy, and defense."

Not everyone was so enthusiastic. Charles Rembar, writing in the March 1981 *Atlantic Monthly,* doubted that "the use of wealth to amplify voices furthers freedom of speech. I suggest it does the opposite. Speech and press must have an audience . . . degrees of audibility have to be considered. First Amendment freedoms are defeated when one of two conflicting arguments reaches a great many people while the other reaches few."

There were many examples where the injection of corporate money seemed to tip the balance unfairly. In 1980 the Media Access Project published a study that found a "strong correlation" between broadcast expenditures and the number of votes received in three initiatives in Colorado in 1976. The Council on Economic Priorities, which studies initiative campaigns on issues directly affecting corporate interest, found that in 1978 eight of 12 such campaigns were won by the side that business had backed. Business had outspent its opponents in some of these initiatives by as much as 100 to 1. And the pattern was continuing in the 1980s. For example, a $5 million war chest was raised by big oil to fight Proposition 11, the proposed tax on oil company profits, which was on the California ballot in June 1981. Backers of the measure had been able to raise only about $314,000. The proposition was defeated.

Traditionally, the Fairness Doctrine, which required radio and TV stations to give equal time to opposing viewpoints on controversial issues, was the principal protection against money tipping the balance where the coverage of issues was concerned. But in September 1981 the new chairman of the

Federal Communications Commission, Mark Fowler, in his push to "unregulate" the industries under his jurisdiction, proposed that the Fairness Doctrine be eliminated.

For good or bad, if there was a market for issue advertising on network TV, it obviously was not in the limited form offered by the ABC experiment. As of November 1981 the network reported not a single taker. Nor was there any sign that either CBS or NBC intended to accept advocacy ads.*

There was, however, evidence that business was getting increasing space across an ever-widening electronic spectrum. The syndicated Independent Network News offered on its nightly newscast a two-minute slot called *Business Report,* sponsored by *The Wall Street Journal* and taken from the Dow Jones wire. The Cable News Network offered three different regular programs on business—*Money Line,* a half hour on weeknights featuring news on world economics, expert commentaries, and financial trends; *West Coast Report,* which offered a half-hour of updated financial news to the western half of the country every weeknight; and *Inside Business,* a weekend half hour in which members of the business press discussed economic issues with corporate and government leaders.

Promising to be even more sympathetic, if somewhat less objective, was the United States Chamber of Commerce's Business Advocate Satellite Network, which was to be produced out of a new $2 million facility in Washington and was scheduled to go on the air five hours a day before the 1982 elections. The Chamber already produced its own half-hour weekly TV show, *It's Your Business,* which was carried on 151 stations. It had a weekly half hour, *What's the Issue?,* heard on 300 radio stations on the Mutual network.

Beginning November 30, 1981, the Financial News Network, launched by Three Ring Productions of Santa Monica,

---

*At an industry forum on advocacy advertising in autumn 1981 former CBS News President Richard Salant responded to a call for advocacy ads as an answer to unfair or unbalanced treatment of issues on network news: "If you need issue advertising to offset perceived journalistic errors . . . you're in trouble." Salant saw the answer in the creation of some kind of "journalistic access," the equivalent of print's letters to the editor or op-ed pages.

California, went on the satellite to UHF and cable outlets in 13 markets from 10 A.M. to 5 P.M. daily.

Treatment of business on the three commercial networks remained a matter of debate. The Media Institute, a nonprofit organization dedicated to righting what it saw as a lack of balance between business and its detractors on the air and in print, brought out a study that analyzed prime-time TV entertainment fare and found that "television almost never portrays business as a socially useful or economically productive activity" and that "two out of three businessmen on television are portrayed as foolish, greedy, or criminal." Although this report dealt with entertainment, the Institute had also produced studies showing that the majority of stories on inflation on the evening newscasts came from government spokesmen and tended to exonerate the government from any role in the growth of inflation. Another Institute study claimed that network evening newscasts from 1968 to 1979 provided insufficient information on nuclear energy for viewers rationally to assess risks and benefits and that there was antinuclear bias in the coverage.

Writing in *TV Guide* in the summer of 1980, sociologist Herbert Gans indicated that any negativity about business, if indeed it existed in TV news, was a comparatively recent and limited development.

The news rarely covers the shortcomings of monopolies or multinationals. Until the latest spell of double-digit inflation, high profits were generally reported as good news, and now spokesmen who blame that inflation on the government seem to appear in the news more often than those blaming private enterprise. . . .

Had newscasters ignored the oil profit stories, viewers might have wondered whether they were incompetents or journalists beholden to the oil companies and their massive television advertising. In fact, the story could have been left out only if the newscasters were prepared to lose their most precious resource, their credibility with the viewers.

Paradoxically, it was public broadcasting rather than the commercial networks that gave the business community its best and most widespread outlets.* In the last two seasons, three series, Ben Wattenberg's *At Large* and *1980* and Milton Friedman's *Free to Choose,* beat the drum for capitalism. (John Kenneth Galbraith's liberal series, *The Age of Uncertainty,* was generally conceded to be a less than adequate balance.)

In fall 1981 Eric Sevareid came on as host to *Enterprise,* dedicated to humanizing the U. S. businessman. "This series," said Sevareid, "will not be Chamber of Commerce boosterism, nor will it reflect the antiestablishment syndrome. It will be an effort to report on how various industrial sectors actually work. The idea is to illuminate, not to advocate. Television news has sometimes done well reporting on macroeconomics and on government policies toward business. It has not done well reporting the story of business itself." The series, which comprised 13 half-hour segments, was carried by 260 stations on the Public Broadcasting Service, 56 more than carried *Bill Moyers' Journal.* In October 1981, *The Nightly Business Report* began broadcasting 30 minutes of news and features each weekday evening over PBS.

Also in public broadcasting's pro-business, free enterprise contingent was its maverick outlet in Erie, Pennsylvania, WQLN-TV, which had produced the aforementioned *Free to Choose* as well as a 90-minute alarm against Soviet expansionism, *The War Called Peace.* "I believe in advocacy journalism," said WQLN President Robert J. Chitester. "In many ways, it's a more honest kind of journalism because any human being has a point of view." Other WQLN projects included a special on government spending, an examination of the health-care industry, and an unsympathetic look at the ecology movement.

A spinoff from public TV was a new half-hour weekly show, *Business Journal,* presided over by Louis Rukeyser of *Wall Street Week*—one of PBS's highest rated shows. It would be syndicated by Viacom and sponsored by, among others, American Express. In mid-November 1981, it was booked in 77 markets.

*The paradox may have been partially explained by the fact that PBS was, with more than $27 million in grants, the country's second largest beneficiary of corporate donations in 1980, after the Red Cross.

As for the other side, supposedly favored by TV, a study by three labor unions claimed network news programs strongly favored corporate or big-business positions on five major issues that involved workers. Even NBC Television's *Nightly News,* cited as the fairest by 2,000 union monitors, tilted toward management's position three times as often as it did toward labor's. ABC favored corporate positions five times more frequently than labor positions, and CBS favored business six times as often as it did labor.

The few TV projects that might lean in labor's favor were having difficulty getting off the ground. A proposed 10-episode series of dramas on the history of the labor movement, *Made in U.S.A.,* was stalled for several months by a funding controversy with PBS President Lawrence Grossman, who felt that it would be wrong to have union money backing a show about labor, although corporations regularly backed shows about business. In July 1980 producer Elsa Rassbach and PBS worked out an arrangement where up to one-third of the financing for the $15 million project would come from unions. As of November 1981 Rassbach had the first episode ready for shooting in the spring of 1982, but was still trying to raise the money. Another series called *Ralph Nader: For the People,* on Showtime pay-TV, featured exchanges between Nader and "corporate titans" as well as reports of business abuses. The program premiered in August 1980 and was off the air in September, after only two shows. To compete with the business media blitz, the AFL-CIO was considering forming a Labor Institute for Public Affairs to produce video programming and explore possible uses of new communications technologies. Meanwhile, the American Federation of State, County, and Municipal Employees began videotaping interviews to be provided to TV news shows.

Not content to leave the coverage of news up to networks and local stations, cable and satellite reports or even such obviously friendly operations as the Chamber of Commerce, individual businesses were offering electronic outlets their own pre-packaged versions of the news of the day that particularly concerned them.

For 17 months in 1979 and 1980 Atlantic Richfield Oil

produced a monthly half-hour news magazine on energy-related topics for all TV takers to do with what they would. Put together by a WCBS-TV alumnus, Anthony Hatch, it emanated from a modern, fully equipped studio in Los Angeles and included, along with the anticipatable features on abalone farming next to oil rigs in the Santa Barbara channel, interviews with oil company critics such as Dan Lundberg of the *Lundberg Newsletter* and John Nesbitt of *Trend Report.* The program, called *Energy Update,* reached 160 broadcast and cable outlets in most of the major U. S. markets and was circulated as far afield as Japan.

The point of entry for *Energy Update* was the small under-staffed station. "Most stations do not have the manpower, the resources or the money—and in some cases even the desire—to cover energy," said Hatch. "They cover it on a spot news basis when there are shortages and so on. If this helps an assignment editor, if this helps the science reporter, then I think it's something worthwhile." There were other motives, of course. "I don't believe oil companies have a great deal of credibility," added Hatch. "What I'm trying to do is give us more credibility."

Other companies, including General Motors, showed interest in starting their own versions, and the American Petroleum Institute adopted a similar format, sending out a quarterly videotape with accompanying script for a voice-over for any station to use.

Viewpoint,* a talk show emceed by a former Miss California and actress in television commercials, offered to interview business spokesmen for $6,000 per five-minute segment, asking them whatever questions they might prefer. The results were beamed to 415 cable TV systems.

Not all the spokespeople for these various special pitches were nonjournalists. Indeed, there were a growing number of on-staff, free-lance, or out-of-work reporters who were willing to take on such assignments.

Besides such regular services there was the electronic press release, another gimmick aimed at giving business access to

---

*No relation of the ABC-TV series of the same name.

broadcast news. Again, it was more frequently used by the hard-up small-market station than the highly competitive big city operation.

Industrial films and corporate promotions ranging from 15 to 90 minutes in length continued to make the rounds, slipping into early morning and late evening schedules in the big cities and around the clock in smaller markets. Privately sponsored and produced and furnished free of charge to any outlet that would take them, they were generally considered to be relieved of stringent journalistic standards of fairness and balance. As in issue and advocacy advertising, special emphasis and selective detail were deemed permissible.

Whether these activities were being passed off as bona fide news and public affairs programs or not, because they adopted journalism's form, mannerisms, and personnel, they were frequently perceived as such by the viewing public. Insofar as they fell short of the highest standards of journalism, which their sponsors, with justified indignation, demanded of radio and TV news people, they tended to degrade the informational environment into which they were being inserted.

Robert Rhody, head of public relations for Kaiser and the man responsible for mounting that company's "Trial by Television" campaign, saw the problem in perspective:

Corporations can no longer afford the luxuries of secrecy and silence. . . . Business must be open and willing to risk controversy. Business has to quit being so insensitive and so insular. And businessmen must, at the absolute minimum, quit being so thin-skinned. There's nothing wrong with criticism. We, and our colleagues in the line operations, must recognize that we are in the public arena almost as much as politicians are in the public arena; and criticism, if it is fair, is not only reasonable but appropriate.

When that criticism isn't fair, though, or when the facts aren't right, we owe it to ourselves, our shareholders, our employees, and the public to set the record straight.

Rhody's reasonable approach, however, was rare on both sides.

A survey of chief executive officers, public relations directors and business reporters, commissioned by the American Management Association, underscored the problem. According to the survey, 36 percent of the business journalists think executives "often lie" to reporters; 7 percent of the public relations directors agree. While 71 percent of the executives felt they were "usually accessible," only 27 percent of the reporters thought so. A meager 25 percent of PR directors claimed to be "very open" on sensitive issues, and only 2 percent of the journalists concurred that they were. 35 percent of the PR directors believed that reporters started out on business stories with a slant; 83 percent thought inaccurate stories came more from sloppiness than bias. 73 percent of the businessmen polled thought less than half of the reporters understood the subject they were writing about.

Although there were evidences of a partial truce between broadcast newsmen and their would-be antagonists in the business community, there were indications that the near future might witness a further deterioration. With deregulation all the fashion, the administration was suggesting that the monitoring of misbehavior might be turned over to the private sector. This could mean that the network and local news operations would find themselves having an increasingly important and unpopular role to play in keeping up with lapses on the part of previously regulated industries, including their own.

Even if an accommodation were reached between broadcasting and business, a reconciliation that would seem to be necessary for the future well-being of society as a whole, the two sectors in consort would still have their work cut out for them.

5

Broadcasters
vs.
the Truth:
Credibility III

O N THE EDITORIAL PAGE of its May 1, 1981 issue, *The New York Times* faced up to one of the thorniest problems confronting any journalist today.

There was a time when to describe a fact as "scientific" meant it was demonstrably true. No longer. In these days of bitter controversy over complex issues of health, safety, and environment, every side marshals platoons of experts to present only a version of scientific truth. A confused, often cynical public has learned that there are as many scientific facts as there are sides in a controversy.

Typically, a union's experts will argue that a small concentration of toxic chemicals in the workplace endangers life; mangement's experts will surely pronounce the same substances benign. Environmental scientists will testify that power-plant emissions cause acid rain that harms lakes and foliage downwind; a utility's experts will dispute the connection. And so on. Is there no way in such disputes to reach consensus at least on the facts?

The answer, so far as dozens of subjects the modern reporter had to deal with every day, seemed to be no. Particularly on TV, with its short attention span, its limited time, and its scattershot approach to the news.

In the pursuit of such stories the differences between business and broadcasting were frequently bitter. For the public the distinction between right and wrong, good and bad could disappear in the mutual distrust of the supposed adversaries.

The story of the Love Canal was a vivid example. This middle-class neighborhood in Niagara Falls, New York, had been the subject of hundreds of network and local news items since early in 1978. It had also been the starting point of dozens of extended investigations on the subject of toxic wastes, coast to coast.

In the first horrified weeks of discovery, reporters estimated the number of similarly hazardous disposal sites at 50,000 nationwide. The threat to citizens living on or near them ranged from cancer and birth defects to skin and psychological disorders.

In December 1980 President Carter signed into law the Hazardous Substance Response Trust Fund, which earmarked $1.6 billion for cleaning up the most threatening dump sites. By then 239 families had been evacuated from the immediate vicinity of Love Canal and their homes boarded up. The Hooker Chemical Company, the corporation that had dumped the deadly chemicals, was denounced as irresponsible and deceptive at the best, murderous at the worst.

After three years of conflicting testimony, the responsibility for the possible effects of the dump at Love Canal was still unresolved.

With fact sheets, taped interviews, and TV appearances, the Hooker Chemical Company had established to some persons' satisfaction that it had left Love Canal with the poisons properly sealed in. It was New York State, to which title to the land was transferred along with the proper warning about what lay under it, that had permitted a school and houses to be built near the site.

In the spring of 1981 New York State, without admitting its culpability, released the results of a study that claimed that the most frightening supposed effects of living near Love Canal seemed to be statistically disproved and that there was no discernible difference between the cancer rate there and elsewhere in the state.*

*Dr. Dwight Janerich, director of the New York State Cancer Control Board and author of the study, admitted that his conclusions were necessarily "tentative" because of the long period during which cancer can develop and go undetected.

Louis Banks, ex-editor of *Fortune* and professor of management at the Massachusetts Institute of Technology, denounced the media for "character assassination" in its Love Canal coverage.

Of the estimated 50,000 toxic sites from coast to coast, the Environmental Protection Agency labeled 1,200 to 2,000 "imminent hazards," with the chemical industry setting the number at 300 to 500. In October 1981, 114 sites were designated dangerous enough to require immediate action. At least 20 sites on the list were rated more urgent than Love Canal.

Meanwhile Hooker Chemical, a subsidiary of the multinational conglomerate Occidental Petroleum, had been accused of negligent waste-disposal practices at five other sites. And so it went.

The Agent Orange, Kepone, acid rain, fluorocarbon, PBB, and PCB stories followed a similarly erratic course, with the journalists reporting the gloomy possibilities and those responsible for the dissemination of the toxic substances questioning the facts and the effects, and dismissing both as inconclusive.

After nearly three years, Three Mile Island remained one of the most persistent and disturbing examples of an indecisive three-way encounter among journalism, business, and government.

Since the original incident, in which ill-equipped reporters faced ill-informed and secretive officials, the Three Mile Island story had never been satisfactorily stabilized. Special panels, research projects, and commissions of inquiry on a local, state, and national level seemed to resolve nothing. Rumors of dire effects from the accident were reported, refuted, reaffirmed. What should have been a matter of fact drifted into a murky middle ground where politics and special interest prevailed over clarity. The media, rather than adding light, were handicapped by their own lack of expertise and further confused by the imperative protestations of pro- and antinuclear factions.

Shortly after the Three Mile Island accident, the utility companies and nuclear manufacturers created the Committee for Energy Awareness to counter the expected erosion of support for nuclear power. By 1981 it had a public relations budget of $4 million.* Its media activities included advocacy ads in 19 key markets, carried by 31 TV and 86 radio stations; two half-hour videotapes on energy sent free to local stations; four multipart "news" series of one-and-a-half to two minutes per segment, aired on more than 140 TV stations; distribution of two half-hour films by the Atomic Industrial Forum to be shown in schools and on cable stations; and a "truth squad" of pronuclear scientists that trailed Tom Hayden and Jane Fonda on their visits to local TV and radio shows cross-country.

The antinuclear groups responded to this barrage by forming their own organization called the Safe Energy Communication Council, a coalition of 16 citizens groups concerned with energy and environment. It had a budget of only $22,500 in 1980, and produced one 60-second and four 30-second spot ads at a cost of $17,000. These were shown on 35 radio and TV stations in 15 cities, with the time provided free under the Fairness Doctrine to answer CEA's original ads.

The arrival of a new admittedly pronuclear administration in Washington further complicated matters. Already the broadcasters seemed to be holding back. Energy, the subject of dozens of major take-outs just five years before, had been put on the back burner with no full-scale documentaries on any of the three networks since January 1980.

None of the continuing major stories that modern reporters were faced with—energy, defense, environment, abortion, welfare, criminal justice, even health—seemed spared the necessity of clearing a double hurdle: first, the contradictory nature of the data itself; next, the politics surrounding each issue, with its vigilant and highly distracting special pleaders. Nor did this include the built-in problems of not enough time, not enough money, not enough expertise to do the job properly.

*This sum did not include the public relations budgets of individual utility companies, which were large even before TMI. For instance, according to figures compiled by Environmental Action Foundation, in 1976 the 100 largest electric utilities spent $60,249,548 on advertising and public relations.

Equally disheartening were those stories whose truth was accepted and action taken only to have it threatened with reversal years later. One of the crowning achievements of NBC's early magazine *First Tuesday* was its revelation of the Defense Department's secret chemical biological warfare maneuvers and the dangers they represented even in peacetime to the population at large. Corrective legislation was passed, eleven years went by, and in 1980 KUED-TV Salt Lake City, in its award-winning *The Deadly Winds of War,* revealed that matters had returned very much to where they had been a decade earlier.

And there were the stories, which, no matter how compelling to watch, seemed to have no appreciable effect on the problems they addressed. A particularly poignant example was *Harvest of Shame,* Edward R. Murrow's classic CBS essay on the sorry lot of the migrant farm workers, which was first broadcast in 1960. Ten years later Chet Huntley and Martin Carr went over the same ground in their hour-long, award-winning *Migrant* for NBC and found nothing changed. In 1980 NBC won a new set of awards when it sent reporter Chris Wallace and producer Morton Silverstein south yet again and a whole new TV generation found the identical conditions to report. Concluded Wallace:

It seems the migrants have always been with us . . . a part of our social conscience. As long as most of us can remember. John Steinbeck and Woody Guthrie told us about them in the '30s; Edward R. Murrow and Chet Huntley spoke of them in recent years.

In this program we have reported what we've found to be unchanged. In 1980 the migrants are still the forgotten people. . . . In a few months, the migrants will be back in Florida for the harvest, back to face the crew chiefs, the corporations, and a government that barely recognizes their existence. How many more harvests will it take before we understand that the migrants' shame . . . is our own?

And then just before the final credits the late Chet Huntley flickered back from a decade earlier to say philosophically, "We hope that no one will need to make a film about migrants ten years from now."

If frustrated TV documentarians were looking for an explanation for the lack of consequences of some of their most eloquent statements, they might find it in a $160,000 study of viewer comprehension made in 1980 by the American Association of Advertising Agencies.

The report, submitted by Jacob Jacoby, a consumer psychologist at Purdue University, found that "the vast majority of TV viewers—more than 80 percent—misunderstand some part of what they see, no matter what kind of broadcast they're watching.

"Normally, the range of misunderstanding is between one-fourth and one-third of any broadcast, whether it is an entertainment-news program, commercial, or public-service announcement.

"Regardless of what they are watching, television viewers seem to misunderstand facts equally as much as they misunderstand inferences in a broadcast."

At the other extreme were the stories that seemed to work too well. At the beginning of the decade, scores of local and national exposés of crowded and inadequate institutions for the care of the mentally ill helped prompt a wave of "deinstitutionalization" nationwide. Scarcely a decade had passed and now the nightmare stories of the horrors of crowded and inadequately staffed state hospitals had been replaced by heartbreaking accounts of released inmates roaming the nation's streets, homeless or holed up in squalid single-room occupancy hotels. Suddenly the actions that dozens of well-meaning documentaries had encouraged were challenged as being worse than useless, ultimately inhumane.

As for crime and justice, a further deterioration of an already impossible situation was described in such superb recent reports as WPLG Miami's *Billion Dollar Ghetto* and *Assembly Line Justice,* and ABC *Closeup*'s "Death in a Southwest Prison" on the riots in New Mexico's state penitentiary. And this after years of exemplary reporting on the causes, prevention, and rehabilitation of the nation's steadily increasing populations of antisocial men and women.

Another admirable example of TV's continued concern for a story television had made particularly its own was Ed Bradley and Philip Burton, Jr.'s two-hour *CBS Reports: Blacks in America—With All Deliberate Speed?*

The program opened with reactions from a white and a black student, elicited by Edward R. Murrow following the Supreme Court decision, which outlawed segregation in the public schools in 1954. The two segments had Bradley first visiting Tupelo, Mississippi, and then schools in his hometown, Philadelphia, to see how things had changed for blacks in the South and in the North—not very much, considering a quarter of a century of court actions, attempted enforcement, and massive media attention.

Minnie Huntley, a member of a Mississippi community-action group, told Bradley: "We have the same problems we had 25 years ago: race, poverty, hunger, the lack of medical attention, and all the things that goes with poverty."*

It was to the broadcasters' credit that despite such discouragements they continued to report the failures and occasional improvements as they saw them. Among the more than 200 finalists selected from 2,500 nominees for the DuPont-Columbia Awards over the past two years, nearly a quarter addressed such persistent problems.

There was, however, the threat that the shifting tides of politics, the antiregulation climate in Washington, and wide concern for a declining economy and loss of income and jobs might make some crucial subjects less attractive to reporters and less acceptable to the public than they had been before. It was also possible that consumer reporting, a popular element on local TV news, might have reached a plateau. David Horowitz, the consumer star of KNBC-TV Los Angeles, said frankly, "I stay away from the stuff that scares people to death and doesn't give them an alternative. Take the asbestos in hair dryers story. A typical glare and scare story. It gets the glare of the headlines and scares people to death, and three weeks later, it's totally forgotten."

---

*On another front, ABC's *Viewpoint* reported that of the three dozen people who prepare the news menu every day for 50 million Americans, none is black. CBS had 10 blacks out of 219 in its producer core. ABC had six out of 206. NBC was reported to have 11 out of approximately 200. NBC had a black woman as head of its Chicago bureau, the only one in network news. There was still only one black news director of a large station in a major city, one national anchor, and no executives.

Lea Thompson, consumer reporter for WRC-TV Washington, D.C., who originally uncovered the asbestos in hair dryers and also delivered an award-winning series of reports on defective baby formula, did not agree. "I personally believe there's more change, both direct and indirect, being brought about by consumer reporting than any other kind of reporting," she said. "The reason is consumer reporting is by definition investigative. When someone calls in and complains, you have to go and uncover what is really happening. Consumer reporters have major impact. Our asbestos hair dryer story led to the recall of 25 million hair dryers around the country and it sent industry back to the drawing board to look at all the consumer products that had asbestos in them—toasters, anything with a heating element, had asbestos. The Consumer Product Safety Commission, Congress, and the National Academy of Sciences are all looking at asbestos now. All that on one story. And we had even more response on our story on the deficiencies in baby formula. That brought about a complete change in the way the Food and Drug Administration looks at things. It had to redefine what is food and what is not food. It looked at the books of individual companies, which it had never done before. And it brought about the Infant Formula Act of 1980. You can't have much more impact than that."

Impact or not, lasting or fleeting, broadcast journalism was obviously involved in an open-ended negotiation between what was possible and what any individual reporter, station owner, and network was willing to risk in money, time, and consequences. Beyond that there was the question of what an audience was willing to listen to and able to assimilate, and what any business or government was willing to acknowledge and attempt to correct.

The embattled reporter, fighting against heavy odds to discover and communicate the truth, was, when he penetrated and hurt, inviting counterattack. Equally hard for businessman or politician to accept—and it would seem the public as well—was the journalist's preference for problems, frequently perceived as an unwholesome fondness for making trouble or an unfair leaning toward the left or right. That journalists were actually performing a function essential to a healthy society, spotting shortcomings and flaws, describing them, and recommending corrective action was a particularly unwelcome notion when those flaws and shortcomings were your own.

What seemed hardest to acknowledge for everyone concerned with broadcast journalism—practitioner, subject, and audience—was that a responsible reporter could not be interested in just two sides of a question. Any journalist worth the name and pay was committed to uncovering the third dimension, which converts a simple controversy into solid, complicated, convincing reality.

That this truth might be gaining currency could be indicated by the dialogue in an episode of *Lou Grant,* a show on prime-time commercial TV with an average audience of 20 million Americans. The interchange was between a frustrated reporter and a harassed businessman.

BUSINESSMAN: We're tired of constantly reading that American business is second-rate, that we're riddled with inefficiency.

JOURNALIST: We'll try to be sensitive to your needs but you be sensitive to ours. Don't duck us. Don't treat us as though we were not entitled to know, and then we'll give you the benefit of the doubt.

BUSINESSMAN: You work on being accurate and we won't need the benefit of the doubt.

Indeed, if broadcast journalists and their subjects should ever exchange doubts and suspicion for accuracy and honesty, credibility need no longer be a problem.

6 🖉
The
Cable
Revolution

On JUNE 1, 1980, Ted Turner, a self-proclaimed media messiah from the deep South, went on the air with a news broadcast, which, if he had his way, would never go off. It made little difference to him that the "air" actually was a transponder on RCA Satcom I or that his news broadcast would be picked up by 172 cable systems, which at the most could deliver him 1.7 million homes. So what if the budget for his Cable News Network, the first all-news TV in history—24 hours a day, seven days a week, 52 weeks a year—was one-fourth what each national TV network spent on its news, or if he had barely half a dozen sponsors paying peanuts to come along for the ride? Said Turner of his new venture: "This will be the most significant achievement in the annals of journalism."

Allowing for the usual Turner hyperbole, there was a morsel of truth in his noisy boast. And a respectable number of his competitors, whether they could get the Cable News Network on their home sets or not, were looking and listening—with good reason.

Already the young Georgian had taken the money he had made by turning around his father's foundering outdoor advertising firm and bought WTCG-TV, an ailing UHF sta-

tion in Atlanta.* He had changed the station's call letters to
WTBS-TV and dubbed it the nation's first "superstation," a
term and concept of his own devising.

The name was a slight exaggeration. WTBS-TV, thanks
again to an early spot on the RCA Satcom I, and the relaxation
of the FCC's regulations on distant signals and syndication
exclusivity, fed its unassuming local program of sports, old
movies, and TV retreads to fodder-hungry cable systems coast
to coast. An essentially schlock enterprise, its potential audience had jumped from 500,000 homes in 1976 to 16.8 million
homes in 1981 with profits to match.

Meanwhile Turner had picked up WRET-TV Charlotte,
North Carolina, another scorned UHF station, by assuming its
$1.2 million liabilities. Again, catching the upward tide that
was lifting the value of UHF stations, he turned the station
into a solid moneymaker. In 1980 he sold it for $20 million to
Westinghouse, a broadcasting giant and future adversary.
That gave Turner the start-up stake he needed to launch
CNN.

On board for CNN's première was President Jimmy Carter
who had taped an exclusive interview. "An exciting and historic thing," Carter described his fellow Georgian's new venture to CNN's first-day viewers.

Present also was Daniel Schorr, the irascible CBS alumnus
who had been hired as Turner's senior correspondent. Schorr
passed his reasons for taking such an apparent gamble on to
his colleagues in the Radio-Television News Directors Association at their national convention in Hollywood, Florida, a few
months later.

. . . CNN is still in its swaddling clothes, and not everything about it is
wonderful. But one thing that is wonderful in an all-news operation
is that there is no fighting for time against the program department,
no conflict of values between news and entertainment. No Fred
Friendly will resign because he couldn't preempt a rerun of "I Love
Lucy." There will be no agonizing, as there was in the networks in

*When Turner bought WTCG in 1970 less than one in three of the nation's
UHF stations realized a profit. By 1978 three out of four were making
money with UHF stations bringing in aggregate annual revenues of $510.3
million.

1973, over whether to drop the soap operas to carry the Senate
Watergate hearings live.

At CNN we lack a lot of luxuries, but one luxury we do have—
every executive we deal with in normal daily operations is a news
executive. And, for audiences, which have come close to confusing
the reality and the fantasy that bombard them from the same tube, it
may be healthy to have separate channels for reality and fantasy.
Maybe it will help to restore some sense of what reality is.

As for Schorr's new audience:

A 24-hour television news service provides a choice. It is like a water
tap that one can turn on when thirsty. It is one of the things—along
with videotape recordings, videodiscs, two-way cable, and text on
command—that will help people regain control of their lives. . . .

People want choices. The technology that gave them the coaxial
cable . . . is now giving them a great and fine chaos of new choices. It
will be a bewildering spectrum, but on that spectrum there will be
room for newspeople to peddle pieces of reality.

There were a fair number of professionals who apparently
shared Schorr's enthusiasm. Reese Schonfeld left the Independent Television News Association to become CNN's president. George Watson left his job as Washington bureau chief
of ABC News to perform the same function at CNN. Former
CBS-TV President Robert Wussler came on as executive vice
president. Jim Kitchell, CNN's senior vice president in charge
of operations, was formerly general manager of news services
at NBC. 380 more professionals, men and women, staffed the
main CNN operations in Atlanta and Washington and the 11
bureaus worldwide.

As special commentators, Turner had signed up a diverse
cast of characters, which included Bella Abzug, Phyllis Schla-
fly, Richard Reeves, William Simon, Barry Goldwater, Ralph
Nader, Rowland Evans, and Robert Novak.

Those who had turned on their sets expecting to see Turner
finally fall flat on his faces, stayed tuned in, if not exactly to
marvel, at least to admit grudgingly that what they saw could
have been much worse. Skeptics still felt that there was little
chance that Turner could keep it up for 24 hours a day 365
days a year either in terms of viewer interest or money. In the
first year there were desertions, most notably George Watson,

who, having returned to ABC in April 1981 as vice president of news, said of the CNN operation, "It's kind of a junk-food diet that may have the illusion of nourishment." Financially, the going was unquestionably rough. Turner restructured his debt and closed down his Atlanta Chiefs soccer team to help cover his 1980 losses of $16 million. But after 18 months and 13,000 news hours the Cable News Network was still on the air. And Turner had scored a respectable number of wins.

When the League of Women Voters refused John Anderson access to the presidential debates, Turner gave him his say for the exclusive benefit of CNN viewers. CNN had stuck with the story of the hostages return not just for 24 hours but for a full four days. CNN was on hand for the entire Senate hearings on Alexander Haig's appointment as Secretary of State while the TV networks, with the exception of PBS which carried a day and a half, were content with brief clips on the evening news. CNN's reporting from San Salvador and Iraq matched the networks for enterprise if not for slickness.

CNN was the first to run the ABSCAM tapes, the first to announce the Reagan assassination attempt on the air, and the first to uncover the Jodie Foster connection with would-be presidential assassin John Hinckley, Jr. The cable network's coverage of the May Day 1981 celebration in Havana was, Turner claimed, the first live telecast from Cuba to the United States CNN sent a crew to cover the explosion at the Titan missile silo in Damascus, Arkansas, and got a Pentagon official to admit that there was still a nuclear warhead on the site. It carried Frank Sinatra's testimony before the Nevada Gaming Control Board live and the full two-and-a-half hour tape of Carter and his staff in the Oval Office on their last night when the hostage settlement was finally hammered out. While the networks were still fighting for a one-hour newscast, CNN's evening news roundup ran a full two hours in prime time.

On several occasions the networks had picked up CNN footage for their own evening news, including interviews with President Carter and Zbigniew Brzezinski.

Still, CNN's relationship with the networks was not all that cordial. In May 1981 Turner filed suit against the networks, President Reagan, and several of the White House staff for excluding CNN from the presidential pool and for "various other predatory and illegal practices" detailed in a 20-page complaint. He also demanded an inquiry into network programming practices, which he called "totally irresponsible" and "criminal." In October 1981, Turner appeared before the House Telecommunications Subcommittee to testify on TV violence and delivered a one-hour diatribe against the networks—fully carried, needless to say, on CNN.

"DDT was heralded as a wonderful miracle substance when it was first developed, and we used it widely," Turner told *Broadcasting* magazine the month before CNN went on the air. "Then after a long period of time, we learned it was going to kill us and we stopped using it that way. TV only came on the scene 36 years ago, and television had a tremendous potential for enlightenment, entertainment, and information. And I think we've gotten the bare minimum out of it. Because of a lack of a sense of responsibility, I think television is the worst pollutant this country has ever seen because it's polluted our minds, our children's minds. It was not responsibly or intelligently used by the people who ran it. We turned it over to three networks who care about nothing but wrenching the last nickel out of everything."

Turner thought the distinction between himself and the networks quite obvious. "I'm not in this to make money. I'm in it to straighten this country out. . . . I want to make it very clear where I'm at. I'm going to improve the quality of the television industry. . . . I'm doing it as a crusade."

If CNN wasn't yet quite in the black, by late fall 1981 it had reduced its monthly losses from $2 million to $600,000 and anticipated turning a profit by the second quarter of 1982. CNN was being offered by 1,850 cable systems coast to coast with 10.4 million potential viewers. Advertising revenues had reached $16 million for 1981.

Perhaps CNN had yet to prove itself the "most significant achievement in the annals of journalism."* However, it could be taken as a forerunner of a new electronic age that promised to change the face not only of journalism but of broadcasting, and if some media prophets were to be believed, of society itself.

*For a report on journalism and the new technology see page 180.

When Turner went on the air in June 1980, the broadcasting establishment was still pretending to hold the barricades against cable and other new technologies, which it had long fought as sinister and un-American threats to "free broadcasting."

Leonard Goldenson, chairman of the board and chief executive officer of ABC, addressing the National Press Club in September 1980, pointed out plaintively that the government had a new favorite. After 50 years of working hard "to foster a climate in which nationwide radio and then television could grow and flourish . . . in the 1970s . . . attitudes toward free television began to change in Washington. Instead of receiving support and encouragement, television broadcasters found themselves confronting an unfriendly government, a government with a different goal: the promotion of new technologies."

Although Goldenson's tone of abandoned favorite was wistful, and his accusation of special treatment for the lawmakers' new darling hard to refute, his recommendations for righting the situation tipped the broadcasters' hand. In addition to demanding better copyright protection for TV programs and the repeal of multiple-ownership restrictions, he suggested that networks be given the right to start up additional over-the-air channels. Furthermore he wanted the FCC to "repeal all rules restricting broadcaster participation in cable ownership. Specifically, it should remove the ban against ownership of both broadcasting and cable facilities in the same market. It also should lift the ban against network ownership of cable." Finally, Goldenson felt the commission "should permit any television station the right to offer over-the-air subscription service."

Goldenson's remarks were not only self-serving, they were prophetic.*

By the time Turner was midway into his second year of operating CNN, his former antagonists had become his customers and his competitors. All three networks or their parent

*Significantly, Goldenson's speech, which received 30 seconds on ABC-TV, was covered in full by cable.

corporations had established cable divisions. ABC had joined hands with Hearst for a woman's programming service, with Warner Amex for the arts and with Getty Oil for sports. RCA, NBC's parent corporation, was backing ex-CBS president Arthur Taylor's Rockefeller Center TV ("The Entertainment Channel"), which had, among other things, purchased first rights to all of the British Broadcasting Company's output. In August 1981 CBS got a variance from the FCC allowing it to buy its own limited cable system. In October it launched its blockbusting, advertiser-supported culture channel, thus becoming the first network to be involved in cable hardware and software simultaneously.

Among the media conglomerates with extensive broadcasting properties that were acquiring or increasing their cable holdings or pursuing allied technologies were Newhouse, Gannett, Knight-Ridder, *The New York Times*, *Post-Newsweek*, Times Mirror, Cox, and Storer.

In October 1980 Westinghouse, the most important U. S. broadcaster after the networks and the proprietor of the nation's first commercial radio station—KDKA Pittsburgh, founded in 1921—announced it would pay $646 million to acquire Teleprompter, the oldest and largest cable system in the country with 1.3 million subscribers in 32 states. Ten months later, Westinghouse announced its partnership with ABC-TV in producing a round-the-clock headline news service to compete with Turner's CNN, plus a second channel that would offer news in depth. It would offer this advertising-supported service free to all subscribing cable systems, while Turner charged his clients 15 to 20 cents for each of the households plugged into their systems. The Westinghouse-ABC services were scheduled to go on line sometime in 1982.

Soon both CBS and NBC were reported to have feelers out to buy Turner's pioneering CNN in an effort to catch up with ABC. Far from selling out, Turner announced he would start a second channel himself—plus an all-news radio service— and get them on the air in January 1982, well ahead of his new competition.

In the wild and wonderful new world of cable it was no

longer possible to tell the red counters from the black, the black hats from the white. Already the industry-wide scramble for new properties had resulted in 38 percent of the cable systems of the nation ending up in the hands of companies that also had broadcast stations. Rockefeller Center TV's acquisition of the BBC output, which for years had been one of the crown jewels of the Public Broadcasting Service's schedule, was just the first of the anticipated raids by cable on conventional broadcasting. Doomsayers predicted a future that would see "free TV" deprived of everything from the Super Bowl and the Olympics* to the Academy Awards and the Emmys.

Not only had the barricades been breached and dismantled, split loyalties in the news business were becoming epidemic, spreading from broadcasting and cable to print with such technological breakthroughs as teletext and videotext. The blurring of the boundaries between print and broadcast journalism brought up the always painful issues of licensing, the Fairness Doctrine, and equal time in a new and uncomfortable way. If broadcasters were not allowed full First Amendment rights, would print entrepreneurs, once their activities spilled onto the home screen, be similarly deprived?

The broadcasters and publishers needn't have fretted. The chaos in their territory was matched by the grinding reversal of gears by the nation's regulators. Already, as Leonard Goldenson had pointed out, the cable industry had benefited from deregulation or at least from an unwillingness to impose regulations in a new field.

Now not only was the FCC moving to make things easier for cable, the commission was responding to conventional broadcasters' complaints by recommending the removal of many regulatory restrictions and the extending of broadcast licenses. Reagan's new chairman of the FCC, Mark Fowler, went to Congress with a proposal that the Fairness Doctrine, equal time, and personal attack provisions all be repealed. He was also on record as being against the limitation of the

*However, against cable competition, ABC still won the 1984 winter and summer Olympics for a whopping $225 million.

number of stations owned by a single entity. Nor did he want any limit set on the size and number of cable systems owned by networks.

In his maiden policy speech, delivered to the Oregon Association of Broadcasters in June 1981, Fowler declared, "When I say that we will reexamine broadcasting rules 'top to bottom,' I mean *every* rule and *every* policy. Unless a rule or policy survives scrutiny in the hard, cold light of current realities, we will get rid of it. I believe that this effort will help us by giving you more freedom to operate as any other business does."

Fowler, however, was not going to play favorites.

"I want each technology to have a fair chance to offer services to the public. Marketplace skills, not massive regulation, should determine your future."

The concern for "the public interest, convenience, and necessity," which had been a part of communications policy since the framing of the Communications Act of 1934, had apparently gone by the boards in Fowler's philosophy. News and public affairs had always been assumed to come under that broad rubric. What would happen to news and public affairs in the new no-holds-barred climate of the Fowler Commission remained to be seen. In the past, when public and business interests disagreed as to whether FM radio should be kept for quality and diversity or given over to more of the same, crass commercialism had won out.

As for the future of the networks, Jack Kent Cooke, chairman of Teleprompter until it merged with Westinghouse in August 1981, had a few words: "There are more than 100 channels that theoretically can be put on cable. The networks are only three channels. . . . It is possible the networks are going to become second-class program conveyors. . . . Perhaps that's too strong. 'Diminished' might be a better word than 'second-class.'"

Not everyone was so ready to write off old-style network broadcasting. Although there was evidence of erosion of TV audiences during the daytime hours and in the prime-time periods, particularly when there was pay-TV competition, projections had over-the-air television still maintaining its hegemony well into the '90s. The reasoning was that while over-the-air broadcasting for the next two decades would get an ever smaller share of the viewing public, the increasing number of viewers, estimated to grow by 25 percent in the next decade, would mean that the actual audience for conventional TV would increase despite the inroads of cable and other technologies. Also, according to broadcasting partisans, the largest audience that the new technologies could hope to reach by the end of the decade was 50 percent of all TV homes while over-the-air TV would be available to 100 percent.

So far, despite Ted Turner's wall-to-wall newscasting,* network and local news seemed less susceptible to the new competition than entertainment programming. Indeed some local news directors felt that cable enhanced rather than diminished their news functions by the mere fact that local news was the one thing the new technologies were unable or unwilling to offer their customers.

From Houston, a news director wrote the survey:

With cable assuredly well entrenched by 1990, local stations have already recognized that local news and news-related programming is their one hope to compete. And staffs will undoubtedly increase as the size of the news hole increases. The doomsayers will ask what is going into these news holes, and I say the news and the issues are there now and they will be there in the future for enterprising producers and reporters to find and explore.

Another from Minneapolis wrote:

The increasing competitive threat of cable television news has proved to be a boon to local newsrooms. Managers are becoming aware that to compete successfully against cable they will have to offer something that cable cannot provide. More and more that is being perceived to be strong local community programming. That, of course, means news.

Not all news directors were so sanguine about cable's impact. When ABC announced its plans to launch its all-news cable service with Westinghouse, ABC affiliates rose up and

*Turner took a full-page ad in September 1981 to claim that 85 percent of CNN's customers preferred its news to the network variety.

complained of the possibility of their own network competing against them.*

So far as network news was concerned, Richard Salant, former president of CBS News and until 1981 vice chairman of the NBC Board of Directors with a special concern for its news operation, was optimistic:

One of the things that networks do best—from my prejudiced viewpoint—and do uniquely, is news and information. If portions of the entertainment schedule and its audience go over to cable and other new technologies, news and information will have a far larger role in the network schedule than they have now, not only because they have the organization and expertise in place but because it makes economic sense.

Simply put, news is less expensive, by a good margin, than entertainment. The costs of entertainment programs are escalating enormously—far outrunning inflation. That escalation can be compounded as the new technologies compete for rights to sports events, to theatrical movies, and to other entertainment programming. And since networks must keep a large news organization in place just to do what they are doing now, if news' share of the broadcast schedule increases, the huge costs of maintaining a network news organization can be amortized over far more news and information broadcasts.

And so my own—perhaps wishful—view is that the odds are not against the demise of broadcast journalism in the face of the new technologies, but rather are in favor of its expansion.

While Salant saw an increase in the importance of national news, he also saw a possible danger in the advent of the new technology and its consequent fragmenting of audiences.

The television viewer's only choice is to turn the news on or shut it off. If the viewer wants to see what is coming next, the viewer must watch what is on *now*. I suspect it is this characteristic which played such a large part in the ultimate shifting of the public's attitudes toward the Vietnam war and the civil rights struggles of the sixties. A *reader* could find those stories disturbing and so skip them. A television *viewer* could not—not if the viewer wanted to see the Charles Kuralt "On the Road" piece at the close of the broadcast. . . .

*Turner, on the other hand, predicted that ABC's service would be handicapped by the necessity of keeping its best stories back for its *World News Tonight*.

The danger, it seems to me, is that our supposedly indivisible nation might be transformed into a nation of tribes. Yet, a successfully functioning democracy depends on a common data base for its people. Some of the new technologies threaten that common data base. Smaller and smaller groups may come to know more and more about less and less.

Cable operators saw a variety of opportunities in the new areas. One from Washington, D.C. wrote to the Survey:

Cable's priority should be to fill the voids that presently exist, not duplicate what is already in place. On the national level, specialized news (such as on foreignaffairs issues) can be covered in depth on a regular basis. At the local level, the cable industry can provide more public access to covering local news and community events.

There are two main ways that the cable industry can best serve the public regarding news and public affairs programming. The first method is for the cable industry to continue to expand and diversify its programming in these areas. The Cable News Network (CNN) and the Cable Satellite Public Affairs Network (C-SPAN) are examples of positive growth in news and public affairs programming. CNN, with its around-the-clock coverage, provides immediacy and greater depth to the news it presents. C-SPAN, through its gavel-to-gavel coverage of the House of Representatives and Congressional Committee action, allows the public to learn more about the governmental process and the issues which are important to the nation.

The second way that the cable industry can serve the public is through local origination. By setting aside a certain number of channels for public access, the public can become more informed about the events in their own communities.

A cable operator in Illinois wrote:

In my opinion, public affairs and news programming will become more and more important to the cable programmer. I see two motivating factors. The local "scene" is the one void in television viewing. To me, this is a cable programmer's dream come true. A relatively unmapped territory, except for local newspapers, it is wide open to program ideas. In general, cable companies will place higher priorities on local news and public affairs as they become aware of the possibilities for local advertising dollars. And there won't be an audience until the programs are quality shows. The priority placed on public affairs programming has to be preceded by extensive training of local volunteers and contagious enthusiasm on the part of the program director.

I think that in five years people buying a home will check the cable channels before deciding on a particular area. There will be more program services then cable channels. There will be differences in cable services offered from one company to another. Cable will be the main artery connecting people to each other. It will be responsible for what people know about their community and the outside world. More viewers will tune away from the redundancy of network news in search of the in-depth coverage cable programming can provide locally and via satellite program sources. Cable in five years will be the main thoroughfare for information transmission and delivery. The networks will continue to cover the sensational and the distant because they have the budget. But the competition could get heavy as more program suppliers start to specialize in news and public interest programming.

From Ohio:

The industry is capable of sustaining responsible journalism or settling for quick-fix, shallow programming. Market forces along with local and federal regulation will settle this dilemma in a few years. In the meantime, industry leaders should be hiring experienced news/public affairs executives. Another problem is taking narrowcasting to the extreme. We may be left with individuals who do nothing but watch tennis news and avoid the national summaries. Consumers of this specialized information must consider how to integrate their viewing patterns.

From New Jersey:

Cable's penetration will have increased significantly by 1986. As a result, viewers will have a supermarket of programming in their homes. This is bound to cut into the traditional viewership of the three major networks as well as local commercial stations. In the areas of news and public affairs, CNN, on a national level, hopefully, will develop into a newsbreaking enterprise instead of an expanded version of the *CBS Evening News*. Locally, I would hope that the systems will devote the time and effort to develop news and public affairs programming for the communities they serve.

The future of cable, the most widespread of the new technologies, was, however, highly uncertain. From a servant of the old technology, it had suddenly become its formidable rival. But it already carried within it, if not the seeds of its own decline, the possibility of a drastically different form for its future. Or several different forms. While billions of dollars were being allocated to wire tens of millions of homes not yet reached by cable, direct broadcast satellites suggested the day when all those wires might be unnecessary, and everyone with the wherewithal could build his own earth station.

Under a headline reading NAB HITS REAGAN ICEBERG, *Advertising Age* columnist Stanley E. Cohen reported back from the National Association of Broadcasters meeting in Las Vegas in May 1981 as if from the bridge of the doomed ocean liner *Titanic:*

Even as they celebrated, the unthinkable was happening. In a letter to the FCC, Secretary of Commerce Malcolm Baldridge spelled out an administration policy that exposes networks and stations to potentially important new competition: direct telecasting from satellites to home. Potentially, it makes networks unnecessary, cuts them off as a source of programs and national advertising revenues for stations and maybe even makes stations a lot less desirable. Broadcasters had been confident they could count on at least six years of regulatory razzle dazzle at the FCC. Now Baldridge was saying that the Reagan Administration wants action now. On the double.

Another potential iceberg was the low-power TV station, with 5,000 applications already in. Intended not only to serve communities within communities but to be within the reach of minorities and small nonprofit special interest groups, already licenses for LPTVs were being applied for by such established operations as NBC, ABC, Frontier Broadcasting, Ted Turner, Gannett, and The American Christian Television System—some of whom were seeking more than 100 stations.

Fiber optics, the magic wire of spun glass that could carry hundreds of signals to existing cable's average of 12, was another option.

And somewhere in the future was complete information retrieval, which would make every homeowner his own programmer and, so far as journalism was concerned, his own

editor with the attendant risks of his choosing nothing but
sports, weather, and gossip. Meanwhile there were teletext
and two-way terminals with their potential for supplanting the
old-fashioned paper-and-ink newspaper and news magazine*
with video yellow pages, video sales, video banks, video security systems and video games. This did not include such luxury items as videodiscs, home videocassette recorders, wall
screens, home earth-receiving stations and "multipoint distribution system microwave receiving discs."

Already most of the above world-of-tomorrow wonders
were technologically feasible. Some obviously would go by the
boards, others prevail. Fortunes would be made and lost. And
there would, perhaps, be other losses as well.

Salant's fear of the loss of a monolithic audience, which
could be assembled by radio and TV in times of catastrophe,
national emergency, and national choice, was worth considering. Returning to the American people the options of picking
and choosing that for over half a century had resided in the
hands of the network news departments could be, as Daniel
Schorr implied, a hopeful possibility. But to some it was also a
frightening one. In a lead story headed "Satellite Era Orbiting
TV News," *Variety*'s Steve Knoll suggested a gloomy outcome.

For decades, networking was the most exclusive club in corporate
America. While that situation left a lot to be desired as far as diversity
was concerned, it nonetheless served to keep national broadcast
news—with its awesome impact—in the hands of journalists forced
by their companies' traditions into a serious and responsible mold.
Now that networking is a game anyone (in a manner of speaking) can
play, the rules are changing, the audience is starting to fragment,
and how it will all come out no one can say for sure. But if radio is any
guide, then more does not automatically mean better, and the
spread of "demographic news," which in the final analysis means
news tailored for the advertiser's target audience, may constitute a
setback to the cause of a well-informed public.

*Addressing the American Newspaper Publishers' Association annual
meeting in May 1981, Ted Turner said with his usual tact, "You're becoming obsolete very rapidly." His recommendation: "I'd be in bed with my local
cable operator. I'd be his best friend. And I'd probably try to sell my paper if
I possibly could."

Another bogy of the new technology was the threat it posed to privacy. The nightmare of *1984*, with its two-way screens peering into the apartments of cringing citizens, was obviously a memorable and recurring one. But it seemed no more justified than apprehension over the uses that a computerized telephone system or mailing list could be put to. Hardware was not at issue. If the American people developed a taste for tyranny, they would find a way to satisfy it, cable or no cable. Meanwhile a properly utilized cable system could be an instrument for enlightening the public and a means of preventing such a day of wrath from ever arriving.

More real than the taking over of the national screens for purposes of tyranny seemed the threat that the new technologies would be appropriated for trivial uses in the interest of profit. Although in order to get their franchises cable operators promised helpings of culture, edification, information, and education in prodigal amounts, there was the possibility and threat that, once enfranchised, the least common denominator of the over-the-air broadcasters would prevail in narrowcasts as well.

Meanwhile, culture and intellect were getting their innings. CBS, which since the days of *Omnibus* and *Playhouse 90* had downplayed culture, was offering on its new cable channel the best of music, dance, and drama. On its cable operation, RCA, which long since had rung down the curtain on the *NBC Opera* and *Symphony,* was promising the best of BBC, which could, as the viewer of PBS well knew, be very good indeed. And ABC had its own cable culture channel called ARTS (Alpha Repertory Television Service).

What would happen when cable's audiences grew larger and advertisers more numerous remained to be seen. Success and large numbers had not been the friend of quality on over-the-air broadcasting. Still the new technologies offered their subscribers another chance to opt for both excellence and diversity. They might indeed go the way of FM radio, introduced as an instrument for diversity, quality, and intelligence forty years ago, and now largely appropriated to the perpetuation of the Top 40. But they could also take their lead from Off Broadway, quality paperback books, classical records, or specialty magazines. If reasonable rather than maximum profits were demanded, quality would seem to have a good chance of surviving among the host of new technologies.

The most ominous indication that something else might happen was the inordinate interest of conglomerates, media and otherwise, in the new forms, the same conglomerate interest which had in the past acquired control of motion picture studios, book publishers, and recording firms, as well as broadcasting outlets, and driven the quality inexorably downward in the search for the bottom line.*

The words of Penny Hawkey, senior vice president of McCann-Erickson, to the Association of National Advertisers Annual Meeting in Hot Springs, Virginia, four months after Ted Turner began his Cable News Network, were cautionary. Midway in a talk entitled "Fast Forward, or How I Lost My Job in the New Electronic Revolution," Ms. Hawkey paused for a parenthesis.

As a personal aside, I think we are losing our audience not only through the splintering technologies but because there is a genuine viewer dissatisfaction with network programming. I believe that in the ratings mania we have broken the camel's back. In our quest for the ultimate far-reaching coverage . . . we forced the networks to stay away from specialized quality programming. We caused them to milk successful shows far too long. And I wonder how many times the folks at the networks have mumbled to each other, "Hey, that was a terrific show last night, really loved it, sorry about the numbers."

Now Fred Silverman insists that network TV will remain the mass audience medium. And to that I say, "Terrific. He can have the mass

---

*A typical conglomerate bidder for cable was Warner Amex, which already owned the fifth largest cable network in the land—144 systems in 27 states, including the experimental Qube systems in Columbus and Cincinnati. It was currently constructing systems in six more markets and was a bidder in four more. In addition, the huge conglomerate included real estate, athletic teams and theatrical film, publishing, record, and videocassette operations—none of them distinguished by a hunger for quality over quantity. Also, Warner had been haunted by rumors of underground connections since its early days as Kinney, Inc. and two of Warner's top executives had recently been involved in the notorious mob-linked Westchester Premier Theater.

audience; I sure can't do a thing with it." Seriously. It's an obsolete direction. . . . We are on the road toward a de-massification of the media. The era of broadcasting is coming to an end, and the era of narrowcasting is upon us.

There is even an outside chance that the competitiveness during this transition stage will finally force a level of quality into network programming that we have never seen before.

At present there is a mind-numbing sameness to everything we see on TV, both in programming and commercials. There is nothing to look for, nothing to study, nothing confusing, nothing open ended, nothing beautiful, outrageous, controversial, or moving . . . and very little that is funny.

It was a chilling picture by an interested insider of an industry old before its time. Although intended for old-fashioned broadcasters and the advertisers who had paid their way, it could also be read as a warning to narrowcasters who were already claiming to have taken over.

7 ✒

Seasons
in
Hell

ON THE AFTERNOON of March 30, 1981, outside the Washington Hilton Hotel where he had appeared at an AFL-CIO meeting, President Reagan was shot. The attack, by a young white male, took place at 2:26. At 2:30 White House correspondent Sam Donaldson on ABC Radio was first to report the act, proving once again that in the crunch the older medium could still be faster. At 2:33 the Cable News Network came on with the first TV report. One minute later ABC-TV broke into its regular afternoon schedule with a bulletin and at 2:42 was on the air with a tape of the shooting. Before 3 P.M., NBC and CBS broadcast tapes of the shooting and stuck with the story until well into the evening. What followed, according to *Time* magazine, "for one draining afternoon ... turned America into a giant newsroom."

Although there had been some delay in getting their pictures on the air, all three networks had cameras focused on the President when the attack took place. NBC actually had three teams covering Reagan: one for the TV pool, which follows the President whenever he leaves the White House and is morbidly referred to as the "death watch," one for unilateral coverage for the network, and yet another for a documentary on "The First 100 Days" scheduled for airing late the next month.

What the television audience saw, beginning in mid-afternoon, was, in the words of *Broadcasting* magazine, "another episode of the country's most engrossing, and horrifying, television show—the assassination attempt, in color. If the show was minutes away from being live, the technology available made up for that, with instant replays, stop action, and freeze frames. And with five ENG cameras rolling, the attempt on President Reagan's life was undoubtedly the most heavily covered assassination attempt in history."*

The graphic footage recorded the shots and then followed a frantic pantomime with the President being shoved into his limousine. Press Secretary James Brady and two other men fell wounded while the assassin was caught and pinned to the pavement. Vivid and specific as they seemed, the tapes were nonetheless capable of misinterpretation. From 2:30 until 3:11 the public was told the President had not been hit. It was not the last error that the TV audience would witness. Never before had the viewer been quite so close to the uncertainties and misapprehensions that accompany the newsgathering process.

The report that the President had escaped injury was finally corrected when Ross Simpson of the Mutual Broadcasting System managed to get inside the George Washington University Hospital where the chief executive had been taken. He called in reports from the third floor of the hospital.**

There followed, however, a long period of vagueness as to just how serious the President's injuries might be, exacer-

---

*Five months before, Beatle John Lennon had been gunned down outside his Manhattan apartment building. Although there were no TV cameras present, the shooting prompted massive media attention and brought forth the predictable comments concerning the violent nature of American society for which television was given its share of blame.

**NBC's Ken Bode also sneaked into the hospital emergency room, talking to presidential advisers Ed Meese, James Baker, and Lyn Nofziger and watching as doctors examined X rays of both the President and Brady. But NBC Washington Bureau Chief Sid Davis did not air Bode's report that the President had, in fact, been shot because it had not been independently confirmed from a second source.

bated by a misunderstanding of Simpson's accurate report that he was undergoing "open chest surgery." Chris Wallace of NBC heard this as "open heart surgery" and the medical consultants called in by the networks and local TV stations immediately predicated a much more dangerous wound than the one that had actually been inflicted. Also the length of time that the President was on the operating table remained unconfirmed, stretching to a full hour longer on TV than it was in reality, further increasing viewer anxiety.

Even more distressing was the report on all three networks that Press Secretary James Brady had died. This error, eventually traced back to press aides and a Secret Service spokesman,* led to premature obituaries delivered on ABC by Frank Reynolds and on CBS by Dan Rather, who was covering his first big breaking story as Walter Cronkite's replacement.

13 minutes later, when the White House issued a correction, reporting that Brady, though seriously wounded, was alive, the TV audience had a rare on-camera glimpse of an apparently unflappable anchorperson losing his cool. Getting the still garbled word over his earplug, ABC's iron-jawed Frank Reynolds began in understandable confusion, "Oh my goodness. I . . . I must apologize. I-I-I hope that what I've been reporting is all wrong, but what I'm now told—people talking in my ear here—that there are conflicting reports, that Jim may well be alive yet. Let's—I—I hope it's true. Obviously we all hope it's true. But we did have reports from the hospital earlier, and from the White House, that, uh—that he had passed away. We know that he was in very critical condition.

---

*ABC's erroneous report arose out of an apparent misunderstanding between correspondent Bill Greenwood and White House Assistant Press Secretary David Prosperi. When Greenwood asked Prosperi if he could confirm a report of Brady's death, Prosperi was on the phone. He said, "Yes, I will," but explained later that he was responding to an earlier request by an AP reporter to "find out" what he could about the report. Greenwood, however, insisted that he heard the words "he died."

Let's get it nailed down," he finally snapped. "Somebody! Let's—find out!"

A different and less easily explained confusion arose when a sweating Secretary of State Alexander Haig appeared before the TV cameras supposedly to reassure the American public and told them that he was "in control here in the White House." Haig's colleagues in the administration, as well as Dan Rather, were quick to challenge this apparent assumption of power (the chain of command actually put Haig after the Vice President, the Speaker of the House, and the President Pro Tem of the Senate), and TV's presence turned what might have been an innocuous imprecision of statement into a political contretemps.

It wasn't until 7:29 P.M. that things really began to sort themselves out, thanks mainly to the appearance of Dr. Dennis O'Leary, a George Washington University Hospital spokesman. O'Leary became "an instant television hero" by the simple expedient of delivering a clear and reassuring bulletin on the President's condition and then answering a half hour of questions from the press in a direct and understandable manner.

At 8:15, NBC was the first to leave the Reagan story (for a broadcast of the NCAA championship basketball game). By 9:00 both CBS and ABC had switched back, CBS to its regular prime-time schedule, ABC to entertainment fillers to replace the Academy Awards, which, in deference to the afternoon's traumatic events, had been postponed until the following evening. All three networks returned later with specials on the assassination attempt.

Since the President's condition continued to be good, the story was effectively wrapped up by these late evening programs approximately ten hours after it broke. The implications of what the nation had witnessed on camera, however, occupied the press for some time to come.

There was general comment, some critical, some sympathetic, about Frank Reynolds' brief on-camera tantrum. *The Wall Street Journal* took exception to Dan Rather's concentration on Haig's slip, charging that he gave it "far greater significance than it deserved." The misinformation concerning the President's condition and Brady's supposed death were alluded to. But, all in all, the networks got high marks from their fellow journalists.*

Broadcasters had dumped all regular programming and all commercials till the President was pronounced out of danger. There was some question as to the advisability of such wall-to-wall coverage, but when CBS, early on, turned the network back to its affiliates the act brought consternation at some local stations and uncertainty as to how best to handle the opportunity given them.

A few affiliates made an attempt to find a valid local angle, most notably WMAQ, NBC's station in Chicago, which sent crews to Jim Brady's home town in southern Illinois, and to Dixon, Illinois, where Reagan was born. Others called on local experts to explain the nature of the President's wound and did the predictable man-in-the-street interviews.

The public reinforced the networks' decision to stick with the story. 130 million Americans tuned in to some or all of the coverage. In New York City early evening viewing was up to 72 percent of all sets in use from 56 percent for the same

---

*Bill Green, ombudsman for *The Washington Post*, was a notable exception. A week after the assassination attempt he wrote: "For the better part of five hours—a long time—national shock had been intensified by contradictory information. Part of it can be credited to the agony of making sense out of chaos, but other blame falls on the pressure of competitive newsgathering, the frenzy to be first. We were getting the raw materials of a developing story with its starts, stops, and blind alleys, and with too many of the facts unconfirmed. The stakes were too high for that, the danger of misinformation too great. We were all swept up in an overwhelming event. It was hardly the time for error.

"I hope the networks worry about the distortions they gave us last Monday afternoon. I hope they ask themselves what would happen if—given the same ratio of mistakes—an emergency of a different nature, say a calamitous natural disaster or, God forbid, an armed attack should come our way with thousands or millions of people approaching panic.

"I hope they understand that their powerful medium, in time of stress, produces a common experience for us all.

"I hope—but after last Monday, I'm not convinced. In all that rush to report I seemed to hear the ominous ticking of a clock."

time period the year before. Once again ABC won in the ratings over NBC and CBS.*

Again there was the usual soul searching as to TV's responsibility in encouraging the kind of violence that it had rushed to cover. Ted Koppel on the ABC *Nightline* followup asked an ex-Secret Service agent how he felt about the increasingly visible press presence wherever the President went. "Well, that always has been a problem," was his answer. "The press has always been given special privileges because they have a special job and the rights of the First Amendment. But because the press is allowed closer many times, and I think this instance was one of them, the general public was also allowed closer. And maybe this gave a little better opportunity to the assailant."

There was no move, however, on the part of the press, print, or broadcast, to reduce its presidential coverage, or by the White House to restrict it.

Perhaps the most sensitive evaluation of the broadcasters' performance and predicament came from the print competition. Daniel Henninger of *The Wall Street Journal* gave a particularly perceptive view of the coverage's deeper implications.

Over the last 10 years I have watched in films and on television countless fictional shooting scenes very much like what we watched here last Monday, and I experienced nearly all the make-believe scenes as gut entertainment. It doesn't surprise me too much now that the Reagan shooting somehow provided a similarly "entertaining" experience. The footage was extraordinary.

We can all say we are appalled, horrified, and dismayed by this shooting and be quite truthful in saying it. But there was a time not long ago, when most of us only read about the violence of death; we stood next to it only rarely. Real knowledge of violence, its texture and look, remained a kind of mystery.

But now we have seen how it looks, again and again and again. Intellectually, one is as shocked as ever by what happened to Mr.

*An unfortunate side effect of ABC's pride in its coverage was the use of footage of the President's shooting to promote its local New York o&o *Eyewitness News,* with the voiceover saying, "*Eyewitness News*: As unpredictable as New York."

Reagan, James Brady, and the other two men. But by the end of the evening Monday, this viewer at least had to admit that in whatever places outside the mind one is supposed to feel the news of a shooting like this, it didn't hurt the way it used to.

Tom Wicker, in his column in *The New York Times,* had other points to make:

A profound difference between broadcast and print reporting always occurs when a "breaking" story, such as a presidential election or an assassination attempt, is important enough to warrant live television coverage. In the former case, when information is speedily provided by impeccable sources, the advantage is all with TV. It can confidently follow the curve of events as soon as they happen, while a newspaper must be sent to press at some fixed point with whatever it then can report—however inaccurate it may be a half hour later.

But for the assassination attempt and its aftermath, a newspaper had time to sift out rumors, mistakes, claims, and the like and to give its readers a reasonably accurate and comprehensive report—but well after the fact. Television, in contrast, was expected to tell the story as it happened, and from whatever sources could be found. . . .

No honest reporter would assert that it's possible to have instant coverage *and* total accuracy; probably no one would want the networks to choose between the one *or* the other. What best serves the public in such a story as the assassination attempt is immediate coverage with the highest attainable degree of accuracy—including a clear distinction between confirmed fact and responsible conjecture, and as much justification for the latter as possible.

The networks did not always meet that standard in covering the assassination attempt, but it's just as well to remember that:

• Finding out what's true is a human, not a technological, problem.

• "Facts" confirmed by two or even three reliable persons may sometimes be false; and vice versa.

• Reports withheld may also do a disservice to truth and can draw as much fire from critics the next day.

And anyway, don't viewers, demanding immediacy as they do, have a responsibility to follow television with some discretion? Those who did during the assassination story were quickly informed and not too often misled.

Newsweek added:

Considering all their problems . . . the newsmen performed with cool, admirable professionalism. . . . Living-room America received a rare inside look into how TV's newsgathering apparatus operates under acute stress. Give it high grades, all told—and hope that it never again has to meet this kind of test.

Another such test, alas, was just six weeks off.

On May 13th, while circulating in an open jeep among a crowd of ten thousand in St. Peter's Square, Pope John Paul II, the spiritual leader of the world's 600 million Roman Catholics, was shot and seriously wounded.

Again the news arrived first by ABC Radio when William Blakemore interrupted a routine report from Rome at 11:30 A.M., EDT to pass on the horrifying word. At 11:35, on CBS-TV, Bob Schieffer broke into *The Price is Right* with a bulletin. Within a minute there were announcements on NBC and ABC-TV.

For a half hour the game shows, frequently interrupted, held the air on all three networks. By 12:35 John Chancellor, a tardy arrival at the Reagan shooting, was the first anchorperson to take over, admitting that he came onto a confused scene. "We are not certain. We are getting conflicting reports."

Frank Reynolds confirmed the confusion when ABC joined NBC with continuous coverage at 1 P.M. Dan Rather, the last to make it on air, asked his audience to "simply bear with us."

With the additional complications of satellite transmission from a foreign country, the confusion and misinformation and corrections were greater and more numerous than with the Reagan shooting. The number of shots reported fired at the Pope ranged from two to six. The location of the wounds varied with each report. The stomach, the chest, and the pancreas—a particularly dangerous spot—were all designated. Finally it was determined that two bullets had hit the Pope, one striking his right arm and left hand, one entering the abdominal cavity.

There was uncertainty about the other victims, finally identified as two women, a 21-year-old American housewife and a retired beautician from Buffalo. The assassin was variously labeled an Arab, a South American, a leftist terrorist, a member of the radical right, a loner, one of a gang of three, a participant in an international conspiracy, thirty years old, in his early twenties.

The first tape from Italian television showed the Pope moving among the crowd and then, following the attack, being rushed out of the teeming square. But there were no frames of the actual shooting. The pictures reached U.S. sets via the Cable News Network at 12:58, some 99 minutes after the assassination attempt took place. Three minutes later ABC showed the same footage to its viewers.

NBC had its first scoop at 2 P.M. when it discovered that the alleged assassin Mehmet Ali Agca, a 23-year-old right-wing Turkish terrorist and convicted murderer, had escaped from prison and threatened to kill the Pope on his visit to Turkey in 1979.

Considering the Pope's international prestige, his symbolic significance, and his enormous popularity in the United States, the network coverage seemed sparse and erratic compared to the attention paid to Reagan. NBC, pursuing its regular schedule of commercials and soaps, alternated brief bulletins with half-hour updates. The thinness of this coverage was intentional. One NBC spokesman explained, "We reached a point at which there was a great deal of repetition and rehash." Another said simply, "We rejected the theory of tonnage."

Newcomer Rather's request for a thoughtful silence followed by an unheard-of ten seconds without sound and motion on the TV screen, the one strikingly different gesture in all the TV coverage, was greeted by editorial sneers and snickers the following day.*

Comparisons of the coverage of the two attempted assassinations and considerations of their cumulative significance and impact were inevitable. Among the most interesting and specific were the comments on the medical aspects by Dr. Lawrence Altman in *The New York Times*.

In the chaos that follows assassination attempts, some confusion about the medical facts is inevitable, if for no other reason than

---

*Rather had made a similar request at the time of Brady's supposed death, which had gone unremarked.

it takes doctors time to assess the damage and to determine prognoses. Also, during the initial phase of an emergency, a doctor's obligation is to the patient whom he is keeping alive, not to news organizations. . . .

A chief reason for having a single source of information about such a patient is to reduce chances for the release of inaccurate and potentially harmful information. But there can be a thin line between issuing reliable information and managing the news. The risk of having a single spokesman is that the leader's aides may impose limitations that are not in the public interest. History is full of accounts of family and doctors who withheld from the public vital facts about a political leader's health.*

There were other questions that arose in connection with the instantaneous and saturation coverage of these events, which might or might not justify NBC's decision to forgo "tonnage" and "repetition" in its handling of the Pope's shooting. Did such intense concentration encourage emulation of the violent act portrayed? What did the endless replaying of the act itself—the slow motion, the freeze frames, the closeups—along with the rehashing and exploring of the background and motives of the assassins accomplish?

The answers seemed at best ambiguous.

Five months after the attack on the Pope in Rome, another major world figure was the object of an assassination attempt, which was neither so ambiguous in its motivation nor so lucky in its outcome.

On October 6, 1981 in Cairo, Anwar el-Sadat, the President of Egypt, was gunned down while reviewing his military forces at a national celebration of the 1973 Yom Kippur War.

Again, so far as the TV viewer and radio listener were concerned, there were long hours of uncertainty in which rumors and unconfirmed reports from unofficial sources overlapped and contradicted each other. When the attack took place, Egyptian TV, like everyone else at the scene, was

*A recent and vivid illustration was the successful five-year cover-up of the Shah's terminal cancer, which, if it had been revealed earlier, could have had international repercussions, including the elimination of the year's biggest story.

focused overhead on a colorful, noisy flight of Mirage jets. With the sound of the first shots the screen went black. From that moment throughout the morning, no certain word got out of Cairo to an anxious world. TV satellites were embargoed. There were no official government statements.

Although at least two reporters from U. S. networks were eyewitnesses—Doreen Kays of ABC and Mitchell Krauss of CBS, who was actually wounded by a piece of shrapnel during the attack—no clear version of what actually took place was available. Nor were the three other network representatives on duty in Cairo, Scotti Williston of CBS and Paul Miller and Art Kent of NBC, able to put together a coherent account.

That there had been an attempted assassination with President Sadat the intended victim was first reported to the American public at 7:11 A.M. by Charles Osgood on CBS Radio. NBC's *Today* was the first to carry the news on TV at 7:22. An audiocassette, recording automatic weapons fire, followed by screams and a confusion of sounds, was repeated throughout the morning. But there were no pictures to accompany it. Nor was anyone able to say exactly what had happened—whether it was a coup d'etat or an isolated incident—or who the assassins dressed in Egyptian army uniforms might be, or why, apparently during the first crucial seconds, they received no answering fire from Sadat's guards.

That Sadat had been wounded and taken to a hospital was finally acknowledged. At the same time his condition was described as "not life threatening."

At 9:57 ex-President Jimmy Carter told CBS that friends in Cairo had reported to him that "President Sadat will be all right." A half hour later Scotti Williston, Cairo bureau manager for CBS, told Dan Rather on the air that her sources had informed her "that the President has passed away." It was the first time the possibility that the assassination attempt had been successful was mentioned.

And still the uncertainty persisted. In one ten-minute stretch shortly after 11 A.M., ABC TV viewers were told by Senator Charles Percy that Sadat was alive. Barbara Walters, a minute later, quoted the semiofficial Cairo newspaper, *Al Akhbar,* as saying Sadat was dead, and then another report followed saying there were two wounds, but that the Egyptian President was in no danger. At 11:20 U.S. State Department sources were reported as saying that Sadat was still alive. At 11:21 Reuters, the international news agency, reported Sadat dead. There was general rejoicing reported in Beirut. In Libya, where people were dancing in the streets, the report was that Sadat had died in a helicopter on the way to the hospital.

There were consistent denials of Sadat's death from the Egyptian Embassy in Washington where the flag was inexplicably taken down and then returned to its mast. At 12:02 P.M., CBS' Mitchell Krauss, waiting at the Cairo airport for a plane to take him to Rome, gave an eyewitness account of the shooting but was unable to clarify Sadat's condition.

As the day wore on, the rumors passed on to the American public by radio and TV grew progressively more ominous. Senator Larry Pressler, visiting his home state of South Dakota, told the Associated Press that he had been informed by the White House that President Sadat was dead. A photo opportunity involving President Reagan and the visiting President of Thailand was canceled. Workmen began setting up a platform in the White House Rose Garden, a sure sign that a statement of prime importance was in the offing. At 11:32 Senator Howard Baker had appeared before the Senate relaying a message from Vice President Bush that Sadat was dead. But the Egyptian authorities refused to confirm. The State Department briefing, traditionally held at noon, was delayed and delayed again. So far as TV, radio and the vast American public were concerned, the watch continued.

There were many signs on air as to the importance the networks assigned the story. In response to the crisis, David Brinkley, who was scheduled to start his job on ABC in mid-November, came on the air for his new employer a month ahead of time. Walter Cronkite, ostensibly retired from regular duties at CBS News, was conspicuously back on board along with his replacement Dan Rather, Bob Schieffer, Lesley Stahl, Diane Sawyer, and most of CBS' first-string reporters. Bill Moyers, not due back at CBS for his second tour of duty for another three weeks, was summoned to do a commentary.

At 9:30 Cronkite was already wisely observing, "I would caution against taking too literally these early reports from Cairo as to the condition of Anwar Sadat. We can be almost certain that the regime is going to cover up whatever his condition is; if it's serious, they're going to cover it up for a period of time."

On ABC, Barbara Walters, seen less frequently in recent months on the network newscast, was back to report on an area where she, like Cronkite, had played a prominent role in Sadat's history-making journey to Jerusalem four years before. Also on hand at ABC were anchors Frank Reynolds and Steve Bell with John Scali, Carl Bernstein, Sam Donaldson, Brit Hume, Sander Vanocur, and Barrie Dunsmore.

Tom Brokaw, soon to be the co-anchor of *The NBC Nightly News,* presided over that network's coverage with incumbent John Chancellor in attendance. Also present were Jane Pauley, Chris Wallace, Marvin Kalb, Bernard Kalb, Tom Pettit, and Richard Valeriani.

When one of NBC's men in Cairo, Art Kent, admitted that he didn't know anything, Brokaw responded, "Art, you're on the air. I don't blame you for not saying something you don't know, but tell us what you don't know." This apparent paradox almost precisely described what Brokaw's network and its competition were trying to do.

To help fill the void, which the official silence from Egypt thrust them into, all three networks gave their audiences the kind of information that day-to-day coverage seldom conveyed. Network appearances were made by ex-Presidents Carter and Ford and former Secretary of State Henry Kissinger. Kissinger was the first to mention, in an interview with ABC, the suspicion that Libyan strongman Muammar el-Qaddafi might have been involved in the attack. Appearing on one or more networks to lend their expertise were Stansfield Turner, ex-head of the CIA; former national security adviser Zbigniew Brzezinski; Professor Edward Said of Columbia University, a member of the Palestine National Council; former Israeli Defense Minister Ezer Weizman; Dan Pattir, former counselor on media affairs to Menachem Begin; and a large assortment of U. S. senators.

In all this talk the possibility of a coup was entertained and dismissed. Estimates of casualties began as low as two killed

and two wounded and went as high as 11 dead and 38 wounded. Those responsible for the incident were variously identified as Muslim fanatics, Libyan hirelings, and simply "The
Brotherhood."

The delicacy of the networks' handling of the central issue
of Sadat—dead or alive?—was demonstrated by Dan
Rather's reaction to the first still photograph of the reviewing
stand surrounded by a confusion of overturned chairs.
Rather's comment: "It is believed, reportedly, supposedly,
allegedly, President Sadat in the lower right-hand corner of
the photograph."

It wasn't until 1:50 P.M., following nearly an hour of readings from the Koran over Cairo radio (the same readings had
preceded the announcement of Gamal Abdel Nasser's death
in 1970), that Vice President Hosni Mubarak, still not visible to
U. S. audiences, made his announcement to the Egyptian
people and the world of Sadat's demise. 40 minutes later a
grim President Reagan, flanked by his tearful wife in the
White House Rose Garden, made his announcement of
Sadat's death to the U. S. TV audience.

Finally, at 2:45 in the afternoon, the raw, violent truth that
had been hinted at for over seven hours was made visible to
the network anchors and the U. S. public at the same time. In
six minutes of unedited footage shot by ABC cameraman
Fabrice Moussos, who had sheltered himself behind the reviewing stand to escape the gunfire, Americans saw it all: the
formation of Mirage fighters roaring across the sky streaming
colored smoke, the camera suddenly dipping to catch six
soldiers running across the open plaza toward the reviewing
stand where Sadat and the other dignitaries were seated,
raking their targets at point-blank range, apparently unchal-
lenged. Next the unsteady camera focussed on the horror and
confusion of the stand itself, the overturned chairs, the dead
and the wounded, the stunned and disbelieving.

Although it was still difficult for the public or professionals
to interpret properly what they had seen, there was no question that this was terrorism at its bloodiest, brutal worst, there
on the screen for everyone to witness.

A moment later all three networks and their chastened
viewers had returned to their regular schedules. On ABC

anchor Frank Reynolds went off saying, "This is the third time in seven months we have been unwelcome messengers of horrible news." Then his network faded into a plug for *Happy Days* and *Three's Company*. CBS was already into *Search for Tomorrow*, which it interrupted to show the assassination footage. On NBC it was back to the serial *Texas*, in progress.

The evening newscasts were devoted nearly 100 percent to the tragedy. CBS, of the three networks, chose to devote an hour of its precious prime time to considering the events of the day, what had led up to them, and what might come next. Both ABC and NBC had late-night specials and all three morning shows were given over almost in their entirety to followups of the tragic event.

To choose among the performances of the three networks in this painful instance was difficult, if not impossible. They all faced the same problems with comparable resourcefulness. They all made similar massive commitments of time, staff, and money. They all sacrificed substantial revenues by cancelling a major portion of their daytime soaps and games and the lucrative commercials that came with them. If CBS Radio was the first to report the news and NBC's *Today* the first TV program to acknowledge it, ABC was the only network that stuck with the story without interruption from beginning to end. NBC had slipped in 20 minutes of *Las Vegas Gambit* between the extended *Today* show and continuous coverage that began at 10:30 EDT. CBS had reverted to its regular schedule from 9 to 9:25 A.M., and then strayed again at 2:38 P.M. after President Reagan's announcement of Sadat's death, thus trailing the other two networks with its airing of the chilling Fabrice Moussos footage.*

For the day, ABC came out, once again, at the top of the

---

*There were two other films of the assassination, one from German TV, which the Cable News Network brought out of Cairo via satellite through Amman, Jordan. The second was the footage that Mitchell Krauss flew to Rome and put on the satellite there. It was finally played on a special six-minute report on CBS at 5:34 that afternoon. Neither was as graphic or shocking as the ABC clip, which would be used by the Egyptian government in its official inquiry into the shooting.

ratings. CBS got high points with the critics, however, for disrupting its prime-time schedule to try to give its viewers some coherent version of what had happened.

Radio's performance was less impressive. After the first bulletins it ran consistently behind TV in its coverage, sticking to the every-once-in-a-while, every-hour-on-the-hour approach.

There were some exceptions, most notably radio station KABC-AM Los Angeles where talk-show host Michael Jackson filled his four allotted hours interviewing an international roster of experts including Ari Rat, editor and managing director of the *Jerusalem Post*, ABC's Pierre Salinger in Paris, psychiatrist Dr. Frederick Hacker, director of the Institute of Conflict Research in Vienna, former KGB agent Vladimir Sakharov, and M. T. Mehdi, president of the New York-based Arab-American Relations Committee.

Four days later the American networks, along with 800 other representatives of the international media, gathered to attend the fallen leader's funeral, which reached the air in the United States at 5 A.M. EDT. Regrouping in Cairo were top broadcast talents including Barbara Walters, Peter Jennings, Tom Brokaw, and Walter Cronkite, the only American newsperson on the Egyptians' official list of funeral invitees.

The roster of world leaders present included American ex-Presidents Carter, Ford, and Nixon, Prince Charles of England (who had spent part of his recent honeymoon in Egypt), heads of government—Mitterrand of France, Schmidt of Germany, Begin of Israel, and such U. S. dignitaries as Alexander Haig, Caspar Weinberger, Henry Kissinger, Jeane Kirkpatrick, Rosalynn Carter, and Sol Linowitz. But the coverage, done exclusively by Egyptian TV, took little advantage of the celebrity turnout. The cameras were kept tight on the Egyptian mourners in the funeral procession, and later on Mrs. Sadat, the Sadat children, and their mates, with a glimpse or two of the former Empress Farah of Iran and her eldest son. The military had embargoed all short-wave transmissions along the course of the funeral procession so that there was no possibility even of voice descriptions of the cortege. The network reporters watching the proceedings from a studio in downtown Cairo saw the same pictures as the viewers in America.

Barbara Walters, as a special friend of President and Mrs. Sadat, had visited the widow and was able to bring back a personal account of her response to the tragedy. Retired or not, Walter Cronkite was given the distinction of being the first non-Egyptian journalist to interview Sadat's successor, Hosni Mubarak. Walters followed with her interview 24 hours later. Lou Cioffi of ABC scored with the first post-assassination talk with Libya's Muammar el-Qaddafi. The interview, which was given three minutes on *World News Tonight,* was conducted in Qaddafi's desert tent where he expressed sober satisfaction at a death some held him responsible for.

The competition between the American networks was a melancholy echo of the exciting days of shuttle diplomacy and Camp David only three years before.

Death and catastrophe hung heavy in the TV schedules of the two seasons under consideration in this survey. The eruption of Mount St. Helens. The earthquake in southern Italy. The multiple murders in Atlanta. The race riots in Miami. The Cuban and Haitian refugees. Even the Reagan Inaugural was given an ominous resonance by the last-minute release of the hostages. And the one totally sunny event of the two years, the British Royal Wedding, took place under the cloud of the death fasts in Ireland and the riots in a dozen cities from Liverpool to Brixton.

Was it that life, indeed, was growing grimmer, or was it just that TV was committed to seeing only the gloomy side of things? Or could it have meant an increased sensitivity to the mixed nature of the real world on the part of a medium that was slowly coming of age?

In June 1981 *CBS Reports* aired a program, *The Defense of the United States,* that seemed to confirm that it was all of the above. "An unprecedented documentary project, more ambitious than any CBS News has undertaken," was the official network description. Dan Rather, who anchored the program, labeled it "the most important documentary project of the decade." Actually *The Defense of the United States* was five programs, the first beginning in prime time on a Sunday night followed by four others at the same hour through Thursday. A staff of 80 had taken nine months and the largest documentary budget in CBS history to put the series together.

"The nation is about to commit itself to the biggest defense spending buildup in our history," Rather stated grimly at the outset, "over the next five years, $1.3 trillion. Yet, for a committment of this magnitude, we have heard little debate about alternatives, about its implications, about the effects on our society."

The first segment, "Ground Zero" was devoted to a description of what a trillion-dollar war might be like and "what would happen to a community [Bellevue, Nebraska]—two miles from Strategic Air Command headquarters, 13 miles from downtown Omaha—if a 15-megaton nuclear bomb hit."

At the end of a disturbing hour Dr. Kosta Tsipis, associate director of the Department of Physics at MIT, said:

In the history of mankind, we've always thought in terms of killing the enemy so we can survive. . . . That is not true anymore. If you attempt to kill your enemy by nuclear weapons, you will also die. It's a way—an entirely new mode, an entirely new environment, an entirely new ecology of survival. For the first time, you cannot insure your own survival by killing the enemy. The enemy surely can be killed, but you will also be killed assuredly yourself.

Given that truth, the viewer was asked to watch four more evenings of programs dealing with (1) nuclear war in Europe—a frightening possibility; (2) the condition of America's armed forces—not very good; (3) the condition of U.S. weaponry—bad; and (4) how things are militarily for the Soviet Union—not all that wonderful.

On Thursday evening Rather said:

We end this series as we began it—in the heartland of America, in a world which can destroy itself in less time than Lincoln took to deliver the Gettysburg Address. We've entered an age of conventional wisdom about very unconventional weapons of war. And we're heading toward the largest military buildup in this nation's history with few questions asked. All of us as Americans want our defenses to be strong and secure. We face a dangerous decade and a resolute enemy. But will we make ourselves stronger by unquestioning faith in new weapons technology? Will our European alliance be strengthened by a strategy that might force us to destroy Europe in order to save it? Will we increase our national security by insisting there is a way to fight a limited nuclear war without mutual destruction? We hope these broadcasts have helped stimulate this debate for, on it, may rest our survival.

The debate was not long in coming. The early reviews were mostly enthusiastic. *The Washington Post* called the series "the first documentary epic in TV history." *Time* magazine said it was not only "the longest and most expensive network documentary ever, but perhaps the most thoughtful and incisive TV examination of the American military as well."

The Economist in London said, "CBS has shown that American television, when freed from the crass commercialism which dominates so much of its output, is a match for anyone." There was some dissent. The American Security Council, a conservative group which had earlier produced such pro-military advocacy documentaries for TV as *Attack on the Americas* and *The SALT Syndrome,* demanded air time for rebuttal.

Accuracy in Media's *AIM Report* was predictably indignant. Under the headline, THE CBS ATTACK ON NATIONAL DEFENSE, and such subheads as CRONKITE TRUE TO FORM and CRONKITE ABETS DISINFORMATION, AIM wrote:

CBS News is in the vanguard of this effort to destroy the new pro-defense consensus. . . . This unprecedented, costly series began with a program that was designed to convince the public that there could be no such thing as a winnable nuclear war.

At the end of its critique AIM added:

This series was sponsored by some of the major businesses in this country. Perhaps they should be asked to explain why they helped underwrite Soviet disinformation on issues vital to our national security.

It then listed the names and addresses of the heads of

Whirlpool, Warner-Lambert, Clorox, General Motors, General Foods, and Chesebrough-Pond's.

The most extended and detailed critique was published in the American Jewish Committee's neo-conservative journal, *Commentary*. Entitled "CBS vs. Defense," it was written by Joshua Muravchik, a research associate at Georgetown University's Center for Strategic and International Studies,* and by John E. Haynes, a former associate staff member of the Senate Armed Services Committee. Its 10,500 words were devoted to the theses that not only had CBS started out with its mind made up, but it had gotten its facts all wrong. Muravchik's and Haynes' conclusion:

A viewer who sat through all five evenings of *The Defense of the United States* would have learned that the United States is not threatened by any external enemy, but rather by the tragic propensity of the two superpowers each to see in the other a mirror reflection of its own fears and hostilities. Guided by these misplaced fears, by the insensibilities of the military mentality, and by the venalities of congressmen and contractors, the United States is about to spend itself into bankruptcy on weapons, which, had we to use them in a real war, would not work, except to kill Western European civilians. Worst of all, our Dr. Strangeloves are pursuing the self-fulfilling idea that nuclear war is indeed possible and are on the way to incinerating us all.

This caricature of U. S. defense policy is a familiar one. It had great currency a decade ago, before it was rejected by most Americans in favor of a more realistic view. Perhaps one reason for its rejection is that it does not stand up to scrutiny, as should be clear from the large number of factual errors, distortions, and misrepresentations to which CBS had to resort in order to bolster its case.

CBS is entitled to its opinions. *The Defense of the United States,* however, was not presented as an editorial but as a news documentary. As the largest information outlet in the Western world, CBS has a responsibility to impartiality and objectivity, which it has seriously failed to meet. For the record (and for the Federal Communications Commission), the network will continue to say that its series presented all sides, but the people at CBS gave every indication that they knew otherwise. They felt that "the opposition wasn't doing its job," so they staged their own guerrilla attack against the emerging consensus in favor of rearming America.

*UN Ambassador Jeane Kirkpatrick was also associated with the Center as a member of its research council.

The debate that the CBS series had hoped to stimulate had obviously been joined. To those who questioned the wisdom of CBS putting such a grim extended series in the heart of their late spring prime-time schedule, there was an emphatic answer in the columns of *TV Guide*:

Along Broadcast Row, it is practically carved in stone that documentaries may be deadly to your ratings. For the top-rated network to schedule one in prime time, the programming gurus thunder, is suicidal. To schedule one over five hours of prime time, they howl, is sheer madness. Well, those seers had better turn in their tarot cards and goat entrails, because this *CBS Reports* proved them wrong, at least in its first two installments, by reaping a 30 percent share of the audience and sweeping its time period. . . .

At the same time, CBS revealed a rather powerful weapon of its own, one that should be kept in mind the next time the merits of free TV, and pay-TV are compared. Anyone with enough money, a satellite and a pipeline to Hollywood can come up with movies and variety hours that are spicier than what ABC, CBS, and NBC will show you. But *not* anyone can muster an army of skilled journalists to attack a subject as terribly complicated, yet vital, as national defense.

The armaments race was reported by the admirable WGBH *World* series, particularly in "The Red Army," which reinforced some of the CBS findings and was once more attacked as "disinformation."

Nuclear warfare was the subject of several programs, both local and network. Notable among them was *Broken Arrow*, a half-hour documentary produced by KQED-TV, San Francisco, which dealt with the possibility of nuclear-weapons accidents in the Bay Area. In the course of the program, reporter Stephen Talbot revealed for the first time that, instead of the 13 previously recorded nuclear-weapons accidents, there had been actually at least twice that number admitted by the Pentagon with more that cannot be discussed for "political and national security reasons."

Also in San Francisco, KRON-TV aired *First Strike*, a 60-minute documentary putting forward the view that America's strategic nuclear arsenal was no longer capable of deterring nuclear war. The station gave a half hour of air time to *First Strike: The Politics of Fear*, a rebuttal that was put together by

Andrew Stern, chairman of the Broadcast Journalism Department at the University of California, Berkeley, and featured antinuclear physicist Charles Schwartz, Wolfgang Panofsky, director of the linear accelerator center at Stanford University, and Vice Admiral (Ret.) John Marshall Lee, former assistant director of the U. S. Arms Control and Disarmament Agency.

The controversy over the deployment of the MX missile received substantial attention on both commercial and public TV, most importantly from *Bill Moyers' Journal,* which devoted two hours to a live debate on the subject from Salt Lake City.

The Day After Trinity, an outstanding independent documentary aired by KTEH-TV, San Jose, and the Public Broadcasting Service, told the fascinating and disturbing story of J. Robert Oppenheimer and the building of the first atomic bomb, giving a strangely homely view of the background for Armageddon that CBS' five-hour blockbuster was to face 40 years later.

8

Preachers, Politics and Public Broadcasting

B ROADCAST PREACHING has been around since the early days of radio. It included the uplift of Harry Emerson Fosdick as well as the rabble-rousing of Father Charles Coughlin in the 1930s. Along the way were the conspicuously successful electronic ministries of such varied clerics as Bishop Fulton Sheen, Norman Vincent Peale, Billy Graham, and Oral Roberts. In most cases, with the obvious exception of Father Coughlin, they limited themselves to spiritual concerns. Occasionally, as with the Reverend Carl McIntire's *20th Century Reformation Hour,* the border between spiritual counsel and political advocacy had been breached and the government had taken corrective action. In the campaign of 1980 a group of religious conservatives known under the rubric "The Moral Majority" suddenly surfaced in force, flying colors of unmistakable political import. So conspicuous had they become in the fall of 1981 that A. Bartlett Giamatti, president of Yale University, made them the subject of his welcoming address to the freshman class, warning young men and women against the "self-proclaimed 'Moral Majority' and its satellite or client groups, cunning in the use of a native blend of old intimidation and new technology. . . ."

Giamatti's characterization of the phenomenon was not flattering. "Angry at change, rigid in the application of chauvinistic slogans, absolutistic in morality, they threaten through political pressure or public denunciation whoever dares to disagree with their authoritarian positions. . . . Using television, direct mail, and economic boycott, they would sweep before them anyone who holds a different opinion." (For another consideration of the problem, see page 236.)

Indeed, the numbers associated with the phenomenon were formidable. Of the more than 50 percent of Americans who acknowledged themselves to be "born again" Christians, 20 percent considered themselves activist fundamentalist evangelicals, the group from which the Moral Majority derived its principal strength. Servicing this group were 1,500 Christian radio stations and 35 Christian TV stations reaching a claimed public of nearly 130 million Americans each week.

In the fall of 1980 the Reverend Marion G. "Pat" Robertson, founder of the Christian Broadcasting Network, headquartered in Virginia Beach, Virginia, launched what he labeled a "wholesome" alternative to the "unethical televison network giants." In addition to religious soap operas, situation comedies and game shows, the network's new round-the-clock schedule would offer up to nine news updates daily, incorporating "Biblical insights . . . the kind of insights you're not going to get, say, from Dan Rather," and documentaries, including a 13-week series on pornography entitled X-posé (hosted by TV star Efrem Zimbalist, Jr.), as well as "a totally revolutionary concept in news" that would concentrate on "soft" or human-interest stories.

Robertson, whose CBN was the first evangelical customer of the RCA Satcom I, claimed to reach 150 TV affiliates including his own four owned-and-operated stations, plus 2,600 cable systems coast to coast. By 1985 Robertson, who boasted he had already reached 13.5 million homes, expected to pass the 35 million mark.*

In addition to such 100-percent Christian outlets, many of

---

*That the televangelists' figures might be somewhat inflated was indicated by A. C. Nielsen's report that Reverend Jerry Falwell's claimed audience of 25 million was closer to 1.2 million as of May 1980.

the nation's radio and TV stations had one or more spokesmen for the religious right somewhere in their schedules. The
evangelists spent an estimated $600 million annually to buy
radio and TV time. Their income from audience donations
and other sources was put as high as $1 billion.

In the election of 1980 the support of the religious right was
given credit by many for Ronald Reagan's landslide victory.
The Christian Voice Moral Government Fund targeted 32
congressional candidates on its hit list for having "poor moral
voting records." The group distributed 2½ million copies of
its "moral report card" to churchgoers, and 23 of its targeted
candidates were defeated. And the Moral Majority was unquestionably instrumental in the defeat of such liberals as
George McGovern, Birch Bayh, Frank Church, John Culver,
and John Brademas.*

Right-wing Christian groups had been the subject of a spate
of radio and TV essays in the weeks preceding and following
the Reagan victory. Among them were an understated but still
alarming essay by WCCO Minneapolis' vigilant *Moore Report*
and a surprisingly objective take-out on book-burning and
censorship by KOOL-TV in Phoenix, Arizona, the heart of
Moral Majority country.** In addition, cautionary segments
of *60 Minutes, 20/20,* and a *Bill Moyers' Journal* were devoted to
the subject.

On its side, the religious right had produced its own share of
advocacy specials that had little or nothing to do with religion
or, in most instances, with legitimate reporting. Conspicuous
among these were the Reverend James Robison's *Wake Up,
America: We're All Hostages!,* which took an aggressive pro-

*Carter and Anderson also had strong ties to the evangelical Christian
movement, but thanks to his conservative stand on such issues as abortion,
defense spending, and the ERA, Reagan—who was demonstrably less
devout—got the Moral Majority votes.
**The station, owned by Tom Chauncey and Gene Autrey, is normally quite
sympathetic to religious causes, sometimes covering religious events up to
five hours at a stretch. For the last 20 years the station identification,
"Blessed is the nation whose God is the Lord," has been aired approximately
ten times a day.

defense, anti-Soviet stance, and *Attack on the Family*. From
Reverend Jerry Falwell, the titular head of the Moral Majority, came *America, You're Too Young to Die,* which gave a documentary picture of moral depravity from coast to coast;
Rescue the Perishing, about the Vietnamese boat people; and
Jerry Falwell in Thailand. These programs were shown on more
than 200 stations nationwide. *Whatever Happened to the Human
Race?,* a 90-minute anti-abortion show, was seen in ten markets. And The Christian Broadcasting Network sold nearly
2,000 copies of its film *Let Their Eyes Be Opened,* a half-hour
broadside against the evils of "secular humanism," a term with
which the Christian right anathematized "liberals" and all
others unfortunate enough to hold divergent views.

To date the admitted thrust of the Moral Majority's pressure groups, the Coalition for Better Television and the National Federation for Decency, was toward the entertainment
sector and particularly that portion of it which they considered violent, profane, or sexually offensive. They threatened
an advertiser boycott, and although polls indicated that most
Americans, whatever their religious allegiances, had little
interest in deleting violent or sexually offensive shows from
the TV schedule, the networks took alarm.*

Top executives from all three networks had gone out of
their way to acknowledge CBTV's potential power and de-
nounce its aim and methods. Gene Jankowski, president of
CBS/Broadcast Group, pointed out that one coalition mailing
piece listed *CBS Reports* and the CBS newsmagazine for young

---

*A Roper poll taken in April of 1981 for NBC found that while 41 percent of
those queried said they were against sex and violence on TV, only two of the
list of 17 shows deemed most offensive got even 3 percent of the respondents to say they would like to see them deleted from network schedules.
ABC commissioned a nationwide study that found 91 percent of Americans
have never boycotted a product because of something on television they
disliked. Of the 6.6 percent of respondents who identified themselves as
part of the Moral Majority, more than half disagreed with the tactic of an
economic boycott. Only 2.3 percent of the respondents supported CBTV's
proposed boycott. And a CBS News investigation found that 30 percent of
the 300 groups listed by Reverend Donald Wildmon as members of his
coalition denied membership.

people, *30 Minutes,* as having aired objectionable segments. "America's largest and most trusted source of news and information is clearly targeted as well," Jankowski concluded. "The Coalition apparently wishes to decide the stories CBS News is to cover."

A traditional opponent of the networks, Action for Children's Television, joined the counterattack, launching an anti-censorship campaign aimed at CBTV with these ominous words:

The Coalition for Better TV . . . is trying to dictate what the American public may or may not watch on television. Perhaps no one will miss the first program forced off the air in the name of morality. But the New Right's censorship crusade will not stop there. What will be the next target? A production of *A Streetcar Named Desire*? A documentary on teenage pregnancy? The news?

After a series of feints and counterfeints, and before the effectiveness of its tactics could be definitely tested, CBTV drew back supposedly to await demonstration of the broadcasters' and advertisers' good faith and called off its boycott until further notice.*

The Christian right, having declared its right to intrude in the selection of the material the U.S. public would be permitted to see, had itself gone on record with highly controversial positions on such varied subjects as abortion, the ERA, the Panama Canal, Taiwan, SALT II and the defense buildup, the Department of Education, and the balanced budget. Having seen its tactics succeed against an impressive list of political candidates, the Christian right might well try to exert pressure on radio and TV news.

Before it simmered down, the dispute involving the net-

---

*Procter & Gamble, the nation's number one TV advertiser with $486.3 million spent on commercial time in 1980, announced in mid-June 1981 that it had canceled its ads on 50 TV movies and series episodes that contained excessive sex and violence, including seven of 10 series cited by the Coalition for Better Television as "top sex-oriented." Representatives of Warner-Lambert, SmithKline, Gillette, and Phillips Petroleum also conferred privately with CBTV.

works, the advertisers, and the Moral Majority prompted considerable comment.

In *The New York Times* conservative columnist William Safire wrote:

Don't be misled: It is not "sponsor pressure" that keeps the networks from tackling important themes on newscasts or documentaries; sponsors can be found who seek courageous reputations, or if not, networks can gain critical stature by sustaining such programs.

. . . That's one reason I do not worry about moral-majoritarian pressure. The boycott, like the strike, is a weapon that can be used for bad ends (to punish gutsy documentary producers) or for good ends (to take some of the profit out of soap-opera sex). But the weapon is in private hands, not government hands, and is thus free speech to be cherished, not deplored . . .

Capitalism's new technology offers a second line of free-speech defense.

Cable's lines are breaking up that old mass media of mine. The admen call it "narrowcasting": many more channels will enable advertisers to reach specific audiences, insuring a place for smut-coms, for ballet, and for Elmer Gantry to pour hellfire and brimstone on the other channels.

The network chieftains protecting the sale of salacious snickering by crying "free speech" are today's dinosaurs and tomorrow's fossils. Free speech finds its safety in numbers—not in masses staring at what a trio of men select, but in the numbers of new channels that will let a hundred flowers bloom amidst a hundred weeds.

Somewhat less apocalyptic was Hodding Carter III's comment in *The Wall Street Journal:*

It is the absolute duty of the television networks to stand fast behind their programs, no matter what it costs, because to succumb to the boycott is to conspire in the murder of "the creative and journalistic spirit."

Or, to put it another way, if what is at stake here is really the principle of free expression in an open society, then television has an obligation that transcends this year's balance sheet, or next year's, or the one after that. It must offer the shows that are distasteful to the coalition, even if major advertisers pull out, until such time as audience surveys determine they are unpopular enough to warrant the same hook given to other programming failures.

But if the principle really at stake, behind all the fine words from television's spokesmen, is the right to make big bucks for schlock shows, then we might as well begin preparation for the funeral. The nets will cave.

For the time being, at least, the networks held out.

The ABC News-Harris Survey of November 24, 1980, reported that the "so-called Moral Majority turned out to vote in handsome numbers, taking away Carter's base in the South and contributing two-thirds of the President-elect's margin nationwide."

The political campaign for 1980 was more than ever skewed toward the electronic media (For a report on politics and broadcasting see page 163). Not only did the Moral Majority have a broadcast-oriented constituency that it delivered intact to Reagan and the adversaries of the nation's most conspicuous liberals, but it was also aided in its task by a new force that was operating with increasing effectiveness in the electronic arena. In 1974 there were 608 so-called political action committees. In 1980 there were 2,551. Devised as a means to get around the Federal Election Spending Act, ostensibly devoted to issues rather than candidates, these groups had no ceiling to the amount they could spend in any given campaign. In the 1980 election they spent $133 million to help elect the candidates of their choice.

The richest and most successful in the field was the National Conservative Political Action Committee (NCPAC). Its executive director, John T. Dolan, had been quoted as saying, "A group like ours could lie through its teeth and the candidate it helps stays clean."

In 1980 four out of six of the liberal senators that NCPAC as well as the Christian conservatives had targeted for extinction —Frank Church of Idaho, Birch Bayh of Indiana, George McGovern of South Dakota, and John Culver of Iowa— went down in defeat.

According to Fred Wertheimer, president of Common Cause, "With no one to answer to and with huge amounts of money to spend, groups such as Mr. Dolan's are seriously undermining the concept of fair competition in our political campaigns."

Richard Richards, chairman of the Republican National Committee, was both critical and skeptical. He contended that NCPAC's Idaho push had backfired and because of its ruthless tactics almost cost the Republicans an election that the unvarnished issues would have delivered to them anyway.

Nevertheless, three months after the inauguration of President Reagan—with Election Day 1982 still 18 months away—NCPAC was back at work, launching a radio and TV campaign against Senator Paul Sarbanes of Maryland and Congressmen Dan Rostenkowski of Illinois, Jim Jones of Oklahoma, and Jim Wright of Texas, four Democrats who had come out strongly against the new administration's economic policies.

A few months later NCPAC had kicked off campaigns against Senators Edward Kennedy of Massachusetts, Lowell Weicker of Connecticut, Robert Byrd of West Virginia, and John Melcher of Montana.

Dolan estimated his budget for the 1982 congressional elections at $8 million—$500,000 more than he had spent in the 1980 elections. Still, his sailing was not completely smooth. A move was afoot to extend the equal-time ruling to cover nonpartisan political action committee commercials, which would seriously cramp NCPAC's style. And in several states Dolan met resistance from TV stations. The three network affiliates and one independent in Tulsa turned down NCPAC's anti-Jones commercials, four stations in Dallas-Ft. Worth refused anti-Wright ads, and three in the Hartford-Springfield market—where Dolan had decided to open his anti-Kennedy campaign—turned him away as well. By December 1981, a total of 13 TV stations had refused to air NCPAC ads. Dolan responded by filing a $5 million lawsuit against seven liberal members of Congress and the 13 stations, charging that they had conspired to block the airing of the ads.

If NCPAC's budget was mounting, so were those of politicians from presidential hopefuls on down. To get the presidential nomination Reagan had spent $26.7 million prior to the Republican convention. In the same period Carter had spent $18.5 million, Bush $22.2 million, Kennedy $12.3 million, compared to Reagan's $16 million in 1976, Ford's $13.3 million and Carter's $12 million.

And if they had their way, at least some of the candidates would have spent even more. In December 1979, thanks to a suit filed by President Carter and Vice President Mondale when CBS refused to sell them 30 minutes of prime TV time to kick off their political campaign, the Supreme Court had ruled that broadcasters must make "reasonable" amounts of time available to legally qualified candidates. The decision was expected to stimulate an even earlier start for the campaigns, with expenditures growing commensurately.

In November 1981, the Republican party had already begun its 1982 campaign, spending the first $2 million of an estimated $12 million advertising budget. The hard-up Democrats, with one-tenth the budget, objected and asked the FCC to call a halt or grant them equal time.

As this rush of gold, local and national, increased, much of it was destined to fall on radio and TV, whether they wanted it or not. Meanwhile there were indications that by 1984 the broadcasting of politics might be drastically different.

In remarks made to the Associated Press Board convention in June 1981, Bill Leonard, president of CBS News, gave a forecast of things to come:

. . . It would seem that we are in a kind of golden age of journalism. We have at our fingertips more ways of gathering and transmitting information than we have ever had. Our profession has a sophistication and luster which is new and flattering. We are making a better living than our predecessors. We are attracting countless numbers of talented young people.

It's a rosy picture. But I wouldn't be a newsman if I couldn't find a few things wrong with it, and I can.

For instance, I am troubled by the fact that no matter how much information we give people, and how often we give it to them, they don't seem to pay any more attention to it than they ever did. There are more facts floating around now than ever, thanks to us. But it is by no means apparent that the public is any better informed in what we consider areas of importance . . . or whether they care much either. Consider national elections. Last year the networks alone spent 75 million dollars covering the presidential campaigns. The political parties spent *175* million. And what do the voting statistics show? Less than 54 percent of the eligible voters went to the polls, which was less than the percentage in the previous presidential election before that. Without the benefit of our superior technology, the island of Malta has a voting percentage of more than 90, and in Iceland more than 80 percent of the citizens vote. Elections in America are attracting more and more reporters and fewer and fewer voters.* The emphasis we put on them seems to mean nothing to the people we are talking to. . . .

The things we place the most emphasis on are the very things they ignore. We keep telling people that something is important and they keep telling us to go soak our heads.

In October, President Thomas H. Wyman of CBS, Inc., in his first public speech after 14 months in the top network job, announced at the International Radio and Television Society in New York that his network, having covered the national political conventions "gavel-to-gavel" since the early days of radio, was no longer going to do so. His reasons:

Unfortunately, over the years the conventions have become far less significant political events. . . . We must ask ourselves whether the public is well served by the availability of long hours when the political process is embarrassed by triviality. The viewers say no. They are watching other programs. . . .

We cannot blame the politicians very much, I suppose, for they are responding in a very natural way to what they perceive as a golden opportunity for a week of national visibility. The blame is ours.

We have been responsible for handling an important step in the political process, and we have done it badly when we were on the air with low-content broadcasts. All of us have witnessed the embarrassment of anchormen struggling in a desperate effort to create broadcasts out of non-events.

As for CBS plans for future conventions:

We do not plan gavel-to-gavel coverage for the 1984 conventions. We will be staffed and equipped to provide coverage as fully as the

*Between 1960 and 1980, the percentage of eligible U.S. voters exercising their franchise dropped from 62.8 percent to 53.9 percent, the lowest in any democracy.

news warrants. We will be there when the conventions open and major developments will be broadcast live. We anticipate that comprehensive summaries will be carried each evening, along with special-subject highlights. It is my expectation that our newspeople will fill our public service responsibilities far better if we approach the conventions with this perspective.

We probably will not enjoy any appreciable financial benefit. An extensive editorial and technical complex still will be necessary to provide this coverage. There will still be inevitable difficulties in scheduling around the portions of the conventions we do carry live.

Wyman, a former Pillsbury flour executive from Minneapolis with no journalistic experience behind him, was also critical of other political coverage. "We must all exercise more editorial judgment than we have in the past, when there was a tendency toward slavishly full coverage of the primaries."

There were those who heartily agreed with Wyman. Fred Friendly, ex-president of CBS News, said of the election and convention coverage of 1980, "It's a bar mitzvah, a coronation, a bore—and a waste of money. That money would be far better spent on real news."

Walter Cronkite was of a different opinion. Before embarking on covering his eighth and last presidential election, he said:

I would agree that some of the drama is gone. You don't have that human confrontation—a winner and a loser determined right there in front of your eyes. But the importance of having gavel-to-gavel coverage is that this is commercial television's one great opportunity—and once every four years is surely not too often—to present the public with one great civics lesson. This is the root, the core of our democratic process. Why not show it to the people? The mere exposure of it forces it into the public consciousness.

As for others, ABC's president of news, Roone Arledge, whose network had gone back to nearly full convention coverage after 12 years of doing what CBS now proposed for 1984, was not convinced that he should revert to this scaled-down approach. Bill Small of NBC was determined to stick with full coverage. "We think it's far too early to write off the conventions as a political institution worthy of live, continuous coverage."

Wyman's stand, brave as it seemed in its calling a dull occasion a dull occasion, had its attendant ironies. Television, which had made the conventions what they were today, was now apparently abandoning its own creation. If it was, as Fred Friendly suggested, in favor of "real news," such a desertion might be justified. But that prospect seemed dim. More likely the long hours spent in convention halls would be exchanged for the boredom and waste of money of run-of-the-mill prime-time TV fare.

And so again the brave new world of cable would be left to pick up the conventions as even now cable was picking up Congress, the United Nations, and many other occasions of local and national importance that broadcasters had long since tuned out.

Public broadcasting, which remained the sector of radio and TV most staunchly committed to speaking out, also continued to be the area most vulnerable to outside attack and to the shifting fortunes of the broadcast industry as a whole.

The arrival of the Reagan Administration heralded a host of cutbacks that directly affected the nation's public broadcasting stations. First and foremost was the elimination of the insulated funding voted to public broadcasting six years before. Already the Carter Administration had planned to cut the Corporation for Public Broadcasting's budget from a peak of $172 million in 1982 and the same in 1983 to $130 million in each of the next three years. Reagan's cutbacks slashed $35 million from Carter's 1983 budget and called for even harsher yearly reductions to a low of $85 million in 1985—less than half of CPB's appropriation for 1982. Although public stations got only 25 percent of their funds from the federal government and some of the bigger stations got as little as 10 to 15 percent, rising costs and a generally worsening economic climate along with the government cutbacks had a definite impact on local news and public affairs programming.

In the 1980–81 season the nation's richest public TV station, WNET in New York, had eliminated virtually all its regularly scheduled local programs except two shows for New Jersey audiences that FCC commitments required. In October

1980 KQED San Francisco canceled its *Evening Edition,* the longest-running nightly news program on public TV.

Cutbacks of state funds had resulted in serious reductions in public affairs programming in Idaho and Wisconsin. Individual projects and series were threatened by the drastic budget reductions at the National Endowments for the Humanities and the Arts and the Department of Education, all heavy backers of public TV fare.

Most seriously affected of all by government withdrawal of funds was the fragile environment of the independent producers. Almost completely excluded from the commercial networks and leaning heavily on federal and state grants for funding, these loners were responsible for some of the most courageous and original informational programming on the air. Their distress was apparent in comments made to the survey.

One award-winning independent producer from New York wrote:

Realistically I don't think independently produced public affairs documentaries will have much of a chance to get broadcast over the next few years. The funding sources that have been a major support are drying up. Cable TV does not seem to hold out much hope. Public TV seems to be in transition, and with fear of offending the Reagan Administration which has a hold on their purse strings, it seems unlikely there will be much outspoken public affairs programming, or much to look forward to in the way of the kind of powerful statements independent producers can create with their documentaries. For people like me, who have been doing this kind of thing for years, it is a holding action, hoping I can survive.

Another independent wrote from California:

There is, unfortunately, very little room for the work of independents in the current world of broadcasting. The commercial networks all have "in-house" production policies, and proposed budget cuts for CPB and PBS threaten recent gains in the arena of public television. Cable has begun to provide some outlet, but the major cable companies are recreating the same situation as commercial broadcasting. In short, considering the depth and quality of the work of many independents, the situation in this country is appalling. Certainly we have a more responsive situation in the European countries, Japan, and Australia.

The distinction between staff producers and independents was indicated by the following two comments:

Independents offer a unique and different perspective from staff producers in that they often have the *access* to a story or situation that most staff producers simply cannot have. Independents have the *time* to cover a story in depth and to explore ramifications. They have no sponsor they must respond to, and need not concern themselves with commercial considerations. For me, the most important difference is the care and attention independents are able to give to a project because they're not covering several stories at one time and do not have to be involved in the internal workings inherent in many staff situations.

And . . .

Staff producers often are in a position . . . of having to follow the edicts or whims of executive producers or their superiors. They may have to drop everything on a production to get involved in some fast-breaking event. They have to deal with internal power politics. . . . Staff producers often are weighed down with bureaucratic procedures, often feel they have to engage in self-censorship because of a belief—mistaken perhaps—that what they would like to do will not be approved by someone higher up. Staff producers fight for assignments and air time and they don't always end up doing what they want. Independents have freedom to take the initiative with an idea and run with it, while struggling with financing along the way.

In addition to a glum financial picture, public broadcasting was faced with a possible rash of defections. Bill Moyers had already left the PBS fold for the second time in five years to take up responsibilities as Eric Sevareid's replacement and other tasks at CBS, including a 20-part series entitled *A Walk Through the 20th Century* for CBS Cable. With his departure, *Bill Moyers' Journal,* one of the principal ornaments of public TV, disappeared.

Robert MacNeil and Jim Lehrer, who had for some years withstood offers from commercial broadcasters, had con-

tracted with Gannett, one of the nation's largest news conglomerates, to produce TV news specials, documentaries, and
cable programming. "We signed with Gannett," Lehrer said,
"because it's a journalism organization. It's also working to
position itself to act and react on the whole information revolution that's taking place."

Although MacNeil and Lehrer intended to continue with
their daily report on PBS through the 1981–82 season, there
was no certainty as to their plans when their contract expired
in June 1982.

In a move in the opposite direction, Gannett launched
America Today, a news and weather service to be offered free of
charge to any public broadcasting station that wanted to plug
it in and give Gannett credit as underwriter.

Another serious blow was the departure of the British
Broadcasting Company from PBS, where its offerings had
long been a staple. BBC's new relationship with RCA's cable
service was just the first of many desertions the public stations
had to look forward to among their prime attractions in
drama, dance, and music.*

Public broadcasters were making some gestures toward
survival in the new age of cable. In 1980, WGBH Boston had
formed an independent company called Novacom to distri-
bute such programs as *This Old House* and Julia Child's *The
French Chef* on videodiscs and videocassettes.

With its head start in the cultural field and a backlog of
5,000 hours of cultural programming, WNET was in a good
position to cash in on cable's need for quality fare. In early
1981 it began a new division called Enterprises specifically to
generate revenues for the station. Its activities included
packaging old programming for cable systems and videocassettes, syndication of non-PBS programs such as Paul Har-
vey's radio commentaries, teleconferencing, and rental of its
studio facilities in New York.

In November 1980, Lawrence Grossman, president of PBS,

---

*To help stay such attrition, the National Endowment for the Arts had given
PBS $7 million in grants for 1981–82, which, with the endowment's 50
percent cut in funds, was not likely to be soon repeated.

invited several hundred cultural institutions coast to coast to participate in a new cultural service for pay TV. Originally called the Public Subscriber Network and later changed to PBS/Cable, the service's principal evening fare would be high-brow offerings from PBS' extensive tape catalogue plus future acquisitions, and adult courses during the day. Its schedule would be presented first via cable for pay, later free over the Public Broadcasting Service. Cluster advertising would be permitted on the original cablecasts. Later, on over-the-air broadcasts, underwriters would be given conventional public TV credit in the form of the special logos and product descriptions recently allowed to public TV funders by the FCC. "A more commercial exploitation of television would be difficult to manage," *Broadcasting* commented.

However, the PBS service was not scheduled to go on cable until 1983.

In April 1982 10 public TV stations were scheduled to be selected for an experiment allowing cluster advertising on the public air. A study entitled "Analysis of Commercial Advertising on Public Broadcasting" predicted that public TV could make as much as $164 million a year. Furthermore, the two- or three-minute clusters of ads with their high-income audience could command 20 percent to 50 percent higher rates per thousand than commercial TV ads with their plebeian demographics. According to the study, it would be years before cable, for all its high-brow pretensions, could offer an equally attractive audience to quality advertisers. However, any decision on the cluster-ad experiment for public TV was not expected before October 1983.

Indeed, even if advertising could save public broadcasting, there was the risk that its salvation would mean the destruction of all the best it stood for. Public TV would be subject to the same pressures and quite possibly make the same questionable responses as the commercial networks. Still without advertising and with generally declining income, public broadcasters could revert to the low-budget documentaries and instructional programming that had characterized its poverty-stricken early years.

Either way, Reaganomics might succeed where Nixon and Agnew had failed, by finally eliminating serious public affairs programming on public broadcasting.

Meanwhile, despite the precariousness of its condition, public TV continued to award high visibility to quality news and public affairs, including among others the outstanding series *Hard Choices* from KCTS Seattle, *World* and *Nova* from WGBH Boston, and WNET's *Independent Focus,* a weekly hour filled by the best available work from independent producers.

National Public Radio was in an even worse way than public TV, with a proposed 50 percent cutback in federal funds scheduled for the next five years. The large proportion of its schedule committed to news and public affairs also reduced its chances for corporate backing.

In its brief 11-year life NPR had built a network of 256 stations to which it delivered some of the nation's most consistently intelligent coverage of breaking news as well as literate commentary, criticism, and the sort of documentary essays that had all but disappeared from network radio with the advent of TV. NPR's exemplary *Morning Edition* and *All Things Considered* totaled three-and-a-half hours of daily news and public affairs.

In addition, the special events covered in recent months included the Senate AWACS debate, the hearings on the Israeli raid on the Iraqi nuclear plant, the House Foreign Affairs Committee hearings on El Salvador, and gavel-to-gavel coverage of the confirmation hearings of Alexander Haig, Sandra Day O'Connor, James Watt, Caspar Weinberger, and David Stockman. The NPR documentary *Father Cares: The Last of Jonestown* was expertly extracted by producer James Reston, Jr. from an overwhelming 900 hours of tape recorded by cult leader Jim Jones in the United States and Guyana. Confiscated by the U.S. government, the reels were secured under the Freedom of Information Act. The resulting 90 minutes was a memorable example of editorial patience and was characteristic of NPR's willingness to devote a long, uninterrupted stretch of time to a serious and sometimes excruciatingly painful subject.

In November 1981, Frank Mankiewicz, president of NPR, announced a plan to save his important operation. He would sell shares in two funds—one for news and public affairs, one for entertainment—to corporate benefactors. In exchange, investors would be given on-air credits at unspecified times throughout the schedule. Other moneymaking plans included the selling of audiocassettes and the subletting of space on NPR's Western Union satellite. (See report on page 231.)

Broadcasting, already incensed over the plans for commercialization of public television, was upset all over again. It expressed its concern editorially:

The corporate underwriting plan that Frank Mankiewicz announced last week for National Public Radio takes the noncommercial system another long step toward commercial operation. It is called by other names. . . . In the frankly commercial radio and television business, it would be called selling spots in a scatter plan.

. . . The truth is that the noncommercial system has been on the fringe of commercial operation all along. The biggest names in public broadcast underwriting are among the biggest names in advertising in all media. They know what they get for their money in whatever medium they buy. . . . No one denies the precariousness of financing in a noncommercial system from which federal funds are inexorably being withdrawn. To survive, public radio and television must find sources for money outside the U.S. treasury.

If, however, the noncommercial system is to compete in the commercial marketplace, it can no longer be called the noncommercial system: the broadcast channels it occupies can no longer be said to be reserved for noncommercial use. As things are going now, there will be one big commercial system, with all its functions responding to the marketplace, including station trading.

Although there was nothing on commercial radio to compare with NPR's news commitment, there were examples of excellence from both the networks and local stations. Representative of the best were Robert Trout's commentaries from Europe on ABC's *Perspective*; a documentary called *The Nuclear Arms Race* from WBBM Chicago; and WHAS Louisville's *Vengeance or Justice,* the story of bigotry in a small Kentucky town reported with chilling exactness. Fred Williams' 40-part series on sexual harassment from WAHT Lebanon, Pennsylvania, was done without support from government entities or other local media and resulted in a conviction of the army officer involved.

The best of these programs proved that where talent and opportunity coincided, radio could still deliver exceptionally effective journalism.

However, the impact of recent developments in Washington on radio news was still uncertain. In April 1981, the FCC eliminated the 18-minute-per-hour limit for radio commercials, relieved radio stations of ascertainment and logging requirements, and removed the nonentertainment programming guidelines (8 percent of total program time for AMs and 6 percent for FMs). All of these deregulation moves would have some effect on the news and public affairs performance of the nation's 9,000 radio stations. But the most threatening was the removal of requirements for nonentertainment programming guidelines, which had furnished the motivation for many station managers to pursue news and public affairs when otherwise they might not bother. Reactions were predictably mixed.

Broadcasting magazine gave its restrained approval:

It is not an emancipation proclamation that the FCC has decreed. Radio broadcasters will still be subject to . . . far more federal control than confronts any other information and entertainment medium, except television broadcasting, whose turn for deregulation should be next if there is any justice in Washington.

Still, last week's deregulation was of meaningful proportion. . . . In practice, stations will continue to ascertain public wants and needs and maintain logs for their own record of performance, but the removal of perpetual government surveillance of those two basic functions creates a new atmosphere of independence. The incentive to experiment will be accentuated, especially if the Supreme Court affirms the FCC's desire, stated earlier, to let broadcasters choose their formats at will.

It may not have been an emancipation proclamation that issued from the FCC last week. It was, however, a writ of new freedom to search for ways to serve the listening public.

Andrew Jay Schwartzman, executive director of the Media Access Project, a public-interest communcations law firm, was less enthusiastic:

This is a sad day for minorities, women, the poor, religious groups and other working people who have relied on the FCC to make sure that radio stations meet the needs of listeners they serve.

Sam Simon, of The National Citizens' Committee for Broadcasting, added:

It's one thing to talk about competition, but it's another to abandon minimum standards that hold all the competitors responsible as a public trustee.

Reactions from news directors were equally contradictory. A sampling:

Since deregulation, radio journalists across the country have had to fight for airtime. In a rock music format geared to a young audience, there is the lingering belief that more music and less talk (e.g. news and public affairs) leads to higher ratings. Despite new research showing that theory to be invalid in the 1980s, programmers tend to still base their decisions on it, rather than trying to brave new frontiers, so to speak, by expanding, rather than reducing, news coverage. Although the feedback from our audience regarding our news coverage is consistently positive, we are still having a difficult time holding on to our pre-deregulation position.   *New York*

Government regulation regarding public affairs programming and the amount of time that must be devoted to local news impacts unfairly on small news departments with small budgets such as ours. Public affairs requirements are often time-consuming and unnecessary. Thank God for deregulation.   *Oregon*

Deregulation means that stations that need news to compete in the marketplace will find better return on their investment because the market won't be saturated. Stations that don't need news won't be required to do *something,* and therefore do bare minimums.

Dereg also means that I don't spend hours filling out forms to justify the existence of some bureaucrat in Washington, D.C.   *Washington*

In radio, it remains much the same. For most stations, news remains an obligatory service. While one or two stations in each of the major markets take pride in the excellence of their product, most seem to consider it something that must be done and do not devote the resources to do it well. With deregulation, I would see fewer stations devoting time and money to their news product. In Boston, there are already many stations doing almost no news at all. I would see that

number increasing. This cannot help but hurt the news product on
radio.   *Massachusetts*

Deregulation concerns me. Not only have we done away with 100
percent of our public affairs, we have cut local newscasts by 50
percent. Our news staff has been cut by one full-time person and a
complete change in attitude has taken place. We are part of a chain
of stations and I am afraid this soon will be the attitude at other
stations. The power structure says: "Why do it when we don't have to
and the people don't give a damn whether we do it or not? Give them
what they want rather than what they need to know when it comes to
news." We also have been forced into happy talk in places and times
where we could be doing hard news.   *Missouri*

Deregulation is a joke which—in the long run—will not benefit
broadcast journalism . . . management and owners of most broadcast operations are not committed to serving their communities with
news . . . they are in it for money and power . . . deregulation only
serves their interests, in the same way permanent licensing does . . .
sounds good, but in the wrong hands, these are dangerous developments.   *Louisiana*

Radio journalism is in a sorry state. News departments are being cut
back at all but the most news-conscious stations nationwide. Radio
journalism lacks true reporting, relying on other sources which it
then edits and summarizes. With deregulation, this stands only to
get worse at a majority of stations, since most are concerned with the
appearance of coverage as opposed to coverage itself. Hopefully,
two things will happen: (1) with deregulation causing reduced news
commitments at music stations there will be a market for heavier
news-emphasis stations and (2) radio news departments will find a
niche—an area or areas in which they can excel and do independent
reporting, separate from their roles as summarizers of "real" reporting.   *Virginia*

   There were other developments in radio that could affect
the health of news operations. While 40 percent of the nation's
radio stations reported financial losses in 1979 (this did not
discourage 287 new stations from starting up between July
1979 and December 1980), network radio, a disaster area for
many years, was showing a resurgence of vitality. In the first
five months of 1981 the national nets reported a 30 to 35
percent increase in earnings. Thanks to satellites, they were
planning to double their programming output during the

1981–82 season, and six new national networks were scheduled to go on the air before the end of 1982.

These developments were not necessarily beneficial to news
and public affairs. NBC, whose 24-hour-a-day Radio News
Information Service went under in 1977 with a $10 million
loss, had replaced it with a strictly demographic approach
represented by The Source, a blend of features, news, and
music aimed at an 18-to-34-year-old audience.

According to a substantial majority of the radio news directors reporting to the survey, their principal sources of
discouragement were public apathy and low professional
standards in the industry. At the same time there was a dramatic increase in the number of directors reporting staunch
support from station management, even when sponsors and
community powers were troublesome.

I sense a fresh wave of managerial support for news and public
affairs throughout the industry. There seems to be an increasing
awareness of how a strong commitment to news and public affairs
adds backbone to a station. The best way to build a successful radio
station is to show your listeners that you care about their welfare.
The message is clear when your news and public affairs effort is a
strong one. With the intrusion of satellite feeds into most of our
markets, local news may soon spell the difference between survival
and oblivion.   *North Carolina*

Most encouraging is the apparent increase in general managerial
support and pride in news. In the past, news was an evil to put up
with for many managers . . . now more news-minded managers are
seeing that news can be a public service . . . and a bottom-line money
maker. It is likewise encouraging to see news directors becoming
general managers.   *Missouri*

With an increasing news audience and a declining prime audience, I
am getting super support from the front office. The realization of
local programming being the answer to increasing national competition is giving news and public affairs a stronger base in station
operations. I'm getting more money for people and equipment and
a larger input to station-wide decisions.

The additional emphasis on news is paying off in audience. The
product is more comprehensive and I feel it is gaining credibility.
                                                           Arkansas

There were other views of radio's continuing importance:

Local broadcast journalism is the only "ace-in-the-hole" that small-market radio stations have against the infringement of powerful metropolitan stations. The local aspect of locally produced newscasts and documentaries can only be customized by using exclusive local knowledge. For this reason and this reason only, local radio will survive the increasing audience fragmentation.   *Alabama*

Radio is better than television at conveying ideas and offering opportunities for lengthy exposition of views or even clashes of views that can be meaningful. But this opportunity is often allowed to disintegrate into the typical call-in program format where ill-informed people respond to misconceptions and half-truths from other ill-informed people. The American public spends a large amount of time every week listening to radio; broadcast journalists should use that access more creatively.   *Washington, D.C.*

We are, I think, about to re-discover radio as a primary information source. The medium has boundless potential to convey ideas and emotions honestly . . . with little potential for manufacturing those things by its electronic presence. Radio really can be a kind of sound "cinéma vérité" in the hands of a skilled professional.   *Washington*

9

The Past
as
Prologue

AGAINST A shuddering backdrop of imminent and monumental change, in the midst of great and intimidating events that they were expected to illuminate and put into perspective, the broadcast news organizations of the nation rolled on, sometimes lurching, sometimes bumbling, but for the most part staunchly on course.

Even drastic changes in the corner offices, control rooms, and studios didn't seem to make that much difference. Nor was anyone much upset when a former adversary suddenly appeared at one's side. Tinker for Silverman, Wyman for Backe. Mudd at CBS at NBC, Moyers at CBS at PBS at CBS, Reasoner at CBS at ABC at CBS. Vanocur at NBC at PBS at ABC. The most dramatic shifts and departures seemed only temporary. Walter Cronkite couldn't stay away. No more could Eric Sevareid. David Brinkley's abrupt departure from NBC after 38 years was followed by his stately reappearance on ABC's new Sunday midday show.

The ratings, however much deplored, continued to send their thrilling and devastating signals—that *60 Minutes* was number one, that ABC's quest for quality news was paying off, that NBC must try again, that for CBS a winning streak might be running out. For the time being dramatic changes at CBS—90 minutes of morning news, Dan Rather in Cronkite's chair, a new late afternoon public affairs program *Up to the*

Minute (taken off the air after two months)—weren't working. A quirky new news president, Van Gordon Sauter, to replace the retiring Bill Leonard might help. Meanwhile *Sunday Morning,* the CBS news department's big unqualified success, was getting an imitator at ABC and possibly at NBC as well.

On a broader field the ratings showed that the network share of viewers had dropped 4 percent in 1980 with ratings down two to three points. A J. Walter Thompson study expected the percentage of TV viewers watching network prime time to drop from 88 percent to 73 percent by the end of 1989. At the same time ratings at independent stations were on the rise. The Independent Network News, which began feeding a half-hour prime-time newscast to 27 stations in June 1980, was up to 72 stations and three million viewers a night by December 1981.

Although a typical household was watching TV a record six hours and 35 minutes daily in 1980, there were indications of a falling off in specific groups. Women from 35 to 54 were watching three hours 40 minutes less every week. Youngsters from two to 11 had cut back by more than three-and-a-quarter hours a week and all people were down in their individual weekly viewing by an hour and a half.

In 1980 the three networks aired more than 2,200 hours of news-related activity. In the same period air time for documentaries was dipping. At CBS they were down to 15 hours from 20 to 24 per season in the mid-seventies.* NBC indicated that it was planning to reduce its 90-minute *White Papers* to 60 minutes by 1982. ABC aired 12 *Closeups* a year, carefully avoiding the sweeps months.

Whatever the threats from the new technologies between 1979 and 1980, the average price of a TV station doubled. In July 1981 Metromedia agreed to pay Boston Broadcasters, Inc. $220 million for WCVB-TV Boston—the highest price ever paid for a single TV station and more than three times the previous record of $65 million for KOVR-TV Sacramento. WCVB, sometimes considered the best TV station in the country with a $4.3 million news budget, was the same

---

*CBS gave itself documentary credit for an additional five hours of election year specials.

station that nine years earlier had been taken from the Herald-Traveler Corporation.

The one-hour network newscast still seemed far away. CBS had announced its historic extension for the spring of 1983 but had yet to convince its affiliates. NBC's latest attempt for expanded news had been defeated in the fall of 1981, and ABC—which had been promising its news talent more space for the past five years—had still been unable to clear the extra half hour.

Dan Rather made an impassioned plea at the Radio and Television News Directors meeting in Hollywood, Florida, in December 1980:

Time—we need time. The evening news ought to be an hour. And I'm not talking about an hour to play with. I don't mean "give us a half hour and we'll do nice, soft mood pieces and entertain you." I mean, we need that time to tell the American public the important things that are going on in the world. There is simply more than a half hour of news each day, more than the 23 minutes an evening news show consists of. I read the wires every day, as most of you do. I try to get a sense of what's going on. And as you do, I see things that are happening that are interesting but that simply don't get told because we don't have the time. Central America is blowing up with deep ramifications for our own peace and security. Most days, Central America winds up on the floor. El Salvador is part of it, and so is what the new government in Nicaragua is up to—the Sandinistas, who kicked out Somoza and created a new government. Remember Nicaragua? Bill Stewart at ABC lost his life covering that story. Now it's on the floor. The Quebec separatist movement—what an extraordinary story—on the floor. Japan's trouble with the Soviet Union on the floor, Cambodia and Namibia—on the floor. I'll tell you, it gets pretty crowded on that floor.

Nevertheless, the quibbling over the 60-minute news continued. In a letter to the CBS-TV affiliate board, Dr. William F. Baker, president of Group W Television Group, wrote:

Local news service faces probable disruption and diminution if the reported CBS plan for expansion of the 30-minute early evening news to 45 minutes in length is put into effect. . . . Certainly we are not questioning the desirability of more national news being made available to the public we serve. . . .

Baker pointed out that 65 percent of the average affiliate's day is already consumed by network-originated programming, then went on:

Westinghouse Broadcasting Company, like many other broadcasters, has invested massive amounts of time, talent, and resources in its investigative, consumer and medical reporting, as well as other important areas of community interest. The proposed CBS plan could, for example, result in substantial time cutbacks of the licensee's local early evening news programs. Such an action would severely jeopardize the licensee's ability to maintain highly diverse, necessary, and important types of news and news-type reporting. Our research also indicates that audiences prefer local news over national news programs.

James Rosenfield, president of CBS-TV, said:

Our position is that the issue of whether viewers receive more local news or more national news is not a factor in local communities. The public generally doesn't differentiate between local and national newscasts. We agree that there is a need for more local news, but we also think it's silly to have two hours allotted to local news, while restricting national and international news to a half hour.

Meanwhile Group W was turning out more of its specialty, the soft news magazine. *PM,* its highly successful half hour of personality, consumer and human interest items that was now in 91 markets, had been joined by *Hour Magazine,* a daytime version aimed at women.

The softening of the news stretched from such popular magazine shows with little or no hard content to prime-time hits such as *Real People* and *That's Incredible!*, where human interest reached its ultimate absurdity.

Happy-talk news was reportedly going out of fashion. But in many cases it had been supplanted by the soft heart-tugging item and the celebrity interview.

WNBC's *Live at Five,* carved out of its two-hour local New York news show, specialized in laughs and nudges while the nation's largest city went inadequately covered. The show's success had encouraged ABC's flagship station WABC to do it one better, going at 4:30 for its *Now on 7.* WCBS, one of the most valuable TV properties in the nation, was not far behind, scheduling its two-hour *Five O'Clock Report* for early 1982.

How did the 100 duPont correspondents and a substantial number of the nation's most conscientious and thoughtful news directors communicating with the survey feel about the current state of broadcast news and public affairs?

The correspondents reported a further decline in the number of local documentaries, an increase in human-interest stories at the expense of hard news, a shortening of item length, and an increase in the number of commercial interruptions. More encouraging was the continued increase in investigative reporting and a marked increase in women and minority producers and on-air personnel.

News directors reporting to the survey represented markets from #1 to #181. Budgets varied from less than $40,000 to nearly $5 million, staffs from one to 65. One station had just purchased its first VTR camera; another had 11 VTR crews in the field.

Large or small, radio or TV, the responses to the survey were surprisingly consistent. Among those negative elements cited as principal impediments to producing quality news, unprofessional behavior by colleagues was mentioned most frequently (60 percent). Public apathy came next with 30 percent of the news directors singling it out as a chronic discouragement. News consultants, came next, mentioned by 15 percent.

As for positive developments, managerial enthusiasm and support, mentioned by 44 percent of the respondents, was rated highest; technological advances came next with 39 percent, and deregulation in third place with 17 percent.

The comments of the news directors give some indication of where broadcast journalism currently stands and the direction it may be going.

Leaving aside the consultants, the haircuts, the beautiful people, and the insatiable thirst for ratings—broadcast journalism is in better shape now than it has ever been. Our equipment is better, our local journalists are better, and local stations are devoting more time and money to covering the news. It is easy to complain about our many mistakes and our "unnewsworthy trends" . . . but the fact remains that television news is a lot better than it was 10 years ago. And it can only get better . . . with numerous bumps along the way.   *Arkansas*

The most encouraging recent development in broadcast news is the emergence of a professional management cadre that is capable of running a journalistically strong organization that can also generate the revenue needed to develop strong resources. As a consequence, the consultant is losing favor with managers who frequently don't understand what the news director is doing. Now, news directors are beginning to move up in station management. The caliber of people getting those jobs indicates that news will have an expanded role in station programming in the next few years.   *Minnesota*

Broadcast journalism is at a turning point. After a long period of evolution from print coverage of events, the technology and substance of broadcasting has reached a stage where issues and events can be brought to the public with dramatic immediacy. The power of television to convey the feel of an event—the slow-motion replay of the attempted assassination of President Reagan, for example—is far beyond that of any previous form of communication, and it is in this direction that the tremendous potential of the medium lies. The danger, on the other hand, is the constant pressure toward the trivial generated by the demands of a mass audience.

In a situation where one or two rating points can mean millions in revenues, the temptation to move the evening news toward *Real People* becomes more and more difficult to resist. This is already happening in local broadcasting as news consultants point out the popularity of features and human interest material over hard news. The kitten-in-the-tree has always been a staple of any form of journalism, but broadcasting has two inherent limitations which exacerbate the problem—length and audience selectivity. As to the first, most public affairs programming is already too short; to further dilute its content would undermine, perhaps fatally, its informative function. The second problem involves the lack of choice open to a viewer, as opposed to a newspaper reader. A reader can approach the paper selectively, reading only hard news, only features, only comics, or some mixture at different times. The evening news, on the other hand, is fixed in the content presented to the viewer and the resulting either/or editorial judgments are significantly more difficult, and important. It is in this context that the ratings pressure can be the most destructive.

The solution to this problem may lie in future technological changes in the medium. The combination of satellites and multiple-channel cable capability may result in a broader range of alternatives open to viewers and a diminution of the importance of the mass audience. The apparent success of the Cable News Network, the various all-news radio stations, and National Public Radio's *All Things Considered* may well be precursors of this development.

In the meantime, we must rely on our own intestinal fortitude as journalists and remain sensitive to the dangers of creeping *National Enquirer*ism. The potential for informing more people better than ever before is a significant challenge; keeping that goal—rather than selling more soap—firmly in mind should help us get from here to there.

Maine

Broadcast journalists, as well as our counterparts in the print media, still seem to be suffering from what has often been termed "The Watergate Syndrome." This is brought about by the media being the story as much as the story itself. Many journalists also suffer from a burning desire to "get Mr. (or Ms.) Big" whether or not Mr. or Ms. Big has done anything. This means many people, especially in the cutthroat level of journalism (major markets and networks) run with a story based solely on rumor and innuendo simply to be first.

Georgia

Two words that I associate with current trends in broadcast journalism are "chilling" and "lifestyle."

Recent decisions by the Supreme Court (and lesser courts), the recent Pulitzer Prize scandal involving *The Washington Post*, the influence of ratings, deregulation of radio, and intimidation of reporters by "officialdom" have all contributed to a "chilling effect" that I believe has discouraged many broadcast journalists from pursuing stories that are harder, less glamorous, more sensitive, and more complex than many others. This, I think, is leading to a kind of "lazy" journalism ethic, in which the harder, more challenging stories are sluffed off to the side and never really dealt with. In many cases, where egos and power are involved, I think reporters are just plain afraid to investigate stories for fear of repercussions.

Although TV and radio are devoting more time to journalism than ever, too often it is "lifestyle" journalism—stories of little substance or import about dimensions of living that have more to do with leisure, idiosyncrasy, and social fads than anything else. The trend is toward the cute, the conversational, the flashy, and the amusing or bizarre. Witness *Real People, That's Incredible!,* and the myriad clones of *PM Magazine* now on television (and other versions on radio). These "small things considered" are conditioning too many people to expect journalism to entertain, rather than challenge and inform. I fear the consequences when that's the expectation.

California

We have in this market a commercial station which has won the duPont-Columbia award twice in a row, and still produces above-average news coverage. But because of pressure from what I believe to be an inferior competitor, but one which has slightly higher ratings, your alumnus has begun to topload its newscast with the traditional tripe: wrecks, fires, and kidnappings. Also, its story length has shortened in order to be more competitive in pacing with the slicker alternative down the dial. It's the same old story which you must have been told countless times.   *Texas*

Because the consultants have made us all look and sound alike in markets big and small, the tie-breaker increasingly will be in the quality of our writing and reporting and unfortunately in the quality of our on-air delivery. I think the challenge of the '80's will be the mad scramble for reporting, producing, and anchoring talent.
Tennessee

Local-level broadcast journalism continues to suffer as emphasis is placed on pleasing personalities and appearances, rather than professional reporting. Perhaps with the advent of all-news television cable capabilities, we will see a diminution of the superficial news program on commercial affiliates or o&o's. Hopefully, competition will upgrade the quality of local news offerings. Thus far, competition for the ratings has not succeeded in increasing the quality of those broadcasts. I don't yet see a trend—only a hope filtered through the critical comments of viewers and listeners willing to communicate their disappointment.   *California*

"Unprofessional behavior" is an important problem at the network and the local level, especially during live coverage of breaking stories. As our technologies improve, we thrust ourselves into positions that demand instant reporting and analysis. Often we come up short; many times glaringly so. In our efforts to fill air time, information goes unchecked and rumors are reported as facts. These situations are made worse by reporters making offhand comments and anchors interjecting their opinions.

Technology has circumvented the editorial process. It has also put an extra burden on management to find competent broadcast journalists who can think on their feet. At our market size, this has proved to be a real problem. Station management is more inclined to spend money on electronics than it is on qualified personnel.
California

As technological advances continue, and as cable and other media change the scope of our business, the importance of good journalism by television stations increases. Narrowcasting has its dangers; what we do in television journalism is an antedote to narrowcasting. We report the issues that affect the large body of citizens, whether on a local, state, or national level. In the years ahead, our responsibility will only increase, and we must be geared up to meet that challenge, in terms of talented people, technology, and air time.   *Michigan*

The one word that captures the state of broadcast journalism in the Pittsburgh market is "commercial." The presentations are slick, chatty, and tend to overplay the disaster/accident type of news and underplay news that has any complexity to it. Thus the stations here are still caught in the "happy-talk" approach to news. They are better at telling "what" has happened—not nearly as good in telling why it happened or what it all means. The future may be affected by the coming of cable television to the urban market—but what that effect will be is by no means yet clear.   *Pennsylvania*

I am becoming less optimistic, perhaps because of personal experience and the experience of others whom I've known, and also because of the increased profits expected from local stations each year by owners and stockholders, regardless of the economic conditions throughout the country. The tenure of the professional news director is still under three years and he/she is still subject to the whim of the general manager, regardless of results, and the qualifications of some news directors being hired in markets of all sizes are becoming open to questions.

It appears the journalistic standards are becoming secondary to budget and ratings and the worth of any effort is predicated, more and more, on the latter. Too many of my colleagues are talking about becoming burned out, or tired of fighting any longer. Some say the hell with it and ride with the tide, others leave the business. I say the former results in the latter, anyway.

Couple this with the loud voice our critics are still given, with very little substantial challenge, and my feelings about the future of broadcast journalism are very mixed.   *Kentucky*

I'm very depressed by the state of local TV news reporting. It is superficial, show-biz, and quite often lacking in the very basics of information. Research is shoddy—attention in local newsrooms is given to style rather than content. "In-depth" stories focus on issues that will bring viewers to the station, controversial but perhaps relatively unimportant things like body searches in the police department, or gay sex in older couples. Heavier, more complicated issues like corruption, housing prices (and where the problem really lies), the crime rate (and what it really means), bigotry, the ethics of the Moral Majority, etc., are overlooked or only superficially treated. Local news has become like radio—stories seldom last more than 90 seconds, and when the newscast runs more than 30 minutes, the stories are repeated in each show ad nauseum. After a newscast, viewers know about "blood, guts, and thunder" but not about substantive issues. Newsmakers, or people involved in news stories, are never given enough time (i.e. more than 20 seconds) to express their views . . . the audience never knows what people in the news really think or what their opinions are. Reporters never are able to in-depth interview newsmakers, so we find politicians and other media-wise officials using the media as sounding boards and plat-forms for their personal views, knowing that follow-up or probing questions will never be asked.   *California*

Broadcast journalism faces some real challenges in the next few years. State-of-the-art technology and instant reporting have clearly strained our ability to apply traditional editorial techniques to our reporting. The quality of that reporting suffers in the process. I think this is beginning to affect audience perception of the accuracy and depth of our coverage. Deadline pressure has always been a factor in journalism, but not to the degree that daily live broadcast-ing of news as it happens makes it today. I think finding ways to cope with this problem is one of the central issues facing broadcast jour-nalism today.   *Oregon*

Unprofessional behavior by both print and broadcast journalists is always the biggest threat we have in our business. . . . With the advances in technology, and the capabilities for live origination, there is also the coupled danger of becoming a party to the event rather than reporting on it.   *Arkansas*

There are currently encouraging and disturbing trends in the field of broadcast journalism. I believe CBS *Sunday Morning* is an example of the finest efforts now underway. The new "reality entertainment shows" such as *That's Incredible!* and *Real People* demonstrate the dangers created by demanding news be more entertaining than informative. The line between news and public affairs has been blurred so much that serious news coverage of issues and events, particularly at local stations, is hard to find, and a "newsy" approach has now been applied directly to strictly entertainment shows, but without any ethical concern for manipulative approaches to stories. For example, a former news cameraman now working on *Real People* tells me sadly that the comments of the "real" people are scripted by show writers but never acknowledged.   *California*

I am concerned that newsgatherers, especially television news, are becoming unwilling but important arms of the legal profession. Specifically, defense and prosecuting attorneys, and the courts, are increasingly abusing the powers of subpoena to obtain scripts, films, videotapes, notes, and testimony about events once covered by tele-vision news crews, and not in litigation. Many of these demands are in the form of "fishing expeditions." I am concerned that the time required to comply with the subpoena affects our ability to gather the news, and that many of our news sources will dry up if the possibility exists that their names could be obtained by the legal system.

New Mexico

Our greatest problem is also our biggest frustration. And that is we have become so reactionary in covering a news event that many times we fail to explain to our audience what the event means. Our reporters are under a lot of pressure to do at least three stories a day. This practice prevents them from having the time to carefully think about a story and go beyond the basic facts. We do not as a rule have time to look into just what effect an issue will have on our community. And this problem is compounded in that many of the broadcast journalists who come our way have never had the time or the training to look below the surface of a news story. So even if we asked them to do a more cerebral piece they would not know how.

Pennsylvania

The danger signs are all around: New competition, declining viewership, fragmenting audiences. A "worst case" scenario assumes that television news will go the way of radio, appealing to an ever smaller and narrowly defined audience, unable to generate the revenue to support the expensive and sophisticated news efforts of years past. New competition *will* force broadcast journalists to settle for a smaller slice of the pie, and maybe smaller budgets in the process. But that same competition will also force us to do more of what we now do best . . . covering what makes news in our own backyard. Nobody is going to get details of the latest tax proposal on Home Box Office, or find out why garbage collection is being cut on DBS. All that new technology aside, people still want to know what's going on next door, down the street, down at the courthouse. That's our business, and that's the reason we'll still be in business in the years to come.

Texas

In recent years, people have come to depend in ever greater numbers on broadcast journalism as either a primary or an exclusive source of news. This dependence was probably created as much by rapid advances in the technology of covering the news as it was by the quality of the reporting, or even by the news itself. More and more, we are able to offer our audiences the opportunity to witness events as they occur, or within minutes of the event. And because of the less obvious nature of the editing process in broadcast journalism, especially television, people come away with the idea that they are closer than ever to experiencing an event firsthand.

This increased trust on the part of our audience increases our credibility, but it also increases our responsibility. Continued improvements in our methods of covering and presenting the news will make it easier to report the "who, what, when, and where." But the less explored avenues of "why, and how" will be one of the important aspects of broadcasting in the future. This would seem to indicate that the demands for growth are as much with the people involved in reporting the news as they are with the machinery. Interpretation and analysis make demands on a continually greater percentage of our news staffs; demands requiring not only massive amounts of background knowledge on a wide range of subjects, but demands that we be able to put an event into perspective on short notice.

New York

PART II ✍

The
Awards

THE ALFRED I. duPONT/ COLUMBIA UNIVERSITY AWARDS, 1979–1980

Carol MonPere, Sandra Nichols, and KTEH-TV, San Jose	*The Battle of Westlands*
Walter Jacobson and WBBM-TV, Chicago	*Perspectives*
Red Cloud Productions and WGBY-TV, Springfield	*Joan Robinson: One Woman's Story*
WLS-TV, Chicago and *Chicago Sun-Times*	*The Accident Swindlers*
Perry Miller Adato and WNET/13, New York	*Picasso: A Painter's Diary*
Mississippi Center for Educational Television	*William Faulkner: A Life on Paper*
Group W and KYW-TV, Philadelphia; WBZ-TV, Boston; WJZ-TV, Baltimore	The I Team
National Public Radio	*All Things Considered* and *Morning Edition*
ABC-TV	*The Iran Crisis: America Held Hostage/Nightline*
Ed Bradley and CBS-TV	*CBS Reports: Blacks in America—With All Deliberate Speed?*
Roger Mudd and CBS-TV	*CBS Reports: Teddy*
Reuven Frank and NBC-TV	*NBC White Paper: If Japan Can . . . Why Can't We?*

156

THE ALFRED I. duPONT/ COLUMBIA UNIVERSITY CITATIONS, 1979–1980

Robert Riggs and WAST-TV, Albany	*Downhill Dollars*
WCCO-TV, Minneapolis	*The Moore Report*
WCVB-TV, Needham	*Denise*
Robert Richter and WGBH-TV, Boston	*Nova: A Plague on Our Children*
Lorraine Gray and WNET/13, New York	*Independent Focus: With Babies and Banners*
Lea Thompson and WRC-TV, Washington	*Baby Formula: The Hidden Dangers*
Alan Griggs and WSM-TV, Nashville	*KKK: The Wizards at Odds*
Public Broadcasting Associates	*Odyssey: Seeking the First Americans*
ABC-TV	*Directions*
ABC-TV	*Closeup: This Shattered Land*
CBS-TV	*Campaign '80*
CBS-TV	*CBS Magazine*

THE ALFRED I. duPONT/ COLUMBIA UNIVERSITY AWARDS, 1980–1981

KCTS-TV, Seattle	*Hard Choices*
Jon Else and KTEH-TV, San Jose	*The Day After Trinity*
WBBM-TV, Chicago	Election Night Coverage
WCCO-TV, Minneapolis	*The Moore Report*
WGBH-TV, Boston	*World*
WPLG-TV, Miami	*The Billion Dollar Ghetto*
Robert Spencer and WTTW-TV, Chicago	*Six O'Clock and All's Well*
ABC-TV	*America Held Hostage: The Secret Negotiations*
David Productions and ABC-TV	*Closeup: Can't It Be Anyone Else?*
CBS-TV	*Sunday Morning*
CBS-TV	*CBS Reports: The Defense of the United States*
National Public Radio	*Father Cares: The Last of Jonestown*

THE ALFRED I. duPONT/ COLUMBIA UNIVERSITY CITATIONS, 1980–1981

KUED-TV, Salt Lake City	*The Deadly Winds of War*
WCBS-TV, New York	*The First Amendment Project*
WFAA-TV, Dallas	*Kelly Air Force Base*
WHAS Radio, Louisville	*Vengeance or Justice?*
Paul and Holly Fine and WJLA-TV, Washington	*Until We Say Goodbye*
William Miles and WNET/ 13, New York	*I Remember Harlem*
National Geographic Society and WQED-TV, Pittsburgh	*Gorilla*
CBS-TV	*CBS Reports: The Saudis*
Betsy Aaron, Joseph DeCola and NBC-TV	*Inside Afghanistan*

PART III

Reports
and
Commentaries

The following essays are done by invitation of the editor. They are written by persons with a special competence and interest in fields relating to broadcast journalism.

𝒯

The 1980
Elections

BY ELMER W.LOWER

AFTER EVERY presidential election, journalists, politicians, academicians, and just plain voters conduct endless post-mortems on television's failures and successes in reporting the campaign. The criticisms receive far more attention than the praise, and the television news executives wind up defending themselves and vowing to do a better job next time. Despite the vast amount of money, air time, and effort the executives throw into campaign coverage, they remain a fat target for those who argue that they should have done better.

Almost all participants in dissecting the political cadaver agree generally with the assessments of Richard M. Nixon ("The tube is what it's all about"), of author Theodore H. White ("Television [is] . . . the playing field of politics"), and of political scientist Thomas E. Cronin ("Television has transformed American politics, presidential elections, and the manner presidents conduct themselves. . . ."). But beyond that, opinions vary on how well television news covers the campaigns and what changes it should make to improve.

In any four-year cycle the biggest, longest, and most important story that the three major television networks cover is the nomination and election of the next American president. They throw all of their personnel (from 500 to 1,000), a huge chunk of their budget (easily $40,000,000 per network for the climactic year), and much special air time into the highly competitive coverage. In 1980 the competition among ABC, CBS, and NBC to outshine each other appeared more important than whether Jimmy Carter, Ronald Reagan, or John Anderson won the four-year ticket to the White House.

The 1980 cycle was little different than the seven previous presidential elections, that television has covered since it went coast to coast in 1952. That summer Americans witnessed their first gavel-to-gavel nominating convention coverage from Chicago's International Amphitheater. And once again in 1980 all three chains provided the tonnage coverage, ABC News—by now better financed—having dropped its edited, abbreviated coverage in effect since 1968.

True, the television coverage of the campaign was much longer, some said endless, but the networks could not be blamed for the mushrooming of the primaries. It was the politicians who had increased the number of presidential primaries from 16 in 1952 to an unprecedented 36 in 1980. Add the caucuses to that and the preliminaries lasted from January 21st (the Iowa caucuses) until the June 4th Super-Tuesday (the primaries in California, Ohio, New Jersey, New Mexico, Rhode Island, South Dakota, Montana, and West Virginia).

Most criticism centered on how the networks covered the day-to-day campaigning, the fairness of how they (and their competitors in print journalism) set "levels of expectations" for candidates in each primary, how they determined who was (and who was not) a viable candidate, when, indeed, did the campaign actually begin, whether the politicians actually manipulated them at the Republican Convention, whether they missed the most important story at the Democratic Convention, and whether they were on sound ground with their election-night projections of an early Reagan landslide.

THE CAMPAIGN OPENING

It was a commercial decision, not a news-coverage problem, that provoked the first argument of the 1980 campaign. In December 1979, the Democratic National Committee wanted to buy 30 minutes of time on the networks to present a Jimmy Carter speech. But the network executives said "no," and, for the moment, they held their ground, arguing that the campaign for the presidency had not started and thus they did not have to sell time that early. They were the ones, the networks said, who should decide when a campaign started, not the national committees or the candidates. (Actually, CBS offered two five-minute periods.)

The Federal Communications Commission told the networks to sell the time to the Carter-Mondale Committee, but the chains appealed to the federal courts. Again, they lost. Again, they appealed, this time to the United States Supreme Court.

It was not until seven months later (July, 1981) that the Supreme Court spoke in a decision, which again upheld the right of the Carter-Mondale Committee for "reasonable access" to the air waves as provided in Section 312(a) (7) of the Communications Act.

Chief Justice Warren Burger in the majority opinion (six to three) warned broadcasters that "willful or repeated violation [of the provision] could lead to a revocation of a station's license."

"When a broadcaster accepts free and exclusive use of a limited and valuable part of the public domain," the Chief Justice wrote, "he assumes with it enforceable public obligations." He added that "it is the right of the viewers and listeners, not the right of broadcasters, that is paramount."

Burger addressed the problem of who had the power to decide when a political campaign had begun. It was the Federal Communications Commission, he said, "on the basis of objective evidence. The matter is not purely editorial."

The networks had argued strongly that their First Amendment rights had been violated, but the high court majority did not agree.

THE PRIMARIES AND CAUCUSES

There were many who cried "overkill" when a horde of national journalists, both television and print media, invaded Iowa on New Year's Day, 1980. Among them, one wondered, were there some of the same critics who, in 1976, faulted all media—television included—for not having spotted Jimmy

Carter's unexpected Iowa success? The networks felt damned both ways, and unfairly.

Des Moines was the scene of the first presidential debate, but, as it turned out, neither of the two leading candidates participated. Neither did the commercial networks on a "live television" basis.

Following his famous "Rose Garden Strategy," President Carter said he was much too busy negotiating for the release of the American hostages in Iran to swap insults with Senator Edward Kennedy of Massachusetts and Governor Jerry Brown of California. So the Democratic debate vanished.

The Republican debate on a snowy Saturday night (January 5th) featured six Republican aspirants, all except Ronald Reagan, who chose to stay in California biding his time. Without Reagan and minus a Democratic encounter, the commercial networks promptly dropped plans for live coverage, leaving the field to the Public Broadcasting Service, which presented two hours in prime time. CBS News carried a delayed -on-tape version of the debate at 11:30 P.M., Saturday night fringe time.

The six Republican debaters were all very kind to each other, content on this first occasion to attack the villainous Democrats, particularly Carter. Any fresh ideas that surfaced came from Congressman John Anderson of Illinois, who later switched to an Independent candidacy.

If the future of presidential debates had hinged on the enlightenment provided by the Iowa encounter, the face-to-face meetings would have ended on that night. There were three Tweedle-dums and three Tweedle-dees. Only the absent Reagan didn't reveal whether he was a "dum" or a "dee."

The mass media, particularly television reporters, like to name a winner and a loser in every race. In Iowa they had no trouble. Jimmy Carter had run away from Teddy Kennedy in the Democratic caucuses and George Bush led the Republican field, starting what the Bush camp called "Big Mo," for big momentum. But New Hampshire, the first primary state, was still five weeks away.

Throughout the primaries, candidates had problems with "levels of expectations" established for them by the "Boys on the Bus." Sometimes these levels hurt them, at other times they were helpful. Both print and television political reporters set them by an unrevealed, subjective formula that is hardly scientific. The standard-setters can be David Broder and Haynes Johnson of *The Washington Post,* Tom Pettit of NBC News, Bruce Morton of CBS News, Sander Vanocur of ABC News, Jack Germond of *The Washington Star,* or Hedrick Smith of *The New York Times.*

Les Crystal, NBC's senior executive producer of political coverage, says that his network was very careful not to exaggerate. "I really don't like to play the 'expectation game,'" he told this writer. "It is very imprecise to determine what percentage of the vote any of the candidates should win in any of the various states."

George Bush observed that television has tremendous power and "does peculiar things that may or may not shape events. I won in Michigan against all predictions of all journalists and all polls," Bush said, "and not only won but won big. The news that night [Michigan primary night], while the polls were still open in Oregon, was that Reagan had it locked up, that he was now over the top, which he wasn't. The fact that we were coming on strong wasn't even reported."

Bush conceded that his Iowa victory and the reporting of it on television did contribute to his "Big Mo." "We did well in Iowa," he said, "and our coverage was disproportionately positive." (Bush pulled 31 percent to Reagan's 29.)

Throughout the primaries and caucuses of the 1980 winter and spring, critics faulted television for concentrating on the "horse race" aspects of the two campaigns at the expense of explaining serious issues. Pollsters Harris, Roper, Gallup, and others received more time on the tube than did candidates' positions on inflation, women's rights, the environment, the future of Social Security, the national budget, and the size of the defense establishment.

Lyn Nofziger, Reagan's press secretary, provided this politician's view of how the reporting and editing process works: "What happens is, reporters write a story once on an issue," he said. "Then they think that everybody has read or heard it, so they decide they will not write about that again.

They run away from the issues after they have written about
them once, even though it might be the most important part of
the campaign."

Television news has a particularly difficult time with issues
because of (1) its lack of air time, (2) its constant demands for
visuals and a new story angle every night, and (3) its tendency
to simplify stories for a mass audience with a limited attention
span. All three networks did present four-minute and five-
minute issue stories in their dinner-hour news programs, but
their run-of-the-mill nightly coverage came in packages closer
to 90 seconds or two minutes.

Roone Arledge, president of ABC News, acknowledged the
problem in a political program on his own network: "There's a
tremendous tendency to report the horse race aspects, and it
frustrates the politicians, and I don't blame them, for us not to
ever be able to get into any substantive issues the way the
political people would like us to. Because we don't have the
time to do it. So what we get is impressions of competence, or
impressions of niceness, or honesty, or whatever."

Perhaps television news' critics expect too much of the
"workhorse" evening news programs that reach the greatest
audiences. A half-hour network news program minus its
commercial breaks has 22½ minutes to report the major world
and national news. A typical lineup will include seven to nine
stories using videotape or film coverage and nine to fourteen
"reader" stories, which the anchorpersons recite. Anyone who
has ever edited such a broadcast knows how many worthwhile
stories wind up on the cutting-room floor and how many of
those that are broadcast get cut to the point of superficiality.
The 1980 campaign coverage was no different in this respect
than earlier races of the television era.

Many critics base their complaints on the assumption that
the half-hour network evening news is all that viewers tune in
to inform themselves about the campaigns. They ignore the
fact that the networks do program specials, that they all carry
morning news, that the Sunday discussion panels are highly
informative, and that local stations carry news programs at
least twice a day, running from thirty minutes to three hours.
Viewers who take the time can be better informed, but they

have become so used to getting their information in short bursts (one to two minutes, whether it is news or advertising time), that they seldom watch the longer programs.

The 1980 campaign—for the fifth time in the television era—unfolded with an incumbent in the White House running for election. And Jimmy Carter, at least in the primary-caucus period, enjoyed a television advantage as had Eisenhower in 1956, Johnson in 1964, Nixon in 1972, and Ford in 1976. The President was able to remain in the Rose Garden, wrap himself in the American flag, and produce his own media shows, especially for television, every day. This proved a decided disadvantage for Teddy Kennedy and Jerry Brown.

James Flug, director of information for the Kennedy for President Committee, was bitter in his comments on the Senator's disadvantage.

"The incumbent could produce his own shows every day for the media," he said, "totally controlled and totally designed to make the President look presidential. On the other hand, you had a large group of the media following Senator Kennedy around 24 hours a day, getting the good and bad parts. In the nature of the television medium, and even to some extent the print medium, the bad works its way to the top. It's much more newsworthy if you do something out of the ordinary than if you give a good basic speech. . . . It is harder to get a positive story on television than it is to get a positive story in print."

Despite Flug's complaints, the Senator had only himself to blame for his worst appearance of the campaign, a late 1979 interview with correspondent Roger Mudd, then of CBS News. His explanation of the Chappaquiddick tragedy, 10 years later, hardly inspired confidence in him as a presidential candidate. It emphasized the truism that television can be of great help to a candidate, but that it can also provide him or her a splendid opportunity to fall on his or her face, as Richard Nixon did in the first of the 1960 Great Debates and as Gerald Ford did in the 1976 foreign-policy debate in San Francisco.

Television is at its best when it covers dramatic events, but participants must be aware that it magnifies them, making them far more important than they often are. The television debate among Republican candidates in Nashua, New Hampshire, in 1980, was a good example, as was Senator Edmund Muskie's tearful breakdown in the same state in the 1972 primaries. It was Ronald Reagan who benefitted in 1980 when he made George Bush look bad for refusing to participate. Reagan went on to win 50 percent of the Republican primary vote to 23 percent for Bush.

THE NOMINATING CONVENTIONS

The presidential campaign lexicon includes one phrase that is a vast misnomer. It is "gavel-to-gavel," which means to the uninitiated that television networks cover the entire proceedings of a nominating convention from the time that the temporary chairman raps the gavel to call the meeting to order until the permanent chairman bangs it to a close four or five days later.

"Gavel-to-gavel" may have accurately described the network coverage in 1952, the first time that the networks presented the proceedings coast to coast. But later, as the state of the television art became more sophisticated, it has been wide of the mark. Armed with portable, wireless cameras and microphones, the networks break out of the four walls of the main convention arena. What is going on within the walls, they say, is *dullsville*.

Television networks do, indeed, start their programs before the gavel falls and they stay with coverage even after the last wilted delegate has left the hall. But there are long stretches of time when they are not presenting the business that the convention is transacting. They may be outside the hall interviewing delegates on the loose, or they may be on the upper floors of one of the convention hotels, reporting the details of a political deal that has just been cut. Or they may be doing a cute feature on the younger party members and their foibles.

For the eighth time the 1980 conventions raised the questions: Do these quadrennial nominating sessions justify the wall-to-wall (some say, yawn-to-yawn) coverage that the networks give them? Do the networks present an accurate picture of what the convention is doing? Do they lend themselves to manipulation by the politicians? Are the conventions, themselves, an anachronism?

The case is strong for at least one network carrying gavel-to-gavel coverage on television, daytime as well as nighttime sessions. What better way is there to inform 230 million Americans about the most important political process touching their lives: nomination of the person who may lead the country for the next four years? Even if the television audience is relatively small, full coverage is still worthwhile.

The full-coverage network should stay much closer to the proceedings—even routine business—than any of the chains have done in the past, but not at the expense of missing important news outside the convention hall. It could dispense with correspondents and anchorpersons interviewing and congratulating themselves.

Some have suggested that public television should undertake the full coverage job. This observer favors one of the commercial networks because of its greater budget, staff, experience, and technical facilities.

If the one-network theory is so good, why haven't the networks adopted it? The answer is competition. For the last eight convention years CBS and NBC have engaged in fierce competition, which they believe leads to television news supremacy for the succeeding four years. ABC News, until recently short of funds, provided edited, abbreviated coverage in 1968, 1972, and 1976 but plunged back into the head-to-head competition in 1980.

The ABC alternative actually provided a public service to that large segment of the public which has no interest in seemingly endless coverage but will watch 90 minutes each convention night. The problem was that the shortened coverage failed to enhance ABC's news image; so in 1980 the network returned to gavel-to-gavel coverage (almost), mainly because of the pressure to compete with CBS and NBC.

On a strictly news judgment basis few quadrennial nominating conventions justify gavel-to-gavel coverage. Some convention buffs extol them as a "national civics lesson" for Americans. Even if they are dull and routine, their importance justifies lengthy coverage. They are potentially too important *not* to cover *in extenso*.

Do the politicians manipulate the mass media, above all, the networks? "Those of us in politics try to manipulate the media," Robert Strauss, chairman of the Carter/Mondale Presidential Election Committee told the *Washington Journalism Review*. "That's a point that ought to be made. There are those who sin, and I've been guilty of it."

Lyn Nofziger of the Reagan camp had a similar view. He said he didn't think that Carter manipulated the press but that he manipulated the news, and that worried him. Now that Reagan is in the White House, presumably Nofziger has the same worries about his President's "tremendous power to make news and shape news."

Television reporting of events unfolding in front of correspondents and cameras has its perils, and all three networks faced those dangers on Wednesday night, July 16, 1980, at the Republican Nominating Convention in Joe Louis Arena, Detroit. When the night was over, the television news industry had not covered itself with glory in building up and later abandoning the Reagan/Ford "dream ticket." For eight hours most Americans in and out of the convention hall thought that former President Ford was going to run for Vice President on a Republican ticket headed by Reagan.

They believed it because they had heard Walter Cronkite say so—with only thin qualification. They had heard him interview Mr. Ford "live" on their screens, and even the former President and his wife didn't utter a flat "no." True, ABC and NBC didn't run with the "dream ticket" story as fast and as positively as CBS. Douglas Kiker of NBC, reporting from the headquarters hotel, said the deal was "cooking but not yet cut." Sander Vanocur of ABC found a Massachusetts congressman on the floor, Silvio Conte, who warned that the combination would never happen. But in the unrestrained rush to be first with the only unexpected story at the convention, the networks abandoned their normal critical caution.

"Television was a disgrace to itself [that night]," said Nofziger afterward. "They were broadcasting rumor as fact, they were running around looking for anyone to say anything, whether or not it was fact. Television did more harm to itself with that story than almost any single television event that I can think of."

Gordon Manning, the veteran, highly respected vice president in charge of NBC's presidential year coverage, provided this rationalization of the night of July 16th.

"We're all storytellers," Manning said, "the cavemen drawing pictures on stone walls, the ballad singers in the Dark Ages, and the writers who came after the printing press. Now it's done electronically, which is quicker. The game stays the same, just the method used to report it is different."

When television is reporting a big story in "real time," the story takes on unusual importance. It did the night of July 16th. "When something happens on television in a big way," observed George Bush's press secretary, Pete Teeley, "it is virtually accepted as gospel truth by the American people and it's very difficult to reverse any established perceptions." Even Bush thought he was off the ticket until Reagan called him at the last minute.

The print media, always quick and eager to point out television's shortcomings, called the night of July 16th "the night that television news ran amok." And worse. Critic John O'Connor of *The New York Times* even suggested that electronic journalists might hold their scoops for 15 minutes to verify them. But some of the morning newspapers had erred, too—notably the *Chicago Sun-Times,* which bannered IT'S A REAGAN-FORD TICKET on page one of one of its editions. So did six other morning dailies, all based on an Associated Press story that, the AP later admitted, should have included stronger qualification.

While the Republican Convention had only one exciting night, the Democratic session in New York's Madison Square Garden had three that were worth watching. Carter had locked up the nomination two months earlier on Super-Tuesday, but the Kennedy forces continued their fight for a more liberal platform more acceptable to them.

The networks emphasized the Carter-Kennedy platform fight and kept pursuing the story of whether Kennedy would campaign for the Carter-Mondale ticket. The Senator did, indeed, endorse the party's candidates and appeared—

somewhat stiffly—on the rostrum with the standard bearers. Only television did justice to that tableau.

But just beneath the convention surface, the Democratic Party, as it had existed for 50 years since Roosevelt put together his victorious New Deal coalition, was falling apart. The networks—and the print media—barely touched that story, which might have provided an advance look at what happened on November 4th at the polls.

LOCAL STATION COVERAGE

The biggest television news at the 1980 conventions was the on-the-spot coverage by 50 or more large, local television stations that sent teams of from five to 25 news people to Detroit and New York. They did this with the encouragement and cooperation of both political parties.

With 1,000 network news people already flooding the two conventions, why would the party managers agree to coverage regulations that increased the horde of electronic journalists and their equipment on the floor, in the surrounding corridors, and in the headquarters hotels? Wasn't that just inviting a bigger headache?

The answer: With networks tiring of gavel-to-gavel coverage, party managers want to fill the void with local coverage. Also, local coverage tends to be less critical than network reporting.

In any event, the local stations considered it successful. At least 50 of the larger stations have followed up their experience by establishing permanent bureaus in Washington. In 1984 they will be even better prepared for local and state coverage from the convention floor.

THE AUTUMN DEBATES

For the primaries Jimmy Carter sneaked by with a Rose Garden strategy: In the autumn campaign—up against both Reagan and John Anderson—he had to come out from the flowers. But he wasn't going to be foolish enough to enter a two-way or three-way debate with Anderson as the possible beneficiary.

Reagan did take on Anderson in a one-on-one meeting, acquitting himself well. Carter's refusal to debate—or really even campaign—in the primaries and his flat "no" to debating Anderson may have cost him votes. There are many independent, undecided voters who think candidates—even incumbents—should campaign for office.

When he did debate on October 28th, Carter was no match for Reagan. While Reagan did not exactly mop up the floor with the President, he is a much better television performer on any occasion. Even in 1976 it was Ford's gaffe that helped Carter and not Carter's greater forensic talent. Against Reagan, the performance gap was wider. And it was that night, October 28th, seven days before the election, that the tide began to run strong in Reagan's favor.

As in 1960 and 1976, there were loud complaints about the formats of the debates and the debaters' avoidance of vital issues. Television, which performed the role as carrier of the message, could not be held responsible for debate shortcomings. The debate sponsor, the League of Women Voters, negotiated the best deal it could with the participants.

THE POLLS

1980 was not a vintage year for pollsters. Track records in predicting the primaries were not of the kind that one brags about in full-page advertisements the next day or week.

As the autumn campaign entered its last week, most polls pointed to a close race on November 4th. The popular vote seemed to divide fairly evenly between Carter and Reagan with Anderson taking 5 to 8 percent. And all that was qualified by the standard 3 percent fluctuation either way.

Louis Harris and his executive vice president, David Neft, sat up late that last week, pondering their figures and running them through the computer over and over again. It was too close for them to stop polling three days before the voting, so they kept up their telephone calls throughout that last weekend; one that, by most accounts, turned out to be volatile.

At 7:45 A.M. on election day, just as early rising voters were drifting into eastern and southern voting booths, Harris told the viewers of *Good Morning America* on ABC-TV that Reagan would win 301 electoral votes, Carter would take 140, and 95 were too close to call at that time. He had spotted the late swing to Reagan.

"My neck was out by a mile," said Harris. His good right arm, David Neft, explained that they had gone to a larger sample of voters.

"We were struck," said Neft, "by how many people were not taken by either candidate. Anything could have happened. The 1976 race was close, but not scary for pollsters."

Unlike other polls, which saturated phone calls into selected "clusters" of voters around the nation, the Harris organization's poll was designed to select one voter in many areas and to keep phoning that area until they reached voters. Otherwise, says Harris, the survey is skewed to the views of people who stay at home—the relatively immobile and nonaffluent who tend to be more Democratic. By assuring contact with the affluent and mobile voters, the Harris poll was able to detect Reagan's conservative sweep.

The poll that created the greatest controversy was the telephone phone-in conducted by ABC News on the night of the October 28th debate between Carter and Reagan. Correspondent Ted Koppel announced that viewers could call one of two numbers to register their votes for the candidate they thought won.

The phone lines were taken hostage. ABC News logged nearly 700,000 call-in votes. The tabloid *New York Post,* which endorsed Reagan, filled its front page the next day with type fonts reserved for the second coming: REAGAN WINS TV POLL 2-1.

"It's unscientific," chuckled anchorman Koppel, "but oh, my, it's enormous."

Associate Editor Reese Cleghorn of the *Detroit Free Press* was one of those who denounced the poll as "one of the most stunning misuses of network power in recent times . . . an extraordinary distortion in public opinion analysis . . . unsound, but good box office."

Roone Arledge, president of ABC News, defended the poll as similar to reporting early election returns and noted that ABC had stressed it was not scientific. Louis Harris expressed his surprise that the network would conduct such a "meaning-less" poll. He and ABC News parted company soon afterward.

One political scientist, Russell Getter of the University of Kansas, raised the question whether the ABC News poll, in itself, had not created a bandwagon trend for Reagan immediately following the October 28th debate. By most later accounts, voters were beginning to swing to Reagan at that time.

ELECTION NIGHT—OVER BEFORE IT STARTED

CBS News introduced UNIVAC to American television viewers on Election Night 1952, surprising even its human masters by an early projection of Eisenhower's landslide that was hard to believe. Ever since, election projections have been controversial. They were even more so on November 4, 1980.

NBC News was first among the networks to call Reagan the landslide winner, at 8:15 P.M., EST, while westerners had almost three more hours to vote. In Hawaii and Alaska the time remaining to vote was from five to six hours.

ABC News followed with a Reagan projection just as Jimmy Carter was walking into the Sheraton Hotel ballroom in Washington to make the earliest concession speech that the most ancient politicians could remember. CBS News weighed in minutes later. All three networks had known since noon that Reagan had won in a landslide. How did they know?

The answer was a technique called "exit interview" polling, asking voters how they voted—and 20 other questions—as they left the polls. Humorist Art Buchwald, who said the election was over before he finished his yogurt course, gave this lighthearted, oversimplified explanation:

"They ask a black man in Buffalo, a Jewish man in Virginia, a housewife in Florida, a med student in Ohio, and a steelworker in Pennsylvania who they voted for, and then they start making the map all blue for Reagan. The network polling methods have become so sophisticated that we don't need anyone west of the Mississippi to decide a presidential election any more."

Actually, all three networks selected about 400 scattered

polling places and stationed one or two interviewers outside.
They asked citizens who had finished about 20 questions, how
they voted and what issues influenced them. Interviewers
phoned in the results to network computers at four different
times during the day, eventually amassing about 25,000 individual interviews.

In 1980 NBC News, which made the fastest use of exit
interviews, took the brunt of the complaints from politicians,
print journalists and irate voters. Both ABC and CBS said that
they had the same statistical information but that their policies
required them to delay projections until they had actual, tabulated votes from their key precincts in each state.

Politicians up and down the west coast cried "interference
with the electoral process" and threatened legislation before
the next presidential balloting in 1984.

NBC News, defending its Election Night "coup," said that
"there is no hard evidence that [broadcast] projections contribute to the problem of declining voter turnout."

William J. Small, president of NBC News, argued, in a
congressional appearance on June 10, 1981, that "one point
remains clear—election night projections have never been
demonstrated to have any measurable effect on either voter
turnout or voter choice."

Acknowledging that congressional legislation was possible,
Small urged: " . . . the scope of such legislation might wisely be
limited to such questions as the day and hours of voting. NBC
urges that this joint hearing reject any measures that would
diminish the public's right to be informed or the news media's
right to report."

The networks knew that they once again were on a sticky
wicket and they hoped to avoid legislation. This was not the
first time there have been cries for legal or voluntary restraint.
They are heard every time one candidate or other wins in a
landslide, for it is in those years that the results are known
early. In the television era we have had landslides for
Eisenhower in 1952 and 1956, for Lyndon Johnson in 1964,
for Richard Nixon in 1972, and, most recently, for Reagan in
1980. In the years of cliffhanger elections, no news medium is
able to make presidential projections while western states are

still voting. Exit interviews, with their wider margin of error, are only useful for projections during a landslide.

BEDFELLOWS—WILLING OR UNWILLING

Network television and presidential elections have been made for each other since television became a national medium in 1952. There may be some changes in 1984, but one observer's guess is that things won't be too different.

This symbiotic relationship is illuminated by an incident that occurred in Kansas City as the Republicans prepared for their 1976 convention. CBS News had a run-in with the crusty convention manager, Ody Fish. The network had grabbed some hotel rooms that had been promised to the Republican National Committee, and Ody Fish demanded their return.

"You know," Fish told a CBS News executive, "if you don't give back those rooms, you could find it very hard to get convention floor passes." Without floor passes, it is true, any network would find it hard to cover the convention.

"You couldn't have a convention without CBS," the news executive sneered.

Fish thought a second, smiled, and said:

"We could try."

𝒪

The New Technology and the News

BY FORD ROWAN

NEWS TECHNOLOGY has been soaring, literally, and not just via satellite. A big fad in the past few years has been for local television stations to buy helicopters for their news departments. The benefits of speed and immediacy aside, the competitive considerations were immense as stations in each city raced to be the first off the ground.

Soon programs like *Action News* and *Eyewitness News* were sporting Copter Cam and Eye-in-the-Sky to match the mobile vans purchased the year before, the Minicam and Instant Eye, out roaming the streets.

This trend toward ever more expensive vehicular hardware worried some news directors like Jon Petrovich of Baltimore's WBAL-TV, who wondered aloud if the next step wasn't for the stations in his market to rush to buy submarines.

We may not descend to Sub Cam or Wet-Eye anytime soon, but the galloping technological race is changing the news profession, both broadcast and print, and poses the serious likelihood that communications may trigger major societal changes. Aside from sweeping implications—to be discussed later—the fascination with sophisticated gadgets sometimes results in editorial decisions based on technical capabilities rather than newsworthiness. Witness the intense pressure on a

180

news department, which has just acquired a helicopter, to include a live airborne report on each newscast or which dispatches its Action Cam van to relay breathless reports on smoldering mattress fires. Electronic news, born only in this century, is still run by technology to an extent its practitioners do not always recognize. Important stories that do not seem immediate, or visual, or confrontational, or which cannot be captured by the Eye-in-the-Sky, seem to get lost in the daily race.

Technology, however, has opened new vistas of communication and the tools it is affording to journalists can improve their craft. The challenge, of course, is to make the technology the tool of the reporter, editor, and producer, instead of vice versa.

But what exciting new tools they are, ranging from new devices for news gathering, transmitting, processing, and broadcasting to whole new systems for communicating, including interactive use of computers. The changes will affect the way journalists, both newspaper and electronic, perform their work.

Newsgathering is being affected not simply by the addition of mobile vehicles but by the increased transmission capacity that makes them an integral part of a broadcast, the microwave capability. It makes little sense to buy an all-terrain vehicle, as one station in Indiana did recently, if all it could do was get five miles per hour in the water but couldn't communicate with the station via the airwaves. It was the growth of ENG, electronic news gathering cameras, married to microwave transmission, that permitted live reports from the field. It is easy to underestimate the distance television has come in just a few years in its ability to broadcast live events. A decade ago newscrews used film cameras that required developing the film back at the lab before use on the air. "Remote" broadcasts from the field required the use of elaborate mobile units, the size of a bus, that carried studio technicians, directors, and cameramen to the scene. The savings in manpower and bulk of equipment have been formidable, not to mention the rapidity with which the ENG crews can be dispatched.

The trend toward speedier, smaller, and smarter is continu-

ing. New ENG cameras, which combine both camera and
recording device in one unit, eliminating the umbilical cord
that connects camera to separate tape recorder, were demonstrated at the 1981 Radio Television News Directors Association meeting. The combo cameras being offered by RCA,
Sony, Panasonic, and Nippon, are revolutionary and aren't
likely immediately to replace the ENG cameras only recently
purchased by news organizations. According to Phillip
Keirstead, in his column in *Broadcast Communications* (August,
1981), "Judging by what we're learning, we'll see a switch to
self-contained camera/recorders in TV newsrooms—but the
pace is likely to be more deliberate." He added, "Nothing to
compare with the helicopter avalanche!"

In the past, radio has had the edge on television in speed. It
was easier to get someone on the phone and hook him right
onto the air. But radio is not relying on Ma Bell's technology to
supply immediacy to its news coverage. Mutual Broadcasting
System has developed a wireless portable system for field
reporters that permits transmission for on-air broadcasting, a
return signal so the reporter can hear cues, and a two-way
capability so the reporter and producer can discuss what to do
next. Radio usually receives less attention in any discussion of
news technology because it is less dependent on heavy mobile
equipment than television, but that has been an asset for radio
news personnel. To maintain their competitive mobility, radio
journalists are moving rapidly to embrace RENG, radio electronic news gathering, a term applied to new wireless microphones, compact audio tape recorders, satellite networking and computerization in the newsroom.

News transmission prior to actual broadcast is also changing
with the greater use of satellites to relay information from
afar. No longer do networks boast "Live Via Satellite" across
the bottom of the screen; it's just too commonplace nowadays.
On the network level, almost daily use is made of overseas
material beamed back to the United States. ABC *World News
Tonight* has established one of its three anchor desks in London and a segment of its newscast originates abroad each
evening. Satellite coverage is most impressive when breaking
news events on the other side of the earth are brought home

instantly, but such coverage depends—as the networks found out in Iran—on the cooperation of foreign authorities in making technical facilities available to "up link" with the satellite. In the future, more portable transmission equipment may make it easier to establish a link, but the need for political approval probably will not diminish.

The real action with satellites in recent years, however, is not with the major television networks, but with local stations that have discovered the "bird." A number of stations dispatched reporters to West Germany, when the American hostages were released from Iran and flown to Europe, so that local talent could be seen putting a local angle on a major story. Even more pervasive is the attention given to Washington news, with an increasing number of stations posting correspondents in Washington or using the services of a group bureau.

"One way or another," according to Jack Gallivan of Salt Lake City's KUTV, "everybody soon will have a Washington news bureau." Satellites have made this feasible, licking the old-time delay problem when material had to be shipped on airplanes and often did not arrive in time for the late newscast. Gallivan says Washington bureaus are the newest rage and "are what helicopters were for news a few years ago."

Groups like Westinghouse, Bonneville, Storer, Cox, King, Chronicle, Fisher, Post-Newsweek, Corinthian, and Gannett have opened or are starting bureaus in the nation's capital. Washington news services like Capitol Broadcasting, Washington Independent Television, and Potomac News Service supply local-angle stories to stations that have no bureaus of their own. Independent stations can obtain news and programming from Independent Network News, Independent Television News Association, Christian Broadcasting Network, and SIN (Spanish International Network).

New technology does not, of course, guarantee quality journalism. The promotional value of having a reporter in Washington may mean more to a station than what's in his news reports. And attention to local angles can disintegrate into boosterism. WDIV-TV, Detroit, regularly uses satellite transmission to receive reports from Washington and elsewhere, including, according to News Director Jim Snyder, the pep rally in Pasadena, which was carried live when Michigan went to the Rose Bowl. With an estimated one out of five commercial television stations now owning earth stations for satellite reception, it is probable that the primary use in the future will not be to relay news produced by the local news department but to accept syndicated programming and sports events. Nevertheless, it is a tool the news organization will find useful.

Radio broadcasters in particular are turning to satellite transmission to avoid the technical degradation of their signal (and the considerable expense) when they use AT&T long lines for network programming.

Satellite capability has made it possible to set up regular, part-time, and special "networks" to beam programs to radio, television, and cable outlets. If the proposal is approved to create a new breed of low power television station (some 5,000 applications for LPTV are on file at the FCC), many would be linked by new networks and may share one attribute with some of the new radio satellite networks—an absence of local programming. Broadcasters contemplating the new competition from additional TV, radio, and cable outlets, are looking for ways to cut costs. Satellite networking and computerized operation offer the easiest way out, but it will be a way that eliminates or reduces local input, including local news.

The bright side of the increased competition coin is that many radio and television stations are upgrading their local news departments to help them compete with newcomers like cable and home video recordings. All-news and all-talk radio seems well established, and the time alloted for local television newscasts seems to grow each year. Specialization can be expected as channels proliferate and the audience is fragmented.

The growth of cable from its old CATV days, when systems served as community antennas to bring in a few stations from just over the horizon, is dependent on satellites to bring in more extensive programming. Where once cable simply relayed the nearest broadcast signals, now a variety of programming from distant "super stations" like WTBS, Atlanta, and WGN, Chicago, is available in many communities, thanks to satellites. Cable systems are carrying pay-TV offerings and all-news programming like Cable News Network and the proposed Group W/ABC effort, Satellite NewsChannels. It cannot be overstressed how economically unfeasible all this would be if only telephone lines and coaxial cables were available to transmit such offerings across the nation. And beyond the use of satellites to relay programming there looms their use to broadcast directly into millions of homes, bypassing the local station or cable system.

News processing has been affected by the onrush of technological developments and it is here that reporters may see some of the most immediate changes in the years ahead. Video Display Terminals, first found in abundance in many newspaper city rooms, are now appearing in broadcast newsrooms. The electronic media have been slower to accept the computer because it does not offer the same labor-saving benefits to a broadcaster as to a publisher. But the economies are very real, as the Cable News Network has found in its use of a BASIS system which permits instant sharing of information among editors, producers and tape operators in CNN headquarters in Atlanta and in six bureaus.

The use of ENP, electronic news processing, can integrate one or more of the following functions: (1) word processing, script editing, and automatic teleprompting; (2) wire copy storage, retrieval, and scripting; (3) organization of stills, tape, film, and graphics with each script; (4) generation of characters and graphics; (5) organization of newscasts with the capacity for easy substitution and deletion of items; (6) timing of newscasts; and (7) cueing the director and/or actually activating tape machines and other equipment during the newscast.

In addition to those program-related functions, the ENP computers can perform other managerial tasks, including: (8) future filing; (9) data storage; (10) research; (11) keeping track of assignments; (12) keeping track of manpower deployment; and (13) monitoring equipment usage. Of course, without wise use, all this can be little more than a fancy garbage compactor.

There's been little rush so far to such multipurpose com-

puters, probably because the costs are high* and the savings
not immediately impressive. The biggest interest among news
directors has been for image-generating computers to prepare graphics and visuals for on-air use. These kinds of devices vary from those that will display words across a screen,
including bulletins, traffic reports, school closings, and the
like to the type that generate animated color images which can
be compressed, expanded, and manipulated. At the 1981
Radio Television News Directors Association meeting, elaborate weather computers were demonstrated that can create
graphics, display satellite weather photos, produce radar images, and even forecast the weather.

Radio is not overlooking the value of computerized operation. Some all-news radio stations are experimenting with
word-processing devices and equipment that will automatically label cartridges from national sources like AP radio and
UPI audio. WRC Radio in Washington is preparing a system
that will help it screen phone calls for its talk shows. Such a
system could keep track of repeat callers and include a quick
display of how pertinent their previous calls had been.

Down the road, the differences between how electronic and
print reporters work may begin to evaporate as computer-
generated news becomes the norm in both parts of the business. For example, newswriters on the print side increasingly
will see their work used on teletext and videotext systems,
which will be aired over TV channels and cable. News stories
will be typed into the computer terminal and then will appear
on television screens in homes or be stored in data banks for
retrieval by viewers. A sample from the KCET teletext experiment gives the headline flavor of the copy. The headline
read, RENT CONTROL 80 and is positioned next to a sketch
showing apartment buildings. Under that are four sentences,
the first of which reads, "Increase limited to annual rise in
consumer price index." After three other brief sentences
these words appear, "More information: pages 20-25," in-
structing the viewer to use the teletext keypad to order up the
text of the longer story if he's interested in finding out more
about rent control.

*$50,000 - $500,000.

It is clear from this demonstration that the writing skills required for radio, television, and teletext are very similar, and that the graphics that can be utilized with teletext will not be very different from the graphics generated for the evening TV newscast.

News communication is experimenting with new ways to integrate sound, sight, and words, and with new methods of bringing the messages into people's homes and offices. The outlets are rapidly expanding as cable systems go on-line around the country and new technologies like multipoint distribution systems, low power television, and direct broadcast satellite are developed.

The immediate attention is on cable, which in September 1981 had achieved a penetration of just under 30 percent of the nation's homes. Some 4,359 cable systems served over 10,000 communities, with an additional 6,500 communities with franchises in the wings waiting to become operational. Although cable in the past has simply relayed programming initially broadcast by others, that is changing. CNN, Home Box Office, Showtime, and the other services are presenting fare that is not available on commercial television stations. For years the growth of cable was retarded by regulations pushed by broadcasters and imposed by the FCC. Several years ago, however, the deregulatory climate took hold and the anti-siphoning rule designed to keep cable and pay TV from taking over big sports events and movies was revoked.

The older cable systems with only a dozen channels are ill-equipped to carry all the new offerings. But newer systems have up to 150 channels available for basic and extra-cost programming. Beyond entertainment and news, the systems offer the exciting prospect of two-way communications, permitting the viewer not only to select from a larger menu of items but to perform research, register opinions, purchase goods, and pay bills. Because the text services will be so revolutionary, it is worth looking at two of these new systems.

Teletext is the transmission of words and graphics across the airwaves on a television signal. In fact, the teletext message can be included along with the usual transmission of a TV station. If the vertical-hold knob is turned on a set, a line

across the top of the picture will roll across the screen; this is
the vertical blanking interval and it can be programmed to
include text. All one needs is a decoder attached to the set to be
able to select the text rather than the normal programming. If
the decoder includes a small computer data bank, some of the
"pages" of material transmitted over the blanking interval can
be stored or "seized," and when a viewer looks at the headlines
or menu board and chooses to read more on a subject, he can
type his instruction into a keypad (which can be as small as a
pocket calculator) and that information will be displayed on
his TV screen. The material that can be stored in a teletext
decoder is limited as is the interactivity permitted on such a
broadcast system.

Videotext is like teletext, except that the wiring that brings
cable into the home can also be used to transmit information
and commands from the home to distant data banks. By
attaching a keypad or a home-computer terminal to the TV
set, a viewer has a much larger selection of data to choose
from. For example, if electronic banking and electronic shop-
ping services are available, he can perform most of his financial transactions at home. Burglar and fire alarms can be
hooked to the cable to warn authorities electronically of
emergencies. Videotext is expected to be a hot item in the
future, but the industry has been waiting for the demand for
home-information systems to rise and for an increased supply
of lower cost computer-terminal equipment.

One challenge is that these text systems combine attributes
of broadcasting, newspapers, and data processing and have
attracted competitors from within each of these industries.
Several television stations are experimenting with teletext systems. Newspapers are eagerly moving into cable, leasing cable
channels and planning news and advertising text services.
Cable systems have purchased the Dow Jones national data
service, which offers impressive amounts of financial information and news.

But the competition that newspapers fear the most is from
Ma Bell. The American Newspaper Publishers Association
has moved vigorously for regulations to keep AT&T from
getting into the text business. AT&T's natural advantage is

obvious. It is already wired into 80 percent of the homes in the nation. It can transmit and receive information from computers over its phone lines or it can assist television stations in setting up hybrid teletext services with the station providing the main textual information and the phone company providing the dial-up retrieval service.

The newspaper interests insist that the monopoly which controls the lines of communication should not control the information that's transmitted and wants to keep the phone company out of the news and electronic advertising business. In fact, it is the advertising that worries newspaper publishers the most, because if an "electronic Yellow Pages" is devised so it can be updated with classified ads, it could replace the printed want ad section and further erode the newspapers' profit base.

Not all newspapers are fighting AT&T's entry. Some see the phone company as an ally in competition with cable systems. One experiment saw the Knight-Ridder newspaper chain teamed with the Bell System to provide text services in Coral Gables, Florida.

The major broadcasters have also cooperated with AT&T in developing a common technical standard for teletext systems.

All the wizardry of two-way communications aside, the success of any medium is not the brilliance of its hardware but the popularity of its software—the programs and services it offers. And the new technology is not without impact on the way reporters work.

Greater mobility influences story assignments. The days when stations felt compelled to use their Minicams to put a live report in every newscast have not passed completely.

Greater speed will increase competitive pressures to be first and will decrease the amount of time available for preparation, including the checking of facts. The difficulties with erroneous information broadcast just after the assassination attempt on President Reagan's life should be kept in mind when racing to cover breaking news.

Greater visual variety will permit more graphic and textual explanation of complex issues, but the danger exists that it could cause oversimplification and distortion.

Greater interconnectivity and the growth of networking could overwhelm local news operations. While many TV stations are expanding their local newscasts to try to establish a community identity and brace for future competition from cable and DBS (direct broadcast by satellite to homes), it is unclear which kind of informational programming will prove most popular. Newspapers will confront similar choices between local and national news in their teletext operations.

Greater pluralism inherent in the proliferation of competing news services may foster a greater variety of viewpoints but not necessarily creative innovation. The growth in the number of radio stations in the United States has resulted in greater diversity of programming in some cities, but there is a sameness of both news and entertainment across the dial. National Public Radio has proved to be a welcome relief from commercial radio, but the all-news and all-talk formats on commercial stations continue to bombard listeners with the same old five-minute news summaries strung together with features, weather, and chatter.

Greater interactivity offered by two-way systems like videotext may reduce the passivity of the news consumer and put new pressures on editors, producers, and reporters. The ability to pick and choose between news stories will give the viewer more control than he can exert while during a newscast of items selected by a producer or scanning through a paper filled with items picked by an editor. If payment is based on what the viewer actually chooses on his home terminal, the videotext computer could keep track of exactly which kinds of news are of interest to the public and which reporters are most popular. Will such a ratings system put new pressures on editors and reporters who now are deprived of such instantaneous feedback? Suppose individual reporters must rely on fees based on how many people choose to read or watch their reports? The current ratings and circulation competitions are largely institutional, or at least confined to major on-air personalities. The impact on story assignments and editorial decisions could be great if competition becomes more individualized throughout the reporting ranks.

Free press values could suffer because of the new technology.

Deregulation is destablizing to any industry, especially one undergoing technological ferment. Despite the recent movement toward deregulation of communications under the past two administrations, the regulatory climate is uncertain. As the status quo is threatened, there may be increasing demands from segments of the regulated industry for protection. For example, the cable industry, itself long restricted by the FCC, isn't eager to see the Commission unleash Direct Broadcast Satellite to compete with cable.

Protection of the cartel in mass communications has long been one of the goals of broadcasters who used the FCC to stifle the growth of cable. As it became more likely that cable and DBS would be primary sources of news and entertainment in the future the three major networks moved to establish themselves in these new technologies as programmers and operators, much to the chagrin of their affiliated stations.

The days when an average city had only three or four TV stations, one or two newspapers, and a dozen radio stations are passing with the advent of cable, low power TV stations, multipoint distribution systems (offering pay TV over microwave channels), and DBS.

The demand for access is not likely to abate as the number of electronic outlets proliferates. Journalists view such demands, when the decision on what is included is ultimately made not by the editor but by government decree, as contravening their First Amendment protections. Broadcasters have endured the Fairness Doctrine, which is less a requirement that they be fair than a means by which those active in controversial issues can demand airing of their viewpoints. The "equal time" rule is no guarantee that stations will adequately cover election campaigns; it is a protection for candidates seeking to equalize the exposure their opponents purchase or are given. Similarly, the personal attack rule and requirements that stations sell time to federal candidates are all designed to afford access to the airwaves. While the FCC has proposed abolishing some of these rules, the prospect for congressional action is uncertain.

As cable has grown, municipalities have imposed public-access requirements designed to open up this new technology to greater participation by the general public. In New York City this has led to the presentation of pornographic programs on public-access channels; viewers can watch such things as *Midnight Blue* and *The Ugly George Hour of Truth, Sex, and Violence.*

In the past the Supreme Court forbade the imposition of access requirements on newspapers while endorsing them for broadcasters. But as print journalism is transmitted electronically, the distinction between print and broadcast will begin to dissolve. Is teletext a broadcast service and videotext a data service? One of the major arguments for regulating broadcasting—the scarcity of the airwaves versus the putative freedom of anyone to publish—is refuted by actual experience. In every major city in this nation there are more radio and television stations than newspapers. Furthermore, the quest for deregulation by the FCC has opened the way for the expansion of cable systems, the development of DBS, and the likelihood of many new low power TV stations. Still, stations and cable systems depend on licenses and franchises to operate, and as the major means of mass communications will increasingly be electronic, it is not unreasonable to expect that politicians and interest groups will continue to insist on rights of access to the tube.

Videotext operations share some of the characteristics of newspaper publishing, broadcasting, and the telephone industry. Cable and DBS contain elements of traditional broadcasting and common-carrier services. They do not fit the old cubbyholes of regulatory activities that treated broadcasting differently than common carriers like the phone company, which are required to make their communications network available to anyone who can pay the fare on a first-come, first-served basis. Cable systems have some of the attributes of a utility. Should they be required to lease their channels? To the highest bidder? To the first in line? At a rate set by regulators? To any newspaper in town? Or should cable operators have the same First Amendment rights as newspaper publishers to carry or reject whatever they choose? Is it possible to separate ownership of the means of communication (the cable common carrier required to provide access) from the users of the channels (the newspapers and TV stations), which could then operate unregulated with complete First Amendment protections?

Whatever the answers to such questions, a stark reality transcending constitutional issues hangs over the new technology. It is the matter of whether society will want to pay for all this news and entertainment, either directly through subscription or indirectly through advertising. Newspaper companies are hedging their bets by getting into cable ownership, leasing channels and establishing text and data services. All three major networks are into cable, with one, ABC, entering a partnership with Westinghouse to produce an all-news service for cable. And the race is on for licenses for DBS channels. Beyond loom the new opportunities presented by fiber optics, digital transmission, and high-resolution television.

But there may not be a sufficient market for all who want to play the game and the landscape could become littered with the remains of failed new ventures and the skeletons of former successes in a simpler era of communications. For those who have watched the demise of great institutions like the *Washington Star,* the prospects are disturbing. For society the stakes can be higher. As information costs more, some consumers will be unable to pay. The public's right to know is enhanced by free TV and cheap newspapers. Will the poor be able to afford to pay $75 a month for teletext?

The intrusiveness of new communications systems could reach troublesome levels if two-way text systems become marketing and surveillance tools. As farfetched as it may seem to journalists conditioned to see the free flow of information as a public good, these new computerized systems could facilitate the organization of information about viewers that reveals personal tastes like what they read, what they watch, and what they buy. If the videotext data bank knows that someone reads a lot about Marxism, watches lots of movies like *Debbie Does Dallas,* and buys many bongs and Turkish waterpipes, the computer might concoct a profile of a drug-crazed, sex-starved bomb thrower. Aside from invasions of individual privacy, such information could permit businesses to develop sophisticated marketing strategies.

There is also the danger that the information distributed on these systems will not be the objective news reports journalists produce but clever documentaries touting commercial messages, "infomercials" which, as former *New York Times* reporter David Burnham has warned, blur the distinction between news and advertising.

And finally, with instant polling via the videotext system, there's always the possibility that democratic institutions could be altered in unexpected ways as the time frame for serious reflection on issues is compressed even further.

Al Goldberg of CBS has said the new communications will lead to a "telepresence," with the viewer actively involved in what he's watching. But will people really want to be involved in all this? Will the cacophony of information cause many to tune out completely?

Man has made several great leaps in communicating, when he went beyond face-to-face speech and learned to write, when he learned to publish what he had written, and when he learned to broadcast what was spoken and written. Now we are on the verge of something new, the ability to communicate through machines, across distance and beyond the horizon.

For those in the enterprise it may be easier to concentrate on today's helicopter mobile unit, tomorrow's graphics generator, or next week's teletext. Richard Wald of ABC News has suggested that broadcast journalism is still in its adolescence and hasn't yet decided what it wants to do. Technology is no longer the toy, the gimmick to attract an audience. The wise use of machines depends on the intelligence of people.

ᐧ᛭

The Cumulative Impact
of News Consultants after
Ten Years in the Field

BY RALPH RENICK

TELEVISION CAME into its own in the '70s as the nation's primary source of information. Network newscasts retained their traditional identities and half-hour formats. There was, however, a revolution in local news.

Local programs were expanded and reached heights not dreamed of by news directors in the '50s and '60s. Back then, local newscasts were limited to fifteen minutes. The newscaster invariably sat behind a desk and read lead-in paragraphs to voice-over-film clips. Some of these programs had a single sponsor. But news was not a hot commodity for the sales department, and station managers budgeted news expense to news income. The product suffered.

Then in the turbulent '60s things began to change. People wanted to know about the Vietnam war, race riots, civil disobedience, the flower children. Politics was in turmoil as leaders were gunned down. Every city and town was affected. People wanted to know at day's end: "What happened?"

Early evening local TV news became a hot property.

As news audiences expanded, advertisers were more inclined to buy spots where the people watched. Local news expanded to a half hour. Longer formats were not far off. News had become a major profit center.

Indeed, with the demise of locally produced programming and the ascension of the syndicated product, news became almost the sole item produced by hometown TV stations.

News rating points, besides being reflected on station rate cards, also established a station's identity. The number one station in news ratings generally led its market with sign-on to sign-off audience share. Rarely was the first overall rated station not the market news leader. The stage was set for the local news revolution. The era of the News Doctors!

Armed with volumes of market studies, tabulated and cross-tabulated in all directions, the news consultants descended on television stations all over the county. They came to woo management with promises of a quick fix for their news programs.

The news consultants had a sure-fire, Catch-22 argument. If you were already number one in the ratings, they had all kinds of insurance policies to keep you there. If you were a trailing number three, they could light the rockets that would boost you quickly to the number one spot. *Washington Post* critic John Carmody described the trend in a February 1977 article entitled "The Image Shapers of TV Journalism":

"Enter the consultant, by now a fixture of the high-risk world of TV talent, a placebo for worried managements, an expert advisor who can help fine-tune a winning newscast or become an indispensable crutch for a faltering or inept news department."

In the early 1970s my station employed a news consultant.

Back then, some of the consultant's recommendations resembled a blockbuster attack on the news department: Replace the sportscaster, the weatherman, the co-anchor; cover these stories and steer clear of others; pare down some stories; emphasize friendliness, warmth, and camaraderie.

The consultant's report even advised that "news personalities should be seated, although the weathercaster will have to stand to point out features on the weather map."

Of the consultant's 42 recommendations for WTVJ, we adopted about half. Most of them dealt with the cosmetics of the newscast: the set, bumper slides, promotion, and the like.

But there was a great pressure on the news department to take the whole loaf; otherwise the consultant couldn't guarantee his promises. Some stations accepted the consultant's report as being chiseled in stone. They adopted whatever the consultant recommended even if the news director felt otherwise. The consultant became the "surrogate" news director.

The consultants took great pride in delivering to client stations volumes of research material upon which their recommendations for change were based. They argued that since the research was tailored to your market and was "scientific," it made perfect sense to drastically revamp your news programs and personalities.

But the amazing thing about the '70s was that despite the consultant's claim that all research was specifically developed for its clients within the station's coverage area, the end result was a similar "happy talk" format that surfaced in cities from coast to coast.

I came to the conclusion that consultants essentially devised a standard news program format and went about "franchising" it across the country under the guise of having tailored an original package for each client station.

In that era of news growth and resultant profits, it was the end result that seemed to matter. Would it make the ratings go up, make the news interesting, enticing, flashy, and talked about? That was the order of the day.

The fact that the order was being given in many cases by an "outsider" and followed to the T by station management raised a further question as to whether some licensees were living up to their responsibility. Were they governing the content of station programming or abrogating that function to a consultant?

In many cases, local news directors found that, in effect, the news consultants from Frank Magid, McHugh & Hoffman, or other organizations had actually become the station's news director.

Some beleaguered news broadcasters—myself among them—tended to describe a news consultant operation in terms like "a plague of locusts . . . a 'liberating' Russian army." They wheel this big, beautiful beast into your newsroom and just when you are about to reach out and pet the animal a lot of little men start jumping out of it and attacking you from all directions.

Possibly as a result of trial-and-error or trial-and-success, the news consultants have developed a sort of blueprint for news show rating success. If a certain type of feature is a smash in Des Moines, the same type of feature is very likely to turn up on the news shows of their other client stations from Tampa to Tacoma.

As a result, if you've noticed, most local television news shows tend to look alike these days. Three people sitting together on the set. Dual anchors. No story running more than 50 seconds. No sound bite over 12 seconds. A lot of warm, friendly interplay between the personalities on the show. They like each other so the audience feels good about listening to them. And, if the local station follows the dictates of the news consultants, it's giving its listeners the kind of news they like to hear, news that is "entertaining."

It's cookie-cutter journalism.

When I was president of the AP Broadcasters last year, I remember that a consultant's survey was distributed to radio stations giving them a list of 50 news topics which were rated in popularity from 1 to 50.

Now, if you were a station manager you could say, "Hey, I've got a hell of an idea. Let's take the top 10. If every newscast includes the top 10, we can't lose. Forget the bottom 40."

Near the top of the list of high-interest stories were taxes, environment, weather, energy, economy, and medicine. Near the bottom were political morality, politics, business, agriculture, music, and the arts.

A radio station manager might be tempted to tell his news staff: "Include a story about taxes in every newscast!" Some years ago it was said a radio station executive in California ordered his news director to have every newscast lead story be connected with the San Fernando Valley, where the 1,000-watter was located.

An out-of-state wire service executive who heard of this incredible directive was driving his rented car on a sales trip to Bakersfield one day and made a point to tune in the hourly news. The newsman led the program by saying "Two high speed trains collided today between Tokyo and Osaka, Japan." The listener thought: "Someone's going to get fired for violating the manager's edict." The newscaster continued: "There were 123 people killed and several hundred have been injured. But, there were *no Valley residents on board!*"

So much for radio's excesses. Now "Let's go to the tape," as Warner Wolf would say.

Wolf utilized sports action videotape replays to make his sports segment of a newscast more appealing, thus gaining a larger audience for the broadcast. WCBS-TV in New York reportedly paid Wolf $400,000 to lure him across town from another network-owned station.

Videotape has not only revolutionized salaries of TV sportscasters in the last decade but new technology has contributed to several offshoot professions, including broadcast news consultants.

Before VTR cassettes became commonplace, a daily newscast vanished into the ether with only 16mm film and script left behind as evidence that a newscast was aired.

The live segments of the show featuring the news talent could not be kept in the newsroom morgue. While it was possible to make a film kinescope at the time of broadcast, the cost discouraged that practice.

But narrowband videotape filled that void. The three-quarter-inch videotape was cheap, reusable and capable of near-instant replay.

A local news revolution was underway. Stations could now record an entire program. This meant that the newscast could be critiqued and analyzed at home or afar.

Consultants as far off as Marion, Iowa, could screen the cassettes and supply detailed critiques. They could also spot promising talent and steer anchorpeople and street reporters from station to station.

A strong competitive anchor against a client station in Jacksonville would be recommended to a client station in Seattle. One anchor move would ostensibly serve the best interests of two consultant customers.

Videotape now makes it possible for news directors to "pipe in" newscasts from stations everywhere and audition on-air talent in a way until recently not possible. Before tape, you hired a reporter on the basis of a resumé and hope. Now, it's possible to see him in action.

Talent agents have proliferated.

There is more opportunity for swift advancement for those in broadcast news. That's on the good side. The reverse problem is that new talent-discovery techniques have greatly increased the mobility of anchorpeople, reporters, producers, and editors. Even news directors move more often. A Radio Television News Directors Association study reports the average TV news director has held his post for only about two years.

The result is more stations with news executives and personnel who don't know the territory. It helps to know a town and its people when it comes to making decisions on what is local news. It is, in fact, essential.

Chain ownership of newspapers has caused veteran hometown editors to be replaced by more inexperienced newcomers. As television news personnel more quickly shift places, it is hoped that the quality, accuracy, and vibrancy of local TV reporting won't similarly suffer.

Satchel Paige, the baseball immortal and curbstone philosopher, once observed: "Don't ever look back, something may be gaining on you."

Local television news directors who did care to look back over the past ten years often found that, sure enough, something was gaining on them: the news consultants.

But what has gone on the last 10 years in this area is past. Like Satchel Paige, I prefer not to look back. And, looking ahead, I'm encouraged by what I see—not only in television news but in the role of TV news consultants.

That last statement may shock some who know me. In the past, because of various circumstances, I have often been in the vanguard of the vocal opposition to the shenanigans of the television news consultants. I have harangued rather loudly and sometimes unreasonably, I suppose. In any case, I hope my message got across.

Believe it or not, though, I do not necessarily equate news consultants with boll weevils in the cotton fields of television journalism. I do not regard Frank Magid or his counterparts with the same lack of enthusiasm with which I would view a dentist poised to do a root canal job on me.

Maybe it's not quite time yet for local television news directors to begin dancing in the streets, but I can see a couple of developments that give us reason to hope.

First, there is beginning to be an increased emphasis on longer, more fully developed television news programs instead of only a machine gun volley of tabloid headlines on the evening news. Second, and this is a purely personal reaction, I believe I detect some news consultants adopting a more realistic stance in their advisory roles.

Make no mistake, I am convinced there are many ways in which a news consultant can become a valuable adjunct to the local news director.

This is just as well, since news consultants obviously aren't going to go away. But perhaps they will address themselves more to areas where they can exercise their talents to achieve benefits of a higher order.

Some of the recommendations they have made at local stations around the country *have* resulted in more interesting news shows, which translate to higher ratings, which translate to more advertising revenue.

Likewise, when a consultant tells a general manager that the station needs a new set, or new electronic equipment, recommends hiring more newscrews for expanded coverage, advises employment of a special business news reporter, this is pretty vital ammunition for a local news director. The persuasive influence of a news consultant can stimulate front-office support of a news operation in the form of increased budget and staff. This can be very heady stuff.

There are distinct and well developed signs that the horizons of television news are broadening. They are evident among viewers as well as station managements.

One recent survey showed that about 60 percent of TV viewers cite news and public affairs shows as their favorites.

Another poll indicated that the public rates television news first in credibility.

As a result, we are now seeing an expansion of local news shows from half an hour to an hour. . . 90 minutes . . . two hours.

From a station management's viewpoint, economics are an important factor in television news. With the diminishment of other types of local programming, local news is what is going to keep a station alive and economically viable. Absent that, there is little reason for a viewer to watch Channel X in preference to Channel Y, when both are showing pretty much the same movies or reruns. Clearly, any local station is well advised to focus on achieving excellence in its news programs. For self-preservation, if nothing else.

The economic benefits are impressive. One network news executive recently estimated that over $1 billion of the network's advertising revenues this year will come from news programming.

A local news program in a large city can generate $35,000 to $50,000 in daily advertising revenues. In my own case, my half-hour news show includes three breaks with two minutes worth of commercials per break. At prime-time rates, it adds up rather quickly in the revenue column.

The question, then, becomes this: How do we achieve the excellence in television news that will attract viewers and thereby attract profit to the fullest extent given the economics involved?

Any experienced professional newsman knows that it is easy to make interesting news sound important. The tough trick is to make important news sound interesting.

As a news director with something more than 30 years of nightly newscasts behind me, I would like to see two things happening in television news in the future.

First, given the expanded opportunities available for local news programming, I would like to see all of us local news directors doing a better job of honestly and intelligently covering the news rather than offering entertainment in the guise of news.

Second, I would like to see greater commitment by local station programming executives to their news operation in the form of budgets and staffing.

There will be tremendous opportunities in the days ahead for local news directors to sharpen and expand the scope of their operations. Cable TV opens up a whole new area of competition in the news field. That competition will be good for all of us. Sophisticated new equipment will permit us to offer live coverage of news at times and in places never before open to us. Satellite communications will give the local television news director the opportunity to cover world events and interpret their significance in terms his local audience will understand and appreciate. With satellite capability and with proper funding of our departments, there is no limit to the impact we can have in bringing home to our listeners in Topeka or Miami or Albuquerque the significance of social and economic happenings in the world around us.

We, as local news directors, have a credibility in our communities that is a priceless asset.

There is indisputably what Walter Cronkite has called "awesome responsibility" inherent in upholding the highest standards of ethical journalism in a free press. This responsibility can be most effectively entrusted to responsible, trained, seasoned news professionals.

It cannot be abdicated. It should not be left in the hands of those who would define "news" as simply something that people like to see and hear and feel good about seeing and hearing.

The First Amendment guarantees freedom of the press.

It doesn't say a thing about "entertainment."

The Regulators
and
Broadcast News

BY LIONEL VAN DEERLIN

IT'S BEEN nearly 50 years since the late Paul White put together the beginnings of network news. His early CBS "stringers" were chamber of commerce staff in the larger cities, eager to volunteer information that might showcase their town. And because news was at best a prestige builder for the network, producing no revenue, White was severely limited on budget for telephone and other expenses. Radio's unique advantage, its immediacy, was sensed only dimly; the technology did not yet exist for fast on-spot coverage wherever news might be breaking. Publishers of newspapers were unworried.

But Paul White was working on something really big. Radio and TV news are now acknowledged to be the main source of information for a majority of Americans, the most important factor in forming their opinions on public issues. It passed long ago from prestige building or public service into a lively source of income, particularly for local television. Many stations have gone to 90 minutes, some to two hours of early evening news, where high ratings return top dollar on the rate card as well as offering stations a leg up in competition for the evening's prime-time audience.

And though it was once assumed that no one could become

a competent news broadcaster without prior training on a newspaper, there have been too many success stories—beginning with Edward R. Murrow—of those who made it without a single day in the print press. Millions of Americans could probably rattle off names of a half dozen newsmen of the air without being able to name a single newspaper writer. And even in a local market, the salaries of broadcast news personalities reflect the star quality of their trade.

But in one fundamentally important respect, those who bring us the news by air are inevitably inferior to their counterparts of pad and pencil: they are not free. Section 315 of the Communications Act, under which broadcasters are licensed to do business, asserts the government's right—indeed, the government's duty—to keep tabs on the even-handedness with which they interpret events. True, the scepter has been waved rarely in recent years. But like a nuclear weapon, it doesn't have to be used to deter the timid.

Reasons for the imbalance between print and electronic newsmen are well known, and rooted in the logic of an earlier time. To avert chaos on the airwaves, government proclaimed them public property and undertook responsibility for assigning their use to private entrepreneurs. Because only one applicant could occupy a given frequency—which by definition, then, was a scarce commodity—government reasoned it should be used "in the public interest, convenience, and necessity" (language deftly borrowed from earlier laws to regulate railroads and trucks). As applied to broadcasters, that meant requiring licensees to render a minimum level of public service. The watchdog at the gate would be the Federal Communications Commission—established when scarcely 500 radio stations were on the air.

Today those same public airwaves are filled with nearly 10,000 commercial radio or TV signals. A middle-size city may have a dozen or more radio stations, five choices in television plus out-of-town stations off the cable—and seldom more than one daily newspaper. Yet that lone publisher basks in the warmth of editorial freedom assured him in the Bill of Rights while the multiplicity of broadcast voices, as if still in "scarce" supply, remain subject to official scrutiny.

Does anyone care? A recent university poll discloses that only one American in four has any idea what the First Amendment says. But the pollsters bring even more dismal news: On having the Fairness Doctrine for broadcasters explained to them, more than half the persons interviewed not only approved it but felt the regulation should be extended to newspapers as well!

"Deregulation" is enjoying a current popularity. Alfred Kahn came to Washington as President Carter's choice to head the Civil Aeronautics Board and helped Congress deregulate his agency virtually out of existence. The trucking industry was freed from mountains of rules that were said to cushion the big haulers against competition. President Reagan has encouraged the trend, seizing countless new opportunities to abolish government regulations.

For radio and TV, the present Congress came through with a change long sought by the broadcast lobby, extending television licenses to five and radio licenses to seven years. And the FCC took what deregulatory steps it could without a new law: It abolished specifications for on-air public service, as well as its requirement that a broadcaster formally "ascertain" the views of a cross-section of the market area he is licensed to serve.

Even this limited loosening of regulatory strings wouldn't have happened if it had been up to some commissioners. Partisan rhetoric aside, the ardor for controls can burn with equal fierceness in both Republican and Democratic breasts. With the entire Commission before our committee for oversight hearings last year, a question was raised about the policy requiring all stations to carry news, regardless of their program format. Commissioner Abbott Washburn, who holds a Republican slot on the FCC, argued that this was necessary and desirable.

"They had a terrible tornado down in Texas this week," he said. "Young people listening to a rock station in Wichita Falls might have had no warning of the danger if we didn't require the licensee to provide a minimum of news."

This, obviously, was one man's conception of broadcast practices as he viewed them from behind the walls of Washington bureaucracy. For me, it conjured up the picture of a disc jockey diving under a studio table, clutching his microphone but saying nothing about the roaring black cloud outside because Commissioner Washburn and cohorts hadn't told him he must.

For those who choose to earn a living as broadcast newsmen, freedom will have to mean more than an easing of paperwork in the front office. Until lawmakers remove the shackles of Section 315, deregulation for them will be meaningless.

In day-to-day practice, it should be noted, good-news departments get their job done with a hard-hitting professionalism that could hardly be different if there were no Section 315, no commission waiting to forward the next viewer complaint for management's immediate attention and response. In the problems they regularly encounter, news staffers are likely to feel greater impact from judicial decisions on libel, or from the views of trial judges about admitting cameras into the courtroom. Reporters occasionally are subpoenaed in connection with crime stories they have worked on—but they're unlikely to be involved in events that place their owner's license in jeopardy.

Yet the law provides a convenient club over the broadcaster's head, and we need look back no more than 10 years to spot politicians who were eager to swing the club. There was the ruckus that followed airing of a CBS summer documentary, *The Selling of the Pentagon,* in 1971. This hour-long program undertook to show how the Defense Department used public funds to promote its image. Film clips depicted sea tours and visits to missile ranges by businessmen, community leaders, publishers, and other opinion molders—persons who, it was hoped, would thereafter help make the case for higher defense spending.

In editing interviews, the program's producers had carelessly spliced the remarks of at least two participants into segments where they appeared to be answering questions other than ones actually put to them on camera. It made little difference in the thrust of the program, but it was all the aggrieved Pentagon officers and certain congressmen needed to attack the show—and CBS.

How well I remember the unpleasant days that followed. The late Representative F. Edward Hebert (D-La.), chairman of the House Armed Services Committee (and a onetime managing editor of the *New Orleans Times-Picayune*, who should have known better) demanded that the House Commerce Committee, with jurisdiction over the FCC, take action against the network. Our Commerce chairman, Harley Staggers of West Virginia, persuaded his investigative subcommittee to order a subpoena served on CBS requiring, among other documents, the film or tape "outtakes" from the interviews in question—portions not used on the air.

The network's president, Frank Stanton, responded that the subpoena went to the sort of materials that a committee of Congress could not constitutionally require of a newspaper or magazine publisher. To comply, he noted, would be to acknowledge that the First Amendment doesn't apply to broadcasters.

Staggers, a thoroughly decent man, had no understanding of the principle Dr. Stanton sought to uphold. Under continued goading, he pressed his full committee for a contempt citation, which only 13 of us on the 43-member committee opposed.

A contempt vote in committee often brings compliance, as the respondent senses his adversaries mean business and may shortly have him in court. But Dr. Stanton remained adamant, and the network prepared for a showdown. In addition to its own governmental relations staff in Washington, CBS retained the special services of high-priced legal and lobbying talent.

It would be pleasant to report that upon sober reflection a majority of House members realized the unseemliness of throwing a citizen like Frank Stanton into jail over a matter of conscience. But Chairman Staggers' headcount showed a 2-1 ratio of support for his contempt resolution as it headed for the House floor shortly before the August recess. He thus refused to listen when Speaker Carl Albert urged restraint. And it failed, finally, only because Albert threw the full weight and prestige of the Speakership against the resolution—an action for which Staggers never forgave him.

From the direction of the White House soon thereafter came added examples of abuse. A particularly shabby segment in the Nixon tapes revealed the President's intent as he started his second term to bring *The Washington Post* to heel by arranging challenges to renewal of the newspaper's TV licenses. At about the same time presidential assistants leaned on a new FCC chairman, Dean Burch, to demand the transcripts of network commentaries following a Nixon news conference. And the first director of Nixon's new Office of Telecommunications Policy (an agency presumably established to monitor technological developments) was used to apply the political squeeze wherever possible: He reminded TV station owners of the obvious—that they could be help responsible under their licenses for the nature of any network programming they accepted; and he sought to discourage educational broadcasters from persisting with strong national programming on subjects the Nixon White House resented.

In Great Britain, whose early experience put broadcasting under total government ownership and operation, it seems safe to assert that the BBC was better cushioned against political interference than commercial broadcasters in this country have been. To assure an uncertain "fairness," we have chosen to rely upon the judgment of politically appointed government officials rather than the discretion of professional broadcast journalists. We have tried to make certain there are no scalawags out there perverting the truth, rather than satisfy ourselves that the truth usually emerges from among conflicting voices. And we have done this in the face of clear First Amendment prohibitions against government abridgment of speech and press. Indeed the general language of Section 315, embodying the concept of fairness, is often implemented by the FCC in a manner that appears to conflict with the ban on censorship in Section 326.

As enforced in recent times, the doctrine can be ostensibly fair but manifestly foolish. The congressional fight over strip-mining legislation in the early '70s was an issue of consummate importance in coal states, hideously pocked from past mining abuses. Yet environmentalists in Clarksburg, West Virginia, were denied air time on a local radio station by a broadcaster

who ignored the issue as if it held no interest for the local folk.
Rep. Patsy Mink (D-Hawaii), a member of the Interior Committee, learned of the situation and filed a complaint with the
FCC. As often happens, the taking of depositions, public
hearings, and legal arguments seemed endless. A little more
than two years passed before the Commission rendered its
decision: The Clarksburg broadcaster had indeed violated the
fairness doctrine—and so he was ordered to editorialize
about strip mining then and there, some 30 months after
enactment of the bill that had sparked the controversy!

Although it's something that riles us only at four-year inter-
vals, Section 315 also provides the underpinning for a
mockery called Presidential Debates. As written, the law
would bar campaign debates that exclude bona fide third- and
fourth-party candidates. The FCC found a way around this,
first by exempting legitimate news coverage of candidates
from application of the stricture, and then asserting that a
debate sponsored by a non-broadcasting third party (the
League of Women Voters) and limited to just the two major
candidates constitutes legitimate news.

The validity of this reasoning was brought home during the
first Carter-Ford debate in 1976. Proceedings broke off for
nearly a half hour when the auditorium's sound system failed.
The interruption could not be dealt with by house technicians
because the system had been installed by ABC network
engineers to be tied in with their network feed.

So much for the debate's legitimacy as an independently
sponsored event taking place with or without broadcast coverage. Let's move to the climactic event of the 1980 election, the
Carter-Reagan debate from Baltimore. President Carter had
insisted that it be limited to himself and Reagan as the major
candidates—and the League of Women Voters obligingly
ruled John Anderson ineligible. Network viewers watched
what the League and FCC rules permitted. But Ted Turner,
brash founder of the satellite-fed Cable News Network, had
an intriguing idea. He seated John Anderson in a remote
studio and cut into the debate with the Independent candidate's responses to the same questions asked of Carter and
Reagan—under the same precise time limits.

Next day a representative of the Socialist Workers Party called the FCC, asking if they could bring a complaint against Turner under Section 315. A staffer explained how to file one, but happily that was the end of it. The courts have recognized FCC jurisdiction over cable insofar as it is "ancillary" to broadcasting. One can only guess how the Commission would have decided the issue raised by Turner's imaginative programming—or indeed whether the rash of new cable services (Westinghouse and ABC both plan news distribution similar to Turner's) are to feel the withering effect of Section 315. Because no one can say, Senator Goldwater, as Chairman of the Senate Communications Subcommittee, has asked the FCC to spell out how equal time rules might be applied to a medium that avoids the spectrum space of broadcasting.

An equally searching question faces the newspaper publisher who may be contemplating new methods of distribution: by going electronic, will he be asked to check his First Amendment rights at the door? Either we change the law or the Bill of Rights could be further whittled away.

And who stands in the way of reform? Just about everyone.

• First, the practitioners who know most about the law—the federal communications bar, 850 strong, all but 150 of whom ply their practice in Washington. Together with slightly more than 300 staff lawyers at the FCC, these men (and a few women) derive their daily bread from the intricacies of a legislative act that began as your typical 90-page major bill and has thickened through rulemaking to the size of a Manhattan phone directory. The more arcane its provisions and the more pervasive its threat to the financial life of their clients, the better the job opportunities for these oracles. Former FCC Chairman Richard Wiley confides that when he sought to shortcut license renewal procedures at the Commission, attorney friends warned in a not altogether joking way that he was tampering with his own future career.

• Second, I regret to note, are the self-styled public interest organizations that have burgeoned over the past decade—including, of course, their lawyers. From the able dean of intervenors, Dr. Everett Parker at the United Church of Christ, down through the Naders, the Nick Johnsons, and others professing to speak for women, for racial minorities, for the elderly, for gays, or maybe for retired sea captains— they cling to the 1934 Act and all its parts. It provides the mechanism they feel they need to gain attention—the attention they can command on the threat of hauling a broadcaster before the Commission or the courts.

At a lesser level, the Fairness Doctrine is their open sesame to planting public service announcements (PSAs) on everybody's air. It makes matters so much simpler than their dealings with the print press, where a hard-nose city editor must be persuaded they deserve publicity.

• A third layer of opposition is found traditionally among those whom the law has chosen as regulators. There being few Alfred Kahns, it is a Washington maxim that your typical government agency will seek to expand, seldom to diminish its authority. However, the FCC's new chairman, Mark Fowler, has shown a commendable willingness to let the marketplace supplant regulation in the field of telecommunications generally. And in mid-September he demonstrated equal concern for the marketplace of ideas by persuading a majority of commissioners to ask that Congress repeal Section 315— equal time, enforced fairness, and all. I confess to a personal sadness that only one Democratic member, Jim Quello, voted with him.

Congress itself is seldom found in the vanguard of change. And when it comes to Section 315, members are impelled by an added motive to keep things as they are. Its "equal access" provision applied to political campaigns means an unfriendly broadcaster cannot easily sponsor a candidate against the incumbent—and that's comforting to an office-holder who must spend 75 percent of his time away from home.

• Finally, and surprisingly, are broadcasters themselves. There are precious few Frank Stantons and Julian Goodmans. Unlike most newspapers, broadcast properties are usually managed by men without news experience. Their orientation having been on the business side, it's rare to find one who senses the importance of editorial independence in a free society. At renewal time they see company lawyers preparing volumes to persuade the FCC how faithfully the station has complied with every last licensing requirement—and invariably attached, a documented litany of public issues with which the station has dealt in faithful adherence to the Fairness Doctrine.

"I don't understand all this criticism of the Fairness Doctrine," the manager of a prosperous TV property told me once at a public meeting. "We operate very well under its provisions. We like it."

You bet he does. Like so much of present law, the Fairness Doctrine provides one more dfensive weapon against license poachers.

And that's fine if the miracle of radio and television is conceived to be the miracle of making back the stockholders' total investment from the profits of a year or two.

Most of us, I hope, see the miracle as more than this.

Business
and
Broadcast News

BY HERBERT SCHMERTZ

FIRST CAME the medieval town crier, one of the earliest of professional "newsmen," who epitomized the era when most people learned of local events by word of mouth. Then came movable type, and the era of the print journalist. Today, in a sense, we have come full circle: As much as 75 percent of the public gets its news from the mouths of television newscasters, and a recent Gallup poll showed that 71 percent of the people believe that the words they hear on network news are accurate and unbiased.

Considering the complex state of the world and nation, this confers on the electronic town criers of our day an awesome responsibility. How well are they handling it? More specifically, how well do they cover the myriad day-to-day activities of that important segment of society we call "business," and which impacts so directly on all our lives?

Despite some glaring lapses (like the recent Pulitzer Prize imbroglio), the newspapers of this country generally do maintain a fair balance in presenting and commenting on the news. Most of the nation's dailies take sides on political issues, and rightly so, because they do so primarily on their editorial pages and by their choice of columnists. They also publish many of the rebuttals they receive in the form of guest columns and letters to the editor.

214

But television, unfortunately, is a different breed of cat; several characteristics distinguish TV journalism from the print media. First, while anyone with sufficient funds can publish a newspaper, the right to broadcast is granted by the government on the grounds that there's a limit to the number of frequencies available. Second, because the license to broadcast is government-given, it cannot be used as freely to espouse political and other causes. Third, as a practical matter, TV journalism lacks the flexibility of newspapers and magazines. Though TV news coverage can be expanded around the clock for earth-shaking events, on the average day it is confined to half-hour segments of national and local coverage. This, however, is a self-imposed restriction. Television news could easily free itself from the time constraints and make its "news hole" as flexible as that of newspapers. And in the daily news mix that gets on the air, business news is covered only superficially and often in a hostile antibusiness way.

Finally, TV news is but an adjunct, albeit an important one, to what is essentially an entertainment medium. This is obvious not only from the salaries paid TV news personalities— equivalent to salaries paid entertainers—but also from the battle for ratings in which network news departments are constantly engaged with each other. And many TV journalists, in their need to entertain as well as inform, may regard business news as crass, or dull, or both.

Because the spectrum of television frequencies is limited, broadcasters have a duty to provide wider, not narrower, access to ideas on the airwaves, even to the ideas of businessmen. In the *Red Lion* case, the U.S. Supreme Court made that clear when it held:

"It is the right of viewers and listeners, not the right of broadcasters, which is paramount. It is the purpose of the First Amendment to preserve an uninhibited marketplace of ideas in which truth will ultimately prevail rather than to countenance the monopolization of that market, whether it be by the government itself, or by a private licensee. It is the right of the public to receive suitable access to social, political, esthetic, moral and other ideas and experiences which is crucial here. . . ."

But the ideas of businessmen, which may seem unimportant, run into another snag: time compression on TV newscasts. Walter Cronkite, still regarded as the dean of American newscasters, complained that ". . . in the compression process forced upon us by the severe limitations of time, the job is incredibly, almost impossibly, difficult. I'm afraid that we compress so well as to almost defy the viewer and listener to understand what we say. And when that becomes the fact, we cease to be communicators." That is particularly true, for example, in a business story as complex as energy.

Cronkite was well aware of the consequences, which he described as "the inadvertent and perhaps inevitable distortion that results through the hypercompression we all are forced to exert to fit one hundred pounds of news into the one-pound sack that we are given to fill each night."

The job of the television reporter is made even more difficult by the pervasive influence of the entertainment side of the medium. John J. O'Connor, *The New York Times* television critic, put it this way: "TV news, no matter how lofty its pronounced aims, is rarely able to escape the clutches of show business considerations." To illustrate his point, one need only observe the frenetic realignments of TV news personalities the moment ratings begin to slip.

Actually, the TV newsperson too often reflects, in his coverage of business, what he sees on entertainment shows. In his book *The View from Sunset Boulevard*, lawyer-journalist Ben Stein points out that "one of the clearest messages on television is that businessmen are bad, evil people and that big businessmen are the worst of all." Based on interviews with some of TV's leading producers and writers, Stein found that what appeared on the screen was indeed a true but narrow reflection of the beliefs of a handful of Hollywood producers responsible for much of what the public sees. They are admittedly antibusiness.

Nor is Mr. Stein alone in this observation. The Media Institute, in a study titled "Crooks, Conmen, and Clowns: Businessmen in TV Entertainment," found that most businessmen are portrayed on TV as "foolish, greedy, or criminal"; that almost half of them are shown involved in illegal acts; and that they are almost never portrayed as useful and productive members of society.

Admittedly, this is the view only of those who fashion TV's entertainment fare, but it is reflected also in the way business-people are perceived when they surface in the news. Couple this image with the adage that it is news only when a man bites a dog and you have the perfect setting for distorted coverage—or noncoverage—of a business event.

To compound the problem, news about business is not ordinarily the first priority. Neither is news about sports. Still, TV journalism has spawned a cadre of specialists who can bring the day's sports action to life. Business coverage, on the other hand, suffers from a lack of reportorial expertise. With few exceptions, TV news departments strongly favor generalists—reporters who can cover any type of story but who may not be sufficiently conversant with business concepts to provide anything but the most superficial information. The time constraint reduces business coverage to no more than two minutes on the average day's newscast. Even if this entire slot is devoted to a single business event because of its preeminence, it hardly suffices to convey enough of the story's nuances to an audience as ill-equipped to comprehend it as the reporter is to explain it. When this kind of coverage then is peppered with an antibusiness slant, it's easy to see how business people can be cast in the role of the dog-biting villain.

In all fairness, the atmosphere has improved to some degree. There has been increased depth in the treatment of business subjects, especially in documentaries. For example, ABC's *20/20* recently devoted a segment to Mobil, which was eminently fair. Since then, CBS' *60 Minutes* opened its 1981-82 season with a self-critique, which, at least in the areas it covered, was even-handed from my viewpoint as a participant in the show. Similarly, I took part in ABC's *Viewpoint* segment dealing with fairness on the air and found it candid and self-searching.

Still, whenever TV news has pointed its stiletto at business, we in the oil industry have probably felt the sting more than most. Fuel shortages on two occasions, and eight years of escalating prices, have made oil companies the perfect foil for this deadly combination of time constraint, reportorial ineptitude and antibusiness bias.

How else can one explain the week-long series on New York's WNBC-TV in 1976, which vilified the oil industry in 17 different ways—literally 17, because Mobil responded in a full-page newspaper advertisement refuting the 17 specific hatchet jobs done during the TV series. Why else would CBS News report Mobil's third-quarter earnings in 1979, admittedly record-high, without any reference points by which viewers could judge them—no explanation of inventory profits and no comparisons with the profitability of other industries, television networks among them?

Presenting oil-industry executives in a villainous light reached a high—or, rather, a low—in 1979, when William P. Tavoulareas, Mobil's president, testified before a congressional committee about the gasoline shortage that then afflicted the nation. Through remarkably adept cutting and editing, the tape shown on ABC News had Mr. Tavoulareas stalking out of what appeared to be the middle of the proceedings, smiling with what viewers just had to conclude was contempt. It never happened. Mobil's president made his exit at the conclusion of the hearings in good humor, shared by others in the committee room. This kind of juxtaposition was obviously not an accident of time compression; it was clearly deliberate in the context of a newscast, which lionized former Representative Andrew Maguire in his antioil tirade.

On another occasion, Mobil's chairman, Rawleigh Warner, spent three hours with a TV reporter expounding the company's position, only to be seen on the home screen for 30 seconds, during which his statements, cut, edited, and out of context, seemed like a string of irrelevancies.

Distortions such as these would be tolerable—though by no means excusable—if television provided a suitable vehicle for rebuttal or clarification. But it doesn't. Not even when a network or station offers the offended company time to state its case can the damage be completely undone, because the editing—the critical choice of what gets on the air—remains in the hands of the same people responsible for the original injustice.

The same attitude holds true in documentaries and public affairs specials—the magazine-format programs of which the networks are so proud. These programs also reflect often dubious broadcast news and entertainment values. The networks select the subjects and the representative viewpoints, establish the formats, provide the film, and do all the editing. There is no room for free, uncensored expression of views on television news and public affairs programming. Thus, when ABC-TV's *20/20* did an unfair segment on natural gas, Mobil had to reply in print and not on television.

The networks' focus is narrow and selective, a systematic exclusion of many viewpoints. This can be especially unfair and dangerous when public attention is focused on a particular issue—when it is most important to hear as many sides as possible, when unwillingness to permit proper debate can result in bad laws or failure to enact good law.

It all boils down to business' lack of access to network television. One solution, of course, is for business to make its voice heard on paid commercial time. Mobil first tried this in 1974 and, for the occasion, created what must have been the blandest commercial of all time. It began with a shot showing a beach and the ocean. Then the camera moved out to show only the water, and this narration followed:

"According to the U.S. Geological Survey, there may be more oil beneath our continental shelf than this country has consumed in its entire history.

"Some people say we should be drilling for that oil and gas. Others say we shouldn't because of the possible environmental risks. We'd like to know what you think.

"Write Mobil Poll, Room 647, 150 East 42nd Street, New York 10017.

"We'd like to hear from you."

NBC accepted it, but ABC and CBS rejected it. CBS said, "We regret that this message addresses a controversial issue of public importance and as such cannot be considered under our corporate policies." In other words, one side of an issue

may never be seen on TV. In subsequent experiences of this
sort, the networks raised the Fairness Doctrine as their defense, arguing that they must allot equal time to those who
disagree. Fairness, it seems, is in the eye of the beholder. So let
us examine the Fairness Doctrine to compare what it was
meant to accomplish with what really happened.

The FCC's Fairness Doctrine owes its existence to the theory
that the airwaves are a scarce resource and must therefore be
allocated among potential users. The doctrine requires owners of broadcast licenses to devote reasonable time to the
coverage of controversial issues and provide reasonable access
to points of view other than their own in the interest of an
informed public. In theory, the Fairness Doctrine does not
preclude anything. In reality, it produces gross unfairness.

Broadcasters are using the Fairness Doctrine to subvert the
Fairness Doctrine. Instead of opening the dialogue to all parties to an issue, they seem prepared to throttle the debate
altogether by telling one side its views can't be heard because
its opponents might also demand to be heard, thus causing the
networks commercial problems. This is precisely the reasoning by which Mobil's advocacy commercials were rejected time
after time.

To overcome the Doctrine's unintended effects, Mobil even
offered on occasion to pay twice the price for airing issue-
oriented commercials, thereby funding the cost of a rebuttal
by any responsible opponent to be selected by the networks.
Even this offer has been turned down.

All this flies in the face of the First Amendment, as interpreted by the U.S. Supreme Court in the now-famous *Bellotti*
case. Though the circumstances of that case had no bearing on
the TV-access issue, it holds some potent lessons for today's
media world.

Expressed or tacit, the argument against permitting business corporations to contribute to the national dialogue via
commercial messages on TV has usually been that they, because of their financial strength, could dominate the debate
unfairly. Chief Justice Burger, however, put that notion to
rest when he wrote in the *Bellotti* case: "It could be argued that
. . . media conglomerates . . . pose a much more realistic threat

to valid interests than do business corporations and similar entities not regularly concerned with shaping popular opinion on public issues."

And Associate Justice Lewis F. Powell, in writing the decision, said that the press, in the form of media corporations "does not have a monopoly on either the First Amendment or the ability to enlighten."

If the news departments of TV networks were to take these words to heart, even though the *Bellotti* case did not involve them directly, it might be possible to give their viewers a broader spectrum of views on current issues. Whether this will happen when viewers will have access to increasing numbers of cable TV outlets remains to be seen. The new technologies are just too young and untested, though it appears they have already made the Fairness Doctrine obsolete in the eyes of the Federal Communications Commission, which recommended its abolition to Congress.

There are some who believe that business can make its voice heard by remote control—by its influence as the commercial sponsor who makes TV news and entertainment possible. Those who hold this view contend that advertisers can withhold sponsorship from networks that fail to give business its due in the news or, even more blatantly, exert direct influence on the contents and tenor of newscasts.

Occasional rumors notwithstanding, there is no evidence that sponsors have, or ever had, any impact on the content or presentation of television news. The reason is simple. TV news departments are probably the most iconoclastic entities to be found anywhere in the business world and are not awed by corporate power, if such a thing exists. In fact, it often seems obvious that TV newspeople are totally oblivious to external influences, including profit-and-loss statements.

For those in the television news field who really fear pressures from sponsors, there is a quick solution: eliminate advertising from news shows.

That leaves only one other area of potential influence—a sponsor withdrawing from entertainment shows to put financial pressure on the station or network whose news department is unkind to business generally or that sponsor in particular. This kind of response poses no philosophical problem to me. Where is it written that any company must spend advertising dollars in a hostile environment? Why feed the hand that bites you?

These, however, are theoretical considerations. In practice, television news must come to grips with the fact that business is a productive component of the society from which all news events emanate in the final analysis. As such, business has a contribution to make to the dialogue that shapes the nation's future and a right to be treated as fairly as any other societal segment. The time has come for the blinders to be removed and the prejudices redressed. The public's demonstrated faith in the accuracy and evenhandedness of TV news deserves to be rewarded in kind.

✑

Investigative
Reporting

BY BILL KURTIS

JOURNALISM'S SHOWCASE success story called Watergate turned investigative reporting into a growth industry. Enrollment at journalism schools increased. Newspapers formed special "task force" units to concentrate time and manpower on investigative targets. CBS News combined four television personalities with its electronic brand of investigative reporting to create the most consistently popular program in the network's broadcast schedule—*60 Minutes.* The competing networks followed with programs of their own. By the end of the '70s local television had also discovered the public preference for investigative reporting over the softer, feature style of the post-Vietnam "happy talk" days. The expanding demand was filled in some instances by a number of independent, nonmedia organizations in exchange for a share of the credit when the story was published.

As the trend spilled into the '80s a new spirit of muckraking, carried by the energy of Watergate, had swept across the entire journalistic spectrum. While commendable for its emphasis on serious newsgathering, the trend was accompanied by some disturbing new issues, both ethical and practical, which reached to the very heart of professional conduct.

It was an examination of these issues that prompted the most controversial debate of 1981, with the exception of the Janet Cooke affair. Television station WBBM-TV, Chicago, broadcast an hour-long documentary in April, 1981, which followed the growth of the Better Government Association, a private, not-for-profit investigative organization based in Chicago.

In the course of examining the BGA's joint ventures with newspapers, local television stations and eventually network news organizations in the post-Watergate escalation of investigative reporting, the documentary criticized a report by the BGA and *20/20* of ABC News. One month after the WBBM-TV program, the network broadcast an hour-long response to the charges and, in turn, criticized WBBM-TV. The resulting confrontation turned attention to the most controversial of the investigative techniques currently being used by both print and electronic media.

MISREPRESENTATION

There are two distinct practices. *The New York Times* represents the belief that falsifying a reporter's identity to gain access to certain facts discredits the attempt to report those facts. On the other hand, many newspapers have endorsed the tactic under strict controls.

Television was slow in adopting the technique because of its need for visual material. However, when the electronic media realized the potential, electronic journalists carried misrepresentation into a new dimension.

Television investigative reports became little "dramas" that fit snugly into the electronic format of telling a story. It wasn't good enough to tell the audience there were undercover reporters on the scene. The television presentation showed those reporters, often either preparing to go undercover or inside the place of business, with the use of hidden cameras. In several instances, to the dismay of company attorneys, a wireless microphone allowed television reporters to interview the subjects without them knowing they were being videotaped.

One such report by a Chicago television station showed a producer disguising his voice on the telephone to gain access for his crew. Then, interspersed between pictures of an unmarked van used by the investigative team, a hidden camera placed inside a briefcase approached a motel room, shakily. The viewer was riding on adrenalin built up by the promise of seeing something "forbidden" inside the motel room. Unfortunately there was no such payoff, but the report demonstrated a key element in making investigative reports interesting for the electronic media—the *Mannix* ingredient. The process itself is interesting. Watching reporters go undercover is better than a sequence of *Mission: Impossible*. So what's the harm? The viewer sees how facts are being gathered, which should give him an insight into any conditions that might affect a subject's answer. The harm comes when investigations place too much emphasis on the entertainment element and forget about the substance that they are pursuing. There are also serious concerns that these techniques might be doing more to distort the truth than reveal it. It becomes most acute in the next application: entrapment.

JOURNALISTIC ENTRAPMENT

The most celebrated post-Watergate journalistic "sting" operation was the Mirage Tavern story in Chicago, conducted by the *Chicago Sun-Times* and the Better Government Association in 1977. A phony bar was set up and the undercover reporters, acting as bartenders and owners, wrote about the payoffs they made to city inspectors. They insist, after strict guidance from their attorneys, that it was short of entrapment—"enticing someone to break the law, which otherwise he would not have done."

But when a *20/20* producer, working with the BGA on the 1979 "Arson for Profit" story, attempted to consummate a bribe on camera, the technique produced questionable results.

Filming from an unmarked van with hidden cameras and a wireless microphone, the *20/20* team caught an exchange of money between an insurance inspector and the ABC producer who had maneuvered the man into position before the camera. It was offered as one more piece of "circumstantial evidence" to support a conspiracy theory that a small group of men in Chicago's Uptown neighborhood were trading buildings among themselves to inflate their paper value so that when the buildings burned the small group of men would collect more insurance money. The report represented the bribe as proof that the "group of men" had special connections with certain insurance inspectors, which made it easy for them to get extra insurance.

The viewer watched the ABC producer ask the insurance inspector if "there was any way in which he might thank him for the favorable report" that the inspector indicated he would write. The inspector suggested 20 dollars and the producer gave him a $100 bill.

What seemed open and shut in the *20/20* report was really a case of deception, although perhaps unwitting. In a subsequent investigation by the office of the United States Attorney for the Northern District of Illinois, agents learned the insurance inspector had never worked for the "small group of men" before. In fact, he was chosen for the job, which appeared on television, strictly by random selection. Although his company fired him immediately after the *20/20* story aired, it was prompted, by the government investigation, to check every report the inspector had ever written. It found that the only erroneous report he had ever turned in was the one he wrote for the *20/20* producers.

The television viewer thought he was seeing a bribe on camera, part of the arson-for-profit conspiracy. In fact, he was watching an insurance inspector with no record of bribe-taking receive $100 when it was offered. Did the television report reveal corruption that advanced its arson story—or create it?

Columbia University professor and former President of CBS News Fred Friendly commented on journalistic entrapment for the WBBM-TV documentary, "When you move investigative journalism to entrapment or anything close to entrapment, and then do that in a media, which, by itself is show business, you're dealing with a witches' brew, and you can destroy a person or an institution by what is so close to entrapment that it is entrapment."

THE AMBUSH OR CONFRONTATION INTERVIEW

Bribery on the television screen has the element of entertainment that makes it "good television," despite the dangers that lurk within the technique. Another investigative technique that is being used in virtually every newsroom in the country touches that dramatic element as well—the ambush interview.

The scene is familiar to television news viewers. A reporter holding a microphone is moving rapidly down a sidewalk, following or chasing a subject who obviously does not want to talk. The reporter shouts his questions but the subject ducks out of sight leaving the impression his silence is evidence of his guilt.

The unpredictability of the situation has created a drama, a tension for the viewer. But is it fair?

Fred Friendly commented again for the WBBM-TV documentary, "That's probably the dirtiest-trick department of broadcast journalism. We have done it so many times that the illusion of somebody being chased down the street—the picture transmitted in our heads—is of the honest reporter asking the honest question, and the crooked interviewee being unavailable, when exactly the opposite could be the case— that the ability of somebody to say 'no' to a television camera is his First Amendment right."

It's debatable whether any reporter could "ambush" a public figure, but it's hardly the forum for a reasoned answer to a question, even for a politician responsible to the people. And when a layman is confronted on the street, the ambush technique runs the risk of making an innocent person look guilty and could result in a terribly inaccurate report. On this point *60 Minutes* gives some guidance. Before Mike Wallace positions himself to catch an illusive subject off guard, the producer makes a minimum of two phone calls and sends one letter. Apparently forewarned is considered fair game.

PRIVATE DOCUMENTS

After the Mirage Tavern story, the *Sun-Times* again joined with the Better Government Association to pursue abortion clinics in Chicago. Undercover reporters gained employment at several clinics and reviewed their observations with the investigative team leader, Pam Zekman. She asked for further corroboration, so the young investigators xeroxed the private medical records of some of the abortion patients. The act of xeroxing is important because the reporters can argue they didn't "steal" any property by taking it out of the clinic. Still, the private files were invaded although none of the names reached print.

The incident is perhaps most instructive in its escalation of investigative techniques. The undercover reporters not only misrepresented themselves to gain employment so they might passively observe the operation of abortion clinics. They actively copied private documents.

Is it unfair to suggest that such a precedent might lead to an easy justification for removing the files from the office next time, even entering the office after hours to obtain them?

TRESPASS

The most notable trespass to date involved a news-camera crew from WCBS-TV in New York. They entered a restaurant without warning to film the premises during the lunch hour. A civil action against the television station resulted in a judgment against CBS of $250,000. The crew was found to be trespassing even though it was an area open to the public. The case was dropped upon appeal.

An ABC News camera crew took the trespass precedent one step further in Harrison, Arkansas, by entering an area not open to the public, a surgical space just outside an operating room. A cameraman and soundman stood at a window filming a doctor charged with performing unnecessary surgery. The ABC producer maintains they were invited by a doctor on the staff. But there was no announcement to the doctors involved in the operation. They claimed the film crew had disrupted the operation. The film crew was found guilty of criminal trespass and fined $100. No mention was made of the transgression when the pictures of the operation were used in an ABC report on the 20/20 program. For the purposes of an

ethical discussion it raises an interesting question: Do television reporters regard such incidents as minor inconven-
iences in the pursuit of visual material for a story, or should
a reporter have hesitated at the prospect of jeopardizing an
operation?

RATINGS

Every local station subject to the competitive system of ratings has experienced the pressure of having to produce its
investigative reports at three specific times during the year,
those months when the rating services are in effect. It goes
without saying that the pressure to conclude investigations
within these "windows" has added additional complications to
a task that requires patient hours of labor to assure accuracy.
Speeding up the process runs the risk of "shaping" the facts
being gathered.

OUTSIDE ORGANIZATIONS

The demand for investigative reports has attracted the services of independent organizations like the Better Government Association of Chicago. A political watchdog group for
some 50 years, it filled the growing demand for source material, manpower, and even investigative expertise in exchange
for little more than a mention of its participation when the
story was published.

The BGA has enjoyed a credible reputation in Chicago, but
several reporters involved in such joint projects have
cautioned that, no matter how reputable the partner, expanding an investigative venture beyond direct editorial control
opens the investigation to the special interests of the outside
group, no matter how subtle.

That fear became more pronounced in two cases involving
partnerships with government agencies.

The *Des Moines Register and Tribune* criticized ABC News for
accepting an invitation from the Iowa Department of Insurance to conduct an investigative report with the aid of the
state's facilities.

A local television station in Chicago was criticized in court for entering into an "unholy alliance" with federal agents. The station provided money for payoffs by the agents, in effect, turning them into "super" reporters. The videotape crew also followed them into private homes to obtain pictures. The line between official federal business and journalism blurred when the journalists and federal agents joined forces.

Investigative reporting will not and should not go out of business following the criticism of the past year. The pressure to produce entertaining investigative reports will not lessen. It is to be hoped that the recent airing of controversial techniques will spark an internal journalistic examination that just might turn the current direction of investigative reporting from an unrestrained to a more responsible path.

For the practitioners of the art, Fred Friendly added a closing thought. "You're not Sam Spade, you're not Dick Tracy, you're not a private eye, you're a journalist and all you've got is your pencil, your imagination, and your shoe leather. That's what God and your profession gave you. All these other trappings don't matter a tinker's damn. It's not the process, it's the substance that matters."

Public Affairs
on the
Public Air

BY FRANK MANKIEWICZ

THE IMPACT on public broadcasting of the substantial reductions in federal funding for the years 1983–86, although these reductions are less than the Reagan Administration had sought, is still difficult to assess. By 1986, given ordinary expectations of inflation, the dollars available to the Corporation for Public Broadcasting will be about one-half of what they are in 1982. The new formula imposed on the Corporation by Congress will at least guarantee that the bulk of the funds will go to *broadcasting*—that is to say, to radio and television stations and programming—but the loss will still be substantial.

How much of that loss can be made up by increased private and foundation underwriting is as yet, of course, unknown. In addition, a serious effort will be made by both stations and national programming entities to *earn* additional funds through a variety of entrepreneurial activities. As this transitional year progresses, more will be learned of how well this will be accomplished, including some assessment of the experiment authorized by Congress in which 10 radio and 10 television stations will test the waters of selling commercial time.

Obviously, the drop in funds will have an impact on news and public affairs programming. In public television, where public affairs programs are generally more difficult to fund by corporate grant than are so-called "cultural" programs, the impact will be significant. At National Public Radio, where daily news programs are a staple of the diet, the impact is also uncertain. Corporate underwriting has been extremely difficult to obtain for either *Morning Edition* or *All Things Considered,* the reason being—as one corporate dispenser of largesse explained—that "we'd rather not underwrite anything that could lead to a director's calling the president of the company the next morning to complain." In plainer English, why pay for news about the MX or the school lunch program when you can have Pavarotti?

But the widespread and increased "market" for news, the obvious public appetite and, if I may say so, the increased awareness of the quality of news programming on public radio may lead to a change. Already there are signs that some companies and foundations are willing to consider the major underwriting of news, public affairs, and documentaries on public radio. It will come, if it does, just in time.

There is, however, another "political" trend in Washington, unconnected to budget-cutting, that could have a serious impact on public radio news programming. There is the trend toward *deregulation,* now fashionable in almost all quarters. It does not seem likely that the end to ascertainment, to the requirement for *some* public affairs coverage, or even to the relaxation of either the Fairness Doctrine or the so-called "equal time" strictures will come to television soon, but that all of these might apply to *radio*—commercial as well as non-commercial—seems quite likely.

The result is almost predictable. Except for a few stations in large markets that now "do news" and do it well, the amount of news and public affairs coverage will decline—and, in many smaller markets, disappear—except where there is an NPR station now functioning. The reasons are obvious. Most radio stations don't like to do news, they do it badly and, if possible, at "off hours." Put more simply, if you don't *have* to teach the DJ's how to pronounce Khomeini or Walesa, or put on a program Sunday morning—*early* Sunday morning—called *Let's Rap,* why do it at all?

That will put a greater burden on those NPR member stations, who not only do news well but also enjoy it and feel it a part of their mandate. But it will mean a need for more news and public affairs coverage by local public radio stations as well as by NPR, and they are all operating on scarce resources now. The Congress which has signalled the commercial sector that it can relax its news coverage is the same Congress that has reduced the noncommercial sector's ability to make up the difference. The losers, if this imbalance persists, can only be the public. You can classify ketchup as a vegetable, but you can't classify the Top 40 as news.

National Public Radio, in response to the cuts in federal funding, is embarking on a novel course that might prove successful—and, if so, point the way for our colleagues in public broadcasting. Briefly put, NPR plans to become independent of government money within five or six years—to "go private" by earning half its budget in a variety of entrepreneurial ways and by gleaning the other half from private donors with a new funding approach.

At the outset of the Reagan Administration it became plain—and has become even more plain with the passage of the amendments to the Broadcasting Act of 1981—that neither the White House nor Congress was in a mood to increase funds for public broadcasting, or to do more, in fact, than *decrease* them, in an orderly way, to about half of where they stood in 1981.

Obscured by the successful battle against rescission of advanced funding for 1982, and by the successful fight in Congress to hold the Reagan administration cuts for 1984–1986 to about half their proposed levels, was the unmistakable evidence that public broadcasting was no one's favorite son; that it was a high priority for even further cuts by conservatives and a low priority for restoration by liberals. By year's end, with a spate of compromise budget resolutions, it became only too clear that in the best and least inflationary of times, public broadcasting stood in a long line, of whose patient members too many were old, sick, hungry, and unemployed.

Faced with these realities, the management and directors of National Public Radio decided to take the President at his word and test whether, indeed, the private sector would make up the difference between declining government funding and budget needs, particularly when coupled with vigorous self-help measures. The result is that NPR has embarked upon a course that, if successful, will yield a stance far more independent of government and unlikely to yield even the dimmest perception of outside influence upon programming—particularly news programming.

The plan is to make available, by 1986, all or nearly all of the federal funds available for public radio solely to NPR member stations, who now receive slightly more than half those funds in the form of unrestricted community service grants. With the decline in federal dollars, modest inflation and a conservative growth in the number of public radio stations, it now appears that the *total* of federal dollars for all of radio in 1986–87 will roughly equal no more than that available for those station grants today.

That will leave NPR seeking—by the same conservative estimates—$35 million to $40 million annually to stay not only independent but healthy. The plans call for about half of that sum to be *earned,* by profit-making subsidiaries, much in the way subsidiaries of public television entities today (of which perhaps the most conspicuous example is the Children's Television Workshop) earn money and turn over the profits to the "public" parent.

These earnings will come, it is thought, from the shared use of the satellite distribution system with commercial interest, the delivery of a variety of nonbroadcast information over the system, and by the member station (everyone turning a profit along the way), and perhaps by NPR's entry into cable audio.

That leaves something on the order of $20 million to be provided by the private sector—businesses, foundations, and other institutions. To that end, NPR has created a new format for underwriting public radio. Instead of seeking funds for individual programs—as is the highly successful model in public television—public radio is shifting to a search for investments in two funds, one for news and the other for performance programs.

Potential underwriters will be asked to buy a full share (or a half- or quarter-share, as the case may be) in the News Fund or the Performance Fund. That will help support not *one* particular program once a week, or even daily, but all the programs fitting each category during a given year. Underwriting credits will be granted "run-of-the-station," as commercial radio puts it, so that the generosity of the underwriter will be reported in all markets at all times during the week, at times selected at random.

In that way, no corporate underwriter can be held responsible for a news program by an irate stockholder, nor can NPR be reasonably or even unreasonably thought of as having turned over a program to an underwriter or group of underwriters. It has all the indicia of fairness and good sense for both the network and the private sector; it will prove ironic indeed if the necessity of hurrying the transition from "public" to "private" radio can be the mother of the invention of a new and adequate financing system. If so, the "pressures" of 1981 on public radio news and information will have created a freedom from government as desirable as it was once thought remote.

IT IS THE BUSINESS of television to deal with, to reflect, and to *report* on the times—so the pressures and tensions touch on this industry in a very special way. America and television face a new brand of monopolists—not monopolists of money or goods but of truth and values. In times of hardship, voices of stridency and division have always replaced those of reason and unity, and the results have always been a deterioration of free and open dialogue, a tension among races, classes, and religions, and the temptation to grasp at simplistic solutions to complex problems.

In our time of hardship, we find the New Right and the Religious New Right—a new breed of robber barons who have organized to corner the market on morals. And who would feel that more keenly than those of us who labor in the marketplace of ideas?

We have lost our way, they say, because, in and out of television, we have turned our backs on God and followed the devices and desires of our own hearts. America's purity and strength can be restored only if the nation submits to the political and moral answers that they see as biblically self-evident.

Our founding fathers never treated the God they worship-

236

ped as the creator of a political platform—or as a rubber stamp to imprint private doctrines on public policy. They all believed, as Abraham Lincoln later warned, that we should never assume God is on *our* side but should always seek, as best we can, to be on God's side.

Lincoln understood the spirit of liberty. So did the late Justice Learned Hand, who defined it as follows:

The spirit of liberty is the spirit which seeks to understand the minds of other men and women; the spirit of liberty is a spirit which weighs their interests alongside its own without bias; the spirit of liberty remembers that not even one sparrow falls to earth unheeded; the spirit of liberty is the spirit of Him who, near two thousand years ago, taught mankind a lesson it has never learned, but has never quite forgotten.

I love those words, ". . . to seek to understand the minds of other men and women" and ". . . which weighs their interests alongside our own without bias." But that is a two-way street. If the television community truly believes in the spirit of liberty, we must seek to understand the minds of those hundreds of thousands—or millions—of people across the country who are currently finding fault with us, and try to weigh *their* interests alongside our own without bias.

I will come back to our responsibility, but, first, let us recognize that the basic principle of tolerance, that principle which allows us to live together as Americans—a people dedicated to achieving consensus through the expression of diverse and conflicting ideas—*that* principle is threatened today.

It is threatened by that extremist coalition of the New Right and some evangelical fundamentalists, who would refuse a hearing to any conflicting opinion because they assume that *their* certainty is the same as absolute certainty. They overlook the fact that every age has held opinions that subsequent ages have deemed not only false but absurd. And so, to disagree with the conclusions of the New and Religious New Right on numerous matters of morality and politics is to be labeled a poor Christian—or unpatriotic—or anti-family.

As communicators ourselves, it should be interesting to look at how well they are able to spread their absolutist views.

There are now over 1,500 Christian radio stations blanketing the country—with approximately one new station being added each week; there are forty-some independent television stations with a full-time diet of religious programming, largely fundamentalist; and three Christian Broadcasting Networks. There are Falwell, Bakker, Robertson, Robison, Wildmon, and others—the "superstars" among TV evangelicals—some taking as much as $1 million a week from their direct solicitations and the sale of religious merchandise.

There are also scores and scores of *local* radio and TV evangelicals, espousing the same absolutist, fundamentalist points of view while attacking the integrity and character of anyone who does not stand with them.

It's important that we not be misled into thinking that these are simply old-fashioned throwbacks—like the Bible-thumping, openly racist, blatantly anti-Semitic, rough-hers whackos of another era. No, sir. These are smooth, buttoned-down, middle-America, business-oriented evangelicals who, borrowing a line Paddy Chayevsky intended for others, are saying: "I'm mad as hell, and I'm not going to take it anymore!" These are revivalistic salesmen—entrepreneurs—who have a genius for responding to the market's desire for stable values. Unlike so many of our leaders who are currently out of touch with their constituencies, these fundamentalist preachers have their fingers *and* their computers on the pulse of the emotional needs of the crowd. And that is power. In the name of these preachers—and as members of secular groups such as the Christian Voice, Religious Roundtable, Christians Concerned for Responsible Citizenship, the Plymouth Rock Foundation, the Heritage Foundation, etc.—here is *some* of what is occurring on the local level across the country:

- The American Library Association reports that libraries in some 40 states are being pressured to remove as many as 126 titles and authors from library shelves. They include John Steinbeck, Kurt Vonnegut, Bernard Malamud, George Orwell, J.D. Salinger, and even William Shakespeare, because in certain communities so-called "concerned parents" don't want their children contaminated by the relationship of Hamlet to his mother.

- In Washington and Virginia, Moral Majoritarians have attempted to secure the names of all those who borrowed books on sex education from the public library.
- Five dictionaries have been banned from use in schools throughout the state of Texas because "concerned parents" objected to such "filth" as the word "bastard" and the word "bed," when used as a verb.
- Textbooks across the country are not being bought by some school boards, under pressure from local groups, until all "liberal dogma and secular humanism" has been excised by a fundamentalist couple in Texas, the Gablers.
- In North Carolina, a social studies test was found objectionable and removed because "seventh graders are not emotionally or intellectually capable of dealing with such complex problems." The problems they didn't want seventh graders dealing with were food shortages, overpopulation, and ecology.
- And the Independent News Service reports that in Anaheim, California recently, there was a high school course for seniors entitled "Free Enterprise." Part of the curriculum included this question: "True or false—the government spends too much money on the environment." The correct answer—the *only* correct answer—was "true."

The New Right organization that could be of most interest to the readers of most interest to the readers of this publication is the Coalition for Better Television and its leader, the aforementioned Reverend Wildmon. I don't know what can be said about the Coalition and Wildmon that hasn't been said—except that it is worth reminding ourselves that they have every legal right under the First Amendment to speak their piece in any way they choose, to threaten boycott, or to engage in boycott if that is their desire. So the Reverend Wildmon, like his evangelical counterparts on TV, does not break the letter of the First Amendment. But they *do* break its spirit. Reverend Wildmon does *not* seek to understand the minds of other men and women and weigh their interests alongside his own without bias. Reverend Wildmon and Reverend Falwell and Reverend Robison and the others see a society out of control, and what they want is a society composed of solid, middle-class, one-morality families leading conventional lives on the model of a colony of ants.

These moralists see the dissonant variety inherent in a pluralistic society; they see people of all races and religions and lifestyles—hotheads, sybarites, and ascetics, the poets, mockers, and madmen—they see people who decline to submit to an ordered morality—and it frightens them.

And so, they would *tame* the dissidents. They would contract this multifaceted land into their own tiny garden of saints. To make us properly moral, they would settle for a nation where there is no way of life that differs from *their* notion of a biblically oriented family.

Ironically, this occurs at a time when the communicaitons industry is witnessing an explosion of new technologies, delivery systems, and satellite networks, promising as many as 100 channels to the home. With this overabundance of sources, there will be room for a diversity of voices, a place for the emergence of cultures and subcultures that have not been heard from before. To insure the broadcast possible access for these voices, consistent with the First Amendment, it might be wise to limit the number of stations, transponders, and channels that may be controlled by any single entity.

The history of network television teaches that the concentration of most of the resources of broadcasting in three companies results in the kind of fierce competition that invites the kind of homogeneous broadcasting which allows for too little diversity and retards the development of new and competing technologies.

The opportunity for those in the creative end of the television business never looked brighter. Narrowcasting may finally become a reality. Channels will exist to inform as well as entertain; to inspire and improve the quality of life. These will be businesses, but smaller businesses, without the need for profit margin that broadcasting is accustomed to today. We will also see new and experimental drama, allowing talents and pieces of our culture to surface that have never before had the opportunity. There will be new approaches to science and to the discussion of issues for which commercial televison, with its concentration on ratings and instant success, has had no time. All of this and more is possible so long as there is sufficient access to the delivery systems for the small communications entrepreneur, wherever he or she may be.

If there are indeed going to be as many as a hundred or more channels to the home, the Tulsas and Orlandos and Perth Amboys must have a crack at them, too. The capital of country-and-western music is Nashville, not Los Angeles. And jazz was born in New Orleans, not New York.

It would also be good for the country to have the dissonant variety inherent in our pluralistic society find its way to the tube—people of all races and religions and lifestyles—the "hotheads, sybarites, and ascetics, the poets, mockers and madmen" mentioned earlier. Let's have them all. We might benefit from the return of the soapbox orator, and since the Pershing Squares and Union Squares of anothe era are gone, perhaps the Fates intend Channels 66 or 81 to be their replacement. The First Amendment says that "Congress shall make no law . . . abridging the freedom of speech." It says "*no law*. . . ." It doesn't say that there will be freedom of speech provided that said speech does not run contrary to popular thought. It doesn't say that there will be freedom of speech provided said speech has no tendency to subvert standing institutions. In the Soviet Union and other totalitarian nations, there may be debates concerning the course of action to follow, but no one is allowed to challenge the government itself nor any activity of the government. How different in America, with the blessings of the First Amendment. But, and this is a very big but, this is not the America of the early 1900s—and today the blessings of the First Amendment cannot be realized fully by every segment of our society without access to the mass media.

Which brings us back to Reverend Wildmon and others who would deny access to those voices, ideas, and attitudes that do not match *their* prescribed morality. Well we know about them. Where they come from is clear. Now what about the people who make television—the creators, the production heads, the news programmers, the network executives—the people responsible for the content of television. How are we responding to Learned Hand's definition of the spirit of liberty? Are we seeking to understand the minds of other men and women, those hundreds of thousands, or millions, of television viewers whose frustration with the content and quality of television is, for them, very, very valid? Are we weighing *their* interests alongside our own without bias?

We know that every born-again Christian is *not* a Biblical absolutist. Every frustrated television viewer is *not* a would-be censor. If we are to weigh their opinions, their feelings, their frustrations alongside our own, then, *without bias,* we must *ourselves* observe those basic principles of tolerance and *listen* to them. But not as they are interpreted to us by their leaders—their leaders may have other axes to grind. We must listen to them *directly,* and the only way to do that is to get out among them!

A professor of sociology and theology at a southern university told me recently that he was visited by a well-known Hollywood director who allowed as to how he had never been outside of California except for visits to New York. That only meant, said the professor, that the director had no real contact with the American people, his viewers, but that those same viewers had no real contact with him, or anyone like him, from television's creative community. The lack of personal contact is the director's loss, the creative community's loss, and in more ways than one. In addition to never really knowing our viewers, except as they are interpreted to us by the likes of Reverend Wildmon, our viewers never, ever get to know us, except as *we* are interpreted to them by such articles as the infamous *TV Guide* cover story on drugs in Hollywood, and the puff and personality pieces that tell the public everything except how hard we may be working and how much we care.

The television industry should make it its business to name its spokespeople and send them out about the country on a regular basis, in whatever forums are chosen, so that America can come to know us as we are: hardworking, family-oriented people, tied to them by the same human umbilicals that connect us all. And we in TV, in turn, can learn at first hand that they are not strangers. They are us.

If we get in touch with our constituents and give them an opportunity to vent their feelings, perhaps they would not wind up in the hands of opportunists like Reverend Wildmon.

And if we *can*—when our spokespeople return to Los Angeles to communicate their experience to us—perhaps then *we* can begin to communicate with each other in new and fundamental ways.

Is there too much gratuitous sex and violence on TV? Let's talk to each other. Directly. How many cars smashed head-on and burst into flames on television last week? How many went through storefronts or over a cliff? Since America is upset about the possibility that there may be too much of this, wouldn't it make sense to get together to discuss it? Not to censor one another, certainly, but to hear ourselves think; to learn from our peers and perhaps to help and influence one another.

Gratuitous sex. Do we really need young women in braless sweaters running and bouncing across a set—and I do mean running and bouncing—because someone has said that dinner is ready? Do we need the same young women jumping up and down in their braless sweaters when they are told that dinner will consist of *lamb chops*? "Not lamb chops?!" Jump, jump. What could we lose if we were to talk together about these things? This sort of TV behavior is not motivated by the artistic needs of the writer or the director or the actress. It is motivated, primarily—in a long, circuitous fashion—by the needs of the three networks to win in the ratings next Tuesday at 8:30; by three networks' obsession with the bottom line. An obsession it shares with all of the rest of American business. And that, of course, includes us.

Not that the quest for monetary gain is wrong at all, but it needn't be the *primary* motivation. It seems to have become that, however, in too many places. It has destroyed Detroit and is eating away at the future of most industries—including ours. It is the greatest societal disease of our time, and it starts at the top. Also, in my opinion, our industry's obsession with ratings and profits, *the bottom line,* which, more than any other factor, including pressure groups, is squeezing the joy out of our efforts.

The pressure to do one's very best, creatively, has been forced, as a result of pressure from the marketplace, to take a back seat to the need for high ratings. And I am convinced that if we could reverse that—if we care enough to reverse that—if the desire to create out of one's own inner vision was the dominant motivation for the existence of a show, chances are that *that* show would rate higher simply because it was *better!* And if everyone, writers, actors, directors, producers, created out of their individual and collective inner visions, the work would still be backbreaking but the joy and the fun would be back!

Now, if all of that is easier said than done—and it always is—let's take our case to the people. With a sense of self-confidence and self-assurance, because we have earned it, let's tell them that the hundreds of thousands of hours of television entertainment that we have provided them with through the years did *not* come out of indifference; that popular art is a great profession, not a way station on the way to the classics; that our work in public affairs broadcasting has enlarged the viewer's vision; that we are *proud* of what we have accomplished; and that if it could have been done better, other people in this free enterprise system would have done it!

And let's listen to the *people*. Learn from what they have to tell us. Show them that we believe in them—that we *value* them—because we really do.

We must. Because there is no way we can get along without them.

ᗐ

Some Information about
the Alfred I. duPont/
Columbia University Awards

EACH YEAR the awards are based upon research done in conjunction with the annual Alfred I. duPont/Columbia University Survey of Broadcast Journalism. There is no set number of awards. Local and network radio, local and network television, as well as syndicated material and the work of independent producers, will be surveyed and considered for awards.

Concerned parties are encouraged to suggest to the jurors examples of broadcast journalism that they feel are particularly worthy of attention. They are also invited to recommend subjects for research.

Suggestions for those wishing to participate:

1. Any person, group, organization, or broadcast station may bring to the duPont/Columbia jury's attention material dealing with performance—one-time or long-term—in broadcast news and public affairs by an individual, a station, or other institutions.
2. The nomination should include the following particulars: a) time, date, and call letters of the station carrying the program; b) the subject of the program; c) the reason the program or the individual is being singled out.
3. Tapes and other supporting material should not be submitted unless expressly asked for by the Director.

4. Although our broadcast year runs from July 1 to June 30, nominations may be made throughout the year.
5. Nominations must be postmarked no later than midnight July 2.
6. All materials submitted will become the property of Columbia University.
7. All inquiries and correspondence should be addressed to:

Marvin Barrett, Director
Alfred I. duPont/Columbia University Survey and Awards
Graduate School of Journalism
Columbia University
New York, New York   10027

Acknowledgments

ONCE AGAIN the generosity of Mrs. Jessie Ball duPont in establishing the Alfred I. duPont/Columbia University Survey and Awards should be acknowledged. The original awards from which the current program has grown were established just forty years ago to honor Mrs. du Pont's late husband, Alfred I. duPont, and to encourage the best in broadcast journalism.

We are also grateful to all those organizations and individuals who have offered us generous assistance in putting together this volume. Unfortunately, it is not possible to list them all. However, we would particularly like to express our gratitude to the news directors and newsmen and women from the networks and individual stations who answered questionnaires, furnished tapes and films, and produced the news and public affairs with which this volume and the Alfred I. duPont/Columbia University Awards are particularly concerned.

We would like to particularly thank the awards and public information departments of ABC, CBS, NBC, PBS, NPR, and CNN, as well as individual radio and television stations, upon whose help, as always, we depended heavily.

Each year the volume of material to be handled in judging the awards and compiling this report increases with a commensurate broadening of reportorial and research chores. These were performed with dispatch and distinction by my assistant editor, Zachary Sklar. Barbara Eddings, Associate Director of the Alfred I. duPont/Columbia University Awards, was once again in charge of the formidable logistics involved in putting this volume together. Invaluable support was given by administrative assistant Dinorah Pineiro.

Again the reporters of *Advertising Age, Broadcasting, The New York Times, The Wall Street Journal, Television/Radio Age, TV Guide, The Columbia Journalism Review,* and *Variety* furnished both individual insights and continuous coverage of the broadcast scene that were invaluable to the editor and to the jurors.

Finally, the network of 100 Alfred I. du Pont/Columbia University correspondents across the country have provided those special insights into local television and radio, which are so important a part of the overall picture of broadcast journalism that we hope this book provides.

We would particularly like to thank the trustees of the Alfred I. du Pont Awards Foundation and the Jessie Ball duPont Religious, Charitable, and Educational Fund who have supported our expanding activities so generously.

MARVIN BARRETT
Editor
January 1982

Index